AWARENESS CODE

			United	Doing the Impossible	Breathtaking	Miraculous	Mastery	Superhuman	Profound	Beyond Incredible (100)
Incredible	90 Grateful	91 Sincere	92 Heartfelt	93 Devoted	94 Thriving	95 Compassion	96 Altruistic	97 Heart-bursting	98 Extraordinary	99 Revealing Grace
Transforming	80 Highest Callings	81 Realizing Power	82 Realizing Value	83 Fellowship Mindset	84 Embracing	85 Spontaneous	86 Off-the-charts	87 Integrating	88 Integrity	89 Inspiring
Opening	70 Receptive	71 Witnessing	72 Open-minded	73 Trustful	74 Connected	75 Collaboration	76 Emerging	77 Agile	78 Wow	79 Flowing
Stepping in	60 Realizing Truth	61 Ready	62 Preparing	63 Releasing	64 Reorientating	65 Positive	66 Adventurous	67 Conviction	68 Fearless	69 Fully In
Egotistical	50 Narcissistic	51 Arrogant	52 Know-it-all	53 Self-centered	54 Dismissive	55 Defensive	56 Pretentious	57 Ego Confidence	58 Complacent	59 Not Buying In
Controlling	40 Malicious	41 Enraged	42 Bully	43 Confronting	44 Deceiving	45 Resentful	46 Passive-aggressive	47 Annoyed	48 Frustrated	49 Sceptical
Wanting	30 Infatuated	31 Perfectionist	32 Addictive	33 Over-ambitious	34 Scheming	35 Competitive	36 Attached	37 Narrowing Down	38 Identifying	39 Ego-requesting
Stressed	20 Numb	21 Terror	22 Dread	23 Trapped	24 Frightened	25 Worried	26 Anxious	27 Over-pleasing	28 Insecure	29 Hesitant
Despondent	10 Inconsolable	11 Hopeless	12 Unfulfilled	13 Lethargic	14 Wounded	15 Hurt	16 Saddened	17 Disconnected	18 Discontented	19 Disinterested
Lifeless	0 Self-loathing	1 Self-hatred	2 Pathetic	3 Unlovable	4 Burden	5 Embarrassed	6 Wrong	7 Regretful	8 Never Enough	9 Inadequate

'Ancestry.com gives people the opportunity to go back in time and understand their heritage. *The Awareness Code* invites people to break life patterns and generational cycles. It allows you to understand who you are now and who you can become in the future to empower the next generation.'

Margo Georgiadis, former President and CEO, Ancestry

'*The Awareness Code* is the *Encyclopaedia Britannica* for leadership in the 21st Century, it is comprehensive and not for the faint hearted. It is insightful and practical with a route map to transformational and incredible leadership and is designed to support development for all leaders. *The Awareness Code* can be the key to reinventing the UK and to bring Britain not back to Great Britain but to an Incredible Britain, playing a vital role in developing an Extraordinary World.'

Paul Drechsler CBE, Chairman of International Chambers of Commerce and former president of the Confederation of British Industry

'An extraordinary leader is the result of higher awareness and diligent self-development. But what does this mean and how do you do it? The Code has helped me understand myself, colleagues, my teams and my family in a way I didn't think was possible and has given me practical solutions.'

Chloe Targett-Adams, Global Director of Race Promotion, Formula 1

'The structure of *The Awareness Code* is revolutionary and the depth of insight contained within each tile extraordinary. It will inspire and challenge leaders in equal measure.'

Angus Kinnear, CEO, Leeds United

'*The Awareness Code* has helped me lead HR in a scale-up, unicorn business, stepping into a field and sector completely new to what I have known in the past with curiosity and greater confidence. *The Awareness Code* is more than a book, it is a movement, a way of life, and it creates endless possibilities for us to truly change society and nations.'

Julia Ingall, Chief People Officer, Bought By Many

'It's mind blowing, *The Awareness Code*. I am sure that it is going to help enhance and rejuvenate both rugby union and rugby league from the Academy through to the first teams as well as the meaning of the game and the communities we play in.'

Kevin Sinfield OBE, Defensive Coach for Leicester Tigers, former captain and Director of Rugby for Leeds Rhinos

'It was fascinating, comprehensive, well written and made a lot of sense. It puts a practical lens upon deep psychological and philosophical thoughts.'

Andy Penn, CEO, Telstra, Fortune 500 Company

'*The Awareness Code* is powerful and I loved it. It is going to lead to massive change across businesses and sport. I really think it's going to help many but particularly looking forward to seeing the impact it could have on sports people.'

Michael Vaughan OBE, former England cricket captain and commentator

'*The Awareness Code* is exactly the right "legacy martial art secret book", which will coach the Chinese business leadership to survive and thrive with their well quenched leadership and better sharpened sword.'

Joe Baolin Zhou, Co-Founder, CEO & CEdO, (Shenzhen) Singularity Education and leader responsible for setting up Harvard in China

'We need to enter a new dawn of retail where we have extraordinary experiences so our customers can fall back in love with stores again. The key to finding this is in *The Awareness Code*, which is incredibly powerful and thought-provoking. It will be fascinating to see this unfold with the next generation of retailers across the world.'

Ian McGarrigle, Chairman, World Retail Congress

'*The Awareness Code* has inspired me to blend technology and higher awareness in ways that expand what I believe is possible in the future. This is a book that can assist humanity to make the quantum shift we desperately need.'

Peter Arvai, Co-founder and Executive Chairman, Prezi

'In today's complex world, leading means being aware of so many matters. But this only works if you are aware of another complex matter: yourself. That's exactly what this important book is all about.'

Stefan Oschmann, former CEO, Merck Group, Fortune 500 company

'There are many books on leadership but I have never read one like *The Awareness Code*. I feel I have been given a gift that integrates ancient wisdom, modern day psychology and best business practice in a wise manual of how to live and how to become the kind of leader I have the capacity to be.'

Kim Krejus, Creative Director, 16th Street Actors Studio

'*The Awareness Code* is a playbook for implementing a personal kaizen or continuous improvement process. It's a wonderful tool that has tremendous potential in application across functions and regions.'

Guenter Butschek, CEO & MD, Tata Motors Worldwide

'Life is a journey of constant learning, development and awareness. *The Awareness Code* offers great insights to help navigate through this journey. It is practical and very insightful.'

Paul Walsh, Executive Chair, McLaren Group

'Having reached the summit of Everest as a double amputee, to me *The Awareness Code* is a tool which can provide the capacity for any human being to climb out of reservations and fear and reach for the summit.'

Mark Inglis ONZM, global mountaineer, researcher and motivational speaker

'I am finding the incredible in the ordinary through my patients' eyes in each consultation and feel as if we are "touching souls". The Code has the potential to radically change not just the way consultations unfold, but also how the health industry is managed.'

Dr Mick Brownstein MBBS FRACGP FACRRM

'I am typically sceptical of new management paradigms that claim to solve everything. With *The Awareness Code*, you get a map and scale to navigate the mental/psychological side of human performance. It is practical, semi-quantitative and full of insights about individuals at different spots on that mediocrity to awesomeness scale.'

Joseph Chen, Chairman and CEO, Renren

'Many organizations are trapped and oscillate between 40–60 in the Awareness Code. What is exciting is to get companies up to 70–80+ and these will be the really high performing companies with great leadership.'

Stephen Murphy, former Group Chief Executive, Virgin Group

'The world is complex and out of balance. We have a leadership crisis and now we need a new set of rules to help inspire and create the future. *The Awareness Code* is extraordinary and will be at the heart of a new global leadership credo which dispenses with power and embraces deep integrity.'

Dr Frank-Jürgen Richter, Founder and Chairman,
Horasis: The Global Visions Community

'In the old paradigm, leaders might have got away with egotistical, even narcissistic, behaviours. In the new paradigm, the end no longer justifies the means – integrity is fundamental, meaning a leader's way of being is even more important than their way of doing. *The Awareness Code* draws attention to the lower states of being and provides a powerful toolkit for transitioning to the higher levels of consciousness.'

Roz Savage MBE FRGS, ocean rower, environmental
campaigner, author and speaker

'*The Awareness Code* is a very thought-provoking and useful book for all leaders that want to develop their leadership skills to the next level. This is a real "work book" and one has to commit to the journey to unlock this treasure trove for leaders and aspiring leaders.'

Dr. Wolfgang Baier, Group CEO, Luxasia

'It is exciting times in Zambia as we move forward under a new government. What an opportunity for people to redefine themselves and their communities using the Awareness Code and drawing on Wayno and Steve's expertise.'

Paul Gates Banda, Zambian author, speaker, banker and philanthropist

'Company boards are very focused on their responsibility to society. Much is talked about what to do – less about how to do it. *The Awareness Code* is a remarkable tool that can guide a new generation of leaders as they build more sustainable, cooperative, responsible and well governed businesses.'

Richard Pennycook CBE, former Chief Executive, Co-operative Group

'*The Awareness Code* is an essential tool for any dramatic artist serious about exploring human motivation and behaviour in very high resolution. The profound and unpretentious skillset of *The Awareness Code* gives the dramatic artist everything they need to build a bridge to their higher selves, to their characters, to fellow artists and the world.'

Iain Sinclair, Head of Acting, 16th Street Actors Studio

'This is a very interesting and useful book. It challenges you first to ask yourself what sort of leader you are compared to the leader you could be. It identifies impediments or traps and has a lot of helpful thoughts to removing these and becoming a better leader.'

Andrew Bassat, Co-founder & CEO, Seek

'*The Awareness Code* is mind-altering. It allows us to empower teammates to take lead roles in running a mine, taking care of our environment, communities, and reinventing mining as a force for good in the world. I'm fully in!'

Rudi Badenhorst, Director of Operations, First Quantum Minerals

'*The Awareness Code* is a real revelation. Bringing together some of the core concepts of meditation, self-care and wellbeing with leadership traps. *The Awareness Code* can help anyone unleash their full potential first as a human being and then as a successful leader. A must read for anyone who aspires to be better.'

Matteo Berlucchi, Co-founder & CEO, Healthily (formerly Your.MD)

'One of the biggest risks for organizations is they are not inclusive. *The Awareness Code* can help leaders and companies become much more diverse by giving us the code to answer the questions behind biases and prejudices, and in doing so helps us to fully understand what's holding our people back.'

Sandra Breene, President Regional Delivery, Croda

'There are so many general leadership books and I have read many of them but this one is so different and it makes you realise the truth about yourself. To read *The Awareness Code*, be ready to have a good look at yourself but if you face into reality and let go of your ego, you can commit to becoming an above-60 awareness leader. It tells you *what* to do in this book and more importantly, it shows you *how* to do it.'

Steve McClaren, former England football manager & senior FIFA consultant

'*The Awareness Code* allows you to both face into yourself and put your hand on the highest mountain. Rugby League for too long has had lower awareness leadership and my goal is to use *The Awareness Code* to help reinvent the game and create an inspiring and unified world of Rugby League.'

Brian Noble, former Great Britain coach of Rugby League
national team with highest win/loss ratio

'*The Awareness Code* is a universally applicable and highly actionable guide to understanding who we are as individuals and as leaders. Our definition of leadership is constantly evolving and *The Awareness Code* puts diversity and humanity at the forefront of our understanding of leadership.'

Zain Masri, Head of Brand & Reputation Marketing, Google, MENA

'If leaders want to have an impact on their organization, they can't do it alone, no matter how smart or how good. One can't deliver results unless the team is sympathetic and understands the strategy and direction. *The Awareness Code* is a wonderful guide that can help leaders at any level, with tangible strategies to improve awareness and ultimately the organization's performance.'

Jose Munoz, Global COO, Hyundai Motor Company; President & CEO,
Hyundai Motor North America

'*The Awareness Code* is a spiritual map that must be adopted by leaders to form the foundation of new technology enterprises and be deployed quickly to measure and enhance existing ones. Steve and Wayno have created a map for modern management which touches all of humanity's frailties and strengths allowing us, as human beings, to embrace our own failings and our abilities, leading us all to a higher level of perception, appreciation and recognition.'

Dan Wagner, Founder, Chairman & CEO, Rezolve Limited

'I think at the core of this book we have a calling that so many are now being driven to think about and find answers for – integrity! Because we are experiencing leadership that exists and seemingly strengthens its hold without it! This is a book of our time. A book with a calling.'

Harriet Green, former CEO & Chair, IBM Asia Pacific

'It really is so good – it allows the reader to dive as deep or stay as shallow as they want to be. The material is awesome and so insightful. For those who dive deep, it can be life changing. *The Awareness Code* shows a path to incredible for every human being, regardless of the starting point.'

Adi Sehgal, former President Nutrition, eRB & Greater China, Reckitt

'This book is a masterpiece and a truly profound body of work. The human awareness table is like a GPS for ourselves as human beings. It helps us understand both ourselves and those we interact with so much better, and at the same time gives us a blueprint on how to get to a much better place – no matter what your starting point is.'

Arjun Purkayastha, SVP eCommerce, Digital & Ventures, Reckitt

'*The Awareness Code* provides a profound yet simple understanding of oneself, a mirror into the complicated, beautiful person you are. Steve and Wayno helped to unleash my highest calling and to be a better colleague, husband and father. Great change starts with Knowing Thyself.'

Enda Ryan, SVP Greater China, Reckitt

'*The Awareness Code* is both intense and impactful. The Code not only describes me as a person, but it's also allowed me to get to the root cause of things for me. It shows me how I can change to lead at a much higher level and I couldn't recommend it any more.'

Patrick Sly, COO Global Nutrition, Reckitt

'*The Awareness Code* is not just a business essential, it's a life essential. Definitely recommend it!'

Jignesh Budhdev, Global VP & GM, Reckitt

'The ability to negotiate effectively is one of the most crucial skills for success, and self-awareness and empathy are the two greatest priorities for good negotiators. *The Awareness Code* provides a pragmatic and inspiring approach to enable the reader to enhance these invaluable attributes.'

Tim Cullen MBC, Chair of TCA Ltd and Founder,
Oxford Programme on Negotiation

'As a lifetime learner, I was further inspired to continue in my quest to become the best leader I can possibly be through *The Awareness Code*.'

Justin Langer, Head Coach and former player, Australian men's cricket team

'This book provides a way to understand and reflect on personal behaviour and leadership. After starting to read the book and I had gained an understanding of the key concepts, I was hungry to understand more.'

Rob Wheals, CEO & MD, APA Group

'There's over 57,000 books on leadership and I've been subjected to many of them over the years. But I found this one really interesting and felt it brought much more "granularity", especially with the entrapments where we have to overcome such behaviours we naturally see in the corporate world.'

Jeff Adams, CEO, Metcash Group

'The keys are brilliant and have huge practical application in my life. *The Awareness Code* is a book whose time has come – I will use this for my team and I, not only to drive transformational leadership but also for us to become better human beings. This is beyond leadership – it is about wholesome wellness.'

Hina Nagarajan, MD & CEO, Member of Global Executive Committee, Diageo

'For any individual seeking to be all they can be this is overwhelming, impressive content - everything you need to know to become an out of this world leader. From two leadership gurus: original concepts, tremendous content and with hands-on reference material drawn from two shared lifetimes work.'

Neil Carr, President Europe, Middle East, Africa and India, Dow Chemicals

'This is a management book like no other. I will buy a copy for all of our current and future leaders as well as recommend it to my fellow CEOs in the Chemical Industry, FTSE 100 and also to Fortune 500 CEOs. As we create the ingredients for the Pfizer vaccine, we get a real sense of how COVID-19 has shaken our world in a way we have never seen before. What we need for leaders is a revolution in awareness. The revolution is *The Awareness Code*.'

Steve Foots, CEO, Croda International, FTSE 100 company

THE
AWARENESS
CODE

The Secrets to Emotional Empowerment for Incredible Leadership

WAYNE LINTON AND STEVE TAPPIN

BLOOMSBURY BUSINESS
LONDON • OXFORD • NEW YORK • NEW DELHI • SYDNEY

BLOOMSBURY BUSINESS
Bloomsbury Publishing Plc
50 Bedford Square, London, WC1B 3DP, UK
29 Earlsfort Terrace, Dublin 2, Ireland

BLOOMSBURY, BLOOMSBURY BUSINESS and the Diana logo are trademarks
of Bloomsbury Publishing Plc

First published in Great Britain 2021

Bloomsbury Publishing Plc does not have any control over, or responsibility for,
any third-party websites referred to or in this book. All internet addresses given
in this book were correct at the time of going to press. The author and publisher
regret any inconvenience caused if addresses have changed or sites have ceased
to exist, but can accept no responsibility for any such changes

A catalogue record for this book is available from the British Library

Library of Congress Cataloguing-in-Publication data has been applied for

ISBN: 978-1-4729-9207-9; eBook: 978-1-4729-9208-6

2 4 6 8 10 9 7 5 3 1

Typeset by Deanta Global Publishing Services, Chennai, India
Printed and bound in Great Britain by CPI Group (UK) Ltd, Croydon CR0 4YY

To find out more about our authors and books visit www.bloomsbury.com
and sign up for our newsletters

'Incredible leaders step in until they are fully in, stay open until they are flowing, create transformation until they are inspiring and bring gratitude until extraordinary things happen.'
Author Wayno Linton

'Knowing oneself is the stairway to Beyond Incredible leadership.'
Sally Louise

Contents

Introduction

So, what is the Awareness Code and what makes its approach unique?

Anywhere two or more people gather for a purpose gives rise for the possibility of a leader taking responsibility. Leaders can be captains, governors, teachers, sporting legends, coaches, school prefects, CEOs, executive and non-executive directors, senior managers, entrepreneurial founders, current and aspiring presidents and prime ministers and commanders. The Awareness Code charts the spectrum of emotional and mental intelligence from our deepest inadequacies through to our heroic best and it offers a blueprint for how to rise up the scale of awareness to create Incredible Leadership and beyond.

Imagine being young and hearing for the first time names like London, Toronto, Sydney and Dubai and hearing about their culture but having no overview of where these places are arranged around the planet. Then you receive a map, a globe of the earth and you are immediately able to plan a 'world trip' with new wisdom and insight as to how you can proceed.

Leadership was in a similar situation with many human qualities or personality characteristics written and spoken about, but how do current and emerging leaders find the bigger picture that will bring all these attributes to life in one table? Chemistry has its Periodic Table. What is the atlas or Periodic Table for psychology? It is called the Awareness Code. Now it is here and about to be revealed to you.

This Code is a map that explicitly names the 100 attitudes, behaviours, thoughts, ideas and concepts that exist at each 100 'tiles' as they are now named. The 0 to 59 tiles are seen as tiles with limitations, Entrapments and lacking true power. Tiles 60 to 100 are empowered, have integrity and contain all the elements a leader aspires to, whereas tiles 0–59 are considered to belong to our Ego.

Let's look at what we mean by the Ego. It is the 'I' or smaller self of a person, the part of a person that separates itself out from the selves of others and from the objects of its thought. The Ego gathers ideas, beliefs, concepts, feelings and selects memories to support the stories that it gathers around these accumulations. In order to build an Ego self-image, the Ego uses its own judgement of itself as well as the judgement of others.

The Ego builds up self-esteem, self-confidence and self-promotion, or the lack of these things. It compares itself endlessly to others and wants to feel good about itself, often at the expense of others. It will defend its behaviours, even when others are affected negatively.

Ego says, 'It's okay to have some anger, worry, scepticism or some arrogance' because it is not aware of the consequences of these Ego traits.

The Ego is centred around getting what it wants, but at a deeper level there is another, wiser humanness that we will call the Higher Self (tiles 60–100). It is also known as the Soul, fundamental self, deeper self, quintessential self, ultimate self or higher conscience. It feels for how to break out of Ego behaviour, emotions and thoughts, and be truly free to express non-Ego that focuses on others' wellbeing.

People see these qualities in others and are inspired to find them in themselves. That is, to move from Ego self-based existence to a higher self-awareness until eventually one can live mostly, if not always, as the Higher Self. Importantly, the Awareness Code shows you a way out of the limited tiles and into the empowered tiles. The more you sit with each of the tiles or dispositions and contemplate how each is present in your life, the more the Code awakens within you so that it goes beyond something to consume as an intellectual endeavour.

It is absolutely clear that there is a fundamental link between the limited tile awareness and political, financial or personal under-performance, toxic cultures and conflicts in companies, organizations and the societies in which we operate.

The Awareness Code promotes a new paradigm of exposing the truth in any situation. Those accessing the above-60 tiles are at the forefront of a new paradigm where relationships and the welfare of our resources are a priority. A paradigm where we do not lose sight of the bigger picture as we negotiate many essential challenges such as:

- Being more ethically minded;
- Promoting transparency;
- Tackling climate change;
- Promoting equality;
- Understanding the impacts of global technology;
- Advocating equitable distribution of wealth and resources;
- Building companies that are not just profit driven;
- Championing solutions that promote the team and humanity.

The Awareness Code provides stepping stones into this paradigm, charting the spectrum of emotional intelligence from our deepest inadequacies through to our heroic best. It offers a blueprint for how to rise up the scale of awareness to improve leadership.

How Can the Awareness Code Improve Performance and Leadership Success?

There have been many attempts at improving leadership success, most focusing on one, two or a few important qualities or behaviours. Now we have 100 identifications of where you are currently at with your behaviour, attitude and performance and importantly, where you can get to and how to get to it. Using the geographic analogy again, an around-the-world trip is not linear – moving northerly, then southerly, perhaps backwards slightly – and big flights forward happen on the Awareness Code too. Another example is the game

Snakes & Ladders. In one day, we can move through many tiles and now we can trace where we are and learn how to live more in the Empowered above-60 tiles.

This book aims to inspire you to action a style of leadership that up until this point has been quite rare and sometimes only witnessed through periods of immense challenge – the springboard for inspirational and unprecedented problem solving. It also provides a map for the inspirational leadership qualities that have the capacity to address the huge challenges currently faced by our global community. This potential does not have to be a rare occurrence. The book exposes the gap in thinking that good leadership is rare and can only occur in often irreversible crisis situations. With over 57,000 books on leadership currently listed on Amazon, the message is pretty clear: we are searching for leaders of integrity and we do not need to wait for an irreversible crisis to create this style of leadership. We are facing challenges that can only be addressed through the unification of the globe beyond national or parochial interests. These challenges of climate, violence, prejudice, slavery and narcissism can all be reversed and it is definitely not too late. The book is a gift to each other and reminds us to move back towards a way of thinking and being that helps us all to flourish.

Where Did the Awareness Code Come From?

This book was born as a result of the combined efforts of the authors, who both come from completely different industries but met with the same questions and interest around why people continue to make poor choices in business or in their personal lives despite the best of intentions. Their collaboration over the last few years has birthed a blueprint that they have used in companies across the globe to transform these organizations by infusing the blueprint through the structure of the companies and solidifying their relationship with integrity. What this integrity looks like, feels like and sounds like has never been so precisely articulated and yet even though the map is explicit, the outcome of the application of the Awareness Code is different according to the needs of the company. It is not prescriptive.

What is Required of Me?

There are many ways to utilize the Awareness Code and we offer it as a lifelong learning tool. It can help you to go to the deepest levels of human nature and assist with any ongoing professional development. There will always be a tile to explore in more depth, always a person entering the team, or your life in general, who is displaying a tile that you realize you would like to know more about. Now that the Awareness Code has been released, its very existence and inherent nature assists those who invest in it to have greater access to the truth of whatever is being investigated.

Incredible Leadership addresses the challenges of the day in dynamic and unprecedented ways and the journey begins with reading this book, but it cannot end there. If you are genuinely committed to becoming an Incredible Leader, the process must go beyond the first reading. We recommend you engage in the suggested activities and programmes that will maximize your engagement with the Code and its potential to transform your leadership. Like any endeavour, any time you invest in the programme is for you and your growth, which translates into being a more aware, compassionate and effective leader. This requires effort and challenging lax belief systems that have become ineffective in directing real change.

Many books on leadership focus on one, two or a few aspects or qualities of a leader. This is useful but now you have the entire 100, all presented in a matrix that opens in direct relation to the degree that you put effort into it. Its deepest secrets require more than just a quick read.

Qualities like devotion, sincerity, altruism, embracing and open-minded will not just be words on a page as you will be shown how to action these dispositions. It starts with a daily practice, as recommended in the 25 keys to living the Code, in Chapter 19 (*see also* pp. 267–295). We also encourage you to actively use the App in order to familiarize yourself with the tiles that can entrap you in weak leadership, and learn how to free yourself from the Entrapments. Reading this book several times while using the App and actively committing yourself to a daily practice that invites mindfulness and contemplation is a starting point that begins your journey towards knowing yourself at levels that unleash your Incredible power. It needs dedicated and devoted effort, and also a passion for leading in a way that inspires people to act with integrity and on behalf of each other's and the planet's wellness. Are you willing to do that?

The Awareness Code charts the spectrum of the psychological intelligence, including emotions, thoughts and behaviours. We can now identify where we are individually and collectively as a team on this spectrum and begin to rise up towards Incredible Leadership.

The Authors Living the Code

The following examples illustrate how the two authors of this book, Steve Tappin and Wayne (Wayno) Linton, use the Awareness Code in their respective lives. The numbers in brackets correspond to the tile numbers, which will all be revealed later in Chapter 2.

Case Study – Wayno

Wayne (Wayno) Linton was three years old when he climbed into a rubbish bin, pulled down the lid and felt a wonderful sensation sweeping through him. His parents called out, but he couldn't be found. He was alone. It felt wonderful to be able to get away from everybody!

Later in life, Wayno felt that as a child he had loved silence. When asked to speak in front of a group, he felt a tension. He avoided groups and requested to be left out. He identified with having only one best friend, or none at all. He felt different to others and became anxious when he had to talk to any more than one person. Family was the exception. As a child, he would dig out an underground shelter and create 'special groups', always with just one other mate.

Wayno stayed mainly silent through school and university. Even when playing the highest level of football for Australia, he was a man of very few words. As a psychology teacher, he would deliver the class to the students and then stay mostly silent.

At 42, he felt adventurous and had a career change. He attained diplomas in hypnotherapy, psychotherapy and kinesiology. He travelled the world to learn directly from experts in many fields of health and healing and leadership. The thing that made him different was coming alive inside as he collaborated with unique people, masters in many parts of the world. He was owning his difference, realizing power, and began teaching about empowerment and being spontaneous as he truly felt these qualities inside of himself finally coming out.

Wayno had an underground room in his house and invited people to a group meeting, much as he had as that child 40 years earlier. He called it 'The Path of the Mystic'. That was 20 years ago and the group is still alive and thriving now, with passionate, dedicated members physically meeting once or twice a week. The teachings were originally given by Wayno but now all members are teachers in their own right. The meetings are based around the Awareness Code (which took 20 years to arrive as it is finally presented in this book) and how to live an Incredible life.

Wayno can still be found spending hours each day in the forest engaging with the Awareness Code Mastery Techniques. He has been able to penetrate deeply into Heart-bursting (97) (*see also* pp. 196–198) and not only talks about it at these gatherings, but radiates from that tile so that others can understand or have direct experiences of what it is like to live there.

From a hesitant boy not knowing what to do with his difference, he is now really enjoying bringing that difference to the group.

Case Study – Steve

Steve's loving mother once told him as a child that he could do anything and Steve still holds faith in that today.

In the early years of his career, Steve was working with the chemical giant ICI. He always wondered why some leaders and institutions couldn't be better in how they led. His life's work evolved to find new ways for leaders to create outperformance, build extraordinary companies, create trusting fellowships, and improve human performance.

ICI's fortunes turned around under the leadership of Sir John Harvey-Jones. After he left, Steve was mentored by his dear friend, Sir John Harvey-Jones.

Steve's mission since his mid-twenties has been to be a CEO's confidant, helping him/her to transform companies. His goal was to meet the world's top leading CEOs and be their confidant, and then coach the next generation of leaders. He has done this for many decades and he has created Xinfu, an award-winning global CEO coaching and consulting firm, and has personally coached, consulted, and interviewed over 500 global CEOs with assets of £8 trillion.

He was asked by the BBC to host the *CEO Guru* series on BBC World which featured him speaking to many of the world's top CEOs on CEO best practice. He also co-authored *The Secrets of CEOs: 150 Leaders on Business, Life and Leadership*, with a foreword by Richard Branson.

Steve is a China expert and an honoured and trusted friend to many of China's domestic entrepreneurs. He has also been a trusted confidant to the CEOs of a number of the fastest growing Chinese multinational companies.

So where did the focus on China start?

Back in 2008, Steve Tappin presented a keynote in New York City. He was then asked to visit China to coach Chinese leaders. They set up a two-way teaching session with Chairman Zhang Renmin, the iconic leader of Haier Group.

At the time in 2008, Steve struggled with making Chinese connections (Anxious, 26), but then he met Joe Baolin, who showed him a new way of approaching China by focusing on their Realizing Power (81). Joe assisted in setting up Harvard Center in China. Joe immediately inspired Steve, as he had suffered a spinal cord injury with a serious paraplegic disability and yet still devoted himself to completing the Gobi Desert 112km walk in Gansu in his wheelchair (Devoted, 93 and Extraordinary, 98). Steve visited China many times and with each visit, he started to feel a Devotion (93) to the people and his ability to help in a real way.

Joe and Steve built a close Fellowship Mindset (83). Joe connected Steve into the heart of the Chinese Entrepreneur Club (CEC), one of the most powerful networks of CEOs in the world. Steve and Joe eventually met over 100 Chinese leaders and together wrote *Dream to Last* in partnership with the CEC (Wow, 78). During the next decade, Joe taught Steve not to focus on what his company, Xinfu, wanted (Requesting, 39 and Attached, 36) but instead to build a deep understanding of China and to love its people (Reorientating, 64). Joe emphasized being a giver first (above 60) and the Chinese would respond to the Heartfelt (92) intention.

In October 2014, the BBC World television series *CEO Guru*, hosted by Steve Tappin, featured the China Entrepreneur Club (CEC). The CEC is a prestigious network of 52 of China's most elite entrepreneurs, whose businesses have a total equivalent wealth that is representative of 4 per cent of China's GDP. Members include Jack Ma of Alibaba Group, Wang Jianlin of Dalian Wanda Group, Liu Chuanzhi of Lenovo, and Li Shufu of Geely Automobile Holdings. Steve was the first Westerner to gain access to the CEC in order to interview Chinese CEOs for his books, *Secrets of Chinese CEOs: On Business, Life and Leadership in China and Dream to Last*. Through his unique experience, he brings to life the motivations of Chinese leaders, understanding how they tick and how best to work with them.

In 2019, Steve and Wayno introduced the Awareness Code to China for the first time, to a predominantly Chinese team working within a Western company. Many Sceptical (49) Westerners questioned whether the benefits of the Revelations in the Code were possible.

Would the translation of the meaning of the words work for them? Could the Chinese build Trust (73) and work collaboratively with Western teachers?

Also in 2019, an opportunity arose to work with another group in China, using the Awareness Code. The company Steve and Wayno worked with is a fast-moving consumer goods (FMCG) business, which had internal below-60 Entrapments to deal with, along with reputational issues working in China. Could the company come back after losing customers, damaging retailers' confidence and creating internal conflicts?

Steve and Wayno started by creating a space for the team to have an honest, courageous conversation about the realities impacting the company (Stepping In, 60s). They helped the team stop making Assumptions (below 60) and took them deeper into Truthful Realizations (60) around issues with the environment, talent and their competition. The fact was the team didn't really understand their competitors, who were changing all the time.

This was not an easy conversation to have and at times caused Chinese 'swirl outs', which occur when Westerners push them too much, or when they need a break but are afraid to voice it. Wayno highlighted that many Chinese women consider being nice, compliant and overly respectful to be great characteristics, but the downside of this way of being is that it can be interpreted as being subservient and submissive and leaders can take advantage of team members displaying these characteristics. Instead, it is much better to give your view from a place of higher awareness, boldly Stepping In with good intention (60s).

They became so Open (70s) that we were able to help the team enter this mindset and to have the confidence to step into a circle of trust. The team expressed who they really are in Chinese names such as 'Good Fairy', 'Big Fortune', 'Rockstar', 'Sufficient Supply'. From their life stories and deep beliefs, they created other messages, including 'Love conquers all', 'Speak from the heart', 'Challenge and with Kindness' and 'Resilience' (Transformating, 80s).

From this place of real conversations, being themselves and moving out of fear they crossed into true Fellowship (83) and explored how they could empower more families across China in a new way. They quickly shifted from a team of wonderful individuals to an incredible team of wonderful individuals. And at the same time, Steve was realizing one of his Highest Callings (80): to bring the newfound Awareness Code into the East and encourage the attainment of Extraordinary (98).

Later on, Steve and one of his closest Chinese fellowship connections, Liu Donghua, founder of the CEC and Z.H. Island Forum, co-created the first East meets West gathering with leaders of the West and leaders of Z.H. Island at Boao Forum for Asia (BFA). Z.H. Island is a China-based, high-end O2O networking platform of over 7,000 entrepreneurs. Together, they represent 16.7 per cent of China's GDP and these leaders all collaborate and support each other's businesses. The Code offers them a powerful technique to continue mapping the way forward for China.

Today, Steve aspires to support CEOs, future Presidents, and sporting and cultural icons all over the world in becoming extra-ordinary leaders.

Let's review

- The authors teach about the Code from a space of authenticity and direct experience.
- Their passion for sharing their life's purpose has transformed – and is transforming – leaders, teams and companies around the world.

PART I

REVEALING THE CODE

CHAPTER ONE

An Overview of the 10 Levels of the Awareness Code

Within all of us there is a deep awareness that there is more to who we currently are and what we do. Humanity has explored many types of external stimuli in order to transcend our ordinary awareness. Examples of this journey towards awareness are music, literature, dance, extreme sports, drugs, alcohol and many more.

Life is very complex. We suggest you see it as a jigsaw puzzle. The Awareness Code has identified the jigsaw pieces that make up the complexity and we call them 'tiles'. They are organized into 10 levels with 10 tiles in each. Therefore, we have 100 tiles or jigsaw puzzle pieces and the Awareness Code has put all these together to complete the puzzle for you. Instead of Wayno and Steve searching for the answer, together, they intuitively pieced together the Awareness Code and where all the tiles were to be located within the Code. Each tile is a way of perceiving the world, living, being, communicating, emoting and thinking. Some tile dispositions have more power, while others are limited in their capacity to drive change.

Your First Team

Think for a moment about when you were first involved in a team. Back at the start, whoever was your caregiver gave you the first experience and conditioning of what it is to be in a team. This is deeply embedded in you and is at a subconscious level. The caregiver(s) presented their style of leadership and you saw and heard it perhaps thousands of times. Did they role model fellowship, where everyone sat around to tell their story of the day, where beliefs or opinions and questions were valid and valued? Did the role modelling celebrate equality and a spirit of fellowship, or was it a top-down approach: 'do it my way or the highway', which is dominating and Controlling? Or perhaps it was something between these two extremes? This subconscious, initial leadership style can be your default when things are challenging or you are asked to deal with a crisis. However, it may not be in your awareness that this initial conditioning is part of who you are as a leader.

Your adult self generates a wiser approach by incorporating things you have read or seen modelled. These can be more caring and more inclusive. However, the original team is at your core. This is what you need to identify, realize and release from your life if this core, initial way of leading is not the best version of yourself. As you read through the next section, be aware of which levels your caregivers were operating from and where you operate from in times when all is going well, and then consider the times when the real challenges occur.

Let's start by looking at the spine of the Awareness Code. It contains 10 levels, each with 10 tiles. Each level has an underlying theme that further indicates what it is like to be operating from that particular level:

AC Level	Tiles
Beyond Incredible	100
Incredible	90–99
Transforming	80–89
Opening	70–79
Stepping In	60–69
Egotistical	50–59
Controlling	40–49
Wanting	30–39
Stressed	20–29
Despondent	10–19
Lifeless	0–9

Every waking moment of each hour of each day will have you operating from one or more of these levels. It is possible to be in one, two or even three levels at the same time. For example, you might be stressed about a public speech but you are still able to complete the task (Stepping In). You move up and down the Awareness Code ladder depending on external influences and inner mental, emotional and physical influences.

Let's take a brief look at each level to get a feel for the spine of the Code. We'll start with the core or the centre of the Ego dispositions: Wanting.

The Entrapment Levels

Which is the best order in which to read the levels and why?

Everybody relates to 'wanting' something. From an early age we want things that give us pleasure and we don't want those that bring displeasure or pain. So, we start here, at Wanting (30s). Now if we are not getting what we want, we have two ways to go in the Code. If we put more effort into Controlling (40s) the situation to get what we want, we go up the Code and if that is successful then we keep going up into pride or Egotistical (50s). Because so many leaders operate this way, we will look at this sequence first. Then we will begin to look at what happens when we don't get what we want and begin to feel disempowered, which is makes us feel Stressed (30s). If this worsens, we can drop into Despondent (10s) and finally, if we continue to not get what we want, we can find ourselves at the bottom of the Code in Lifeless.

All of these situations arise as a function of your Ego (as explained earlier in the introduction, *see also* p. 2). To break out of the Ego, we then look at the level of Stepping In (60s), where we really examine our wants and the degree of suffering they cause to self or others. We then ascend up through the Code from 70s, 80s, 90s to Beyond Incredible, finding more empowerment as we go.

Wanting, 30–39

This is all about trying to get what I think I want. Having a want is a type of personal motivation. There are potentially hundreds of wants that a leader generates in any given day. I can want others to improve, others to change, others to be more for the team. Interactions with others can be very transactional, where I see them as a means to an end. That end is what I want/don't want.

This may be to get something (money) or to not get something (retrenchment). If I can get what I want, it can become addictive. It can feel good to create harder and harder challenges to get what I want. There are two directions on the spine I can go when the start point is Wanting: up or down. One direction if I use pressure and manipulation to get what I want is to go up to Controlling.

Controlling, 40–49

This level is all about manipulation, consciously or subconsciously, to get what I *think* I want. Many controlling patterns are learned from a person's upbringing in early life. I learn to become agitated, disgruntled and irritated when I am denied getting things. This eventually builds so I need to blame others for things not working out in my life. It may be that I want something from the team or they want something from me. When that doesn't manifest, I blame them or someone else to take the heat off me, such as others' incompetence, ignorance, lack of intelligence or organization. If that works, and I get away with it, I will learn to do it more and may include nastiness and aggression to make my point.

Egotistical, 50–59

Having manipulated the situation to get what I want by being Controlling, I can sit back feeling pleased with myself that this is what I do to get what I want. I can justify and defend whatever it takes. I don't have to look at myself or how it affects others as my primary focus is on results that support my Ego. My Ego Confidence (57) grows as I learn to control more and more people or situations and my beliefs and opinions solidify and become 'me' and what I think is best. Without empathy, I become self-centred and even a 'know-it-all'. I am not open to being told any of this. Why should I change as I have learned how to get what I want? What's the problem?

Stressed, 20–29

The other direction I can go when I don't get what I want is downwards, towards being unsure, indecisive and stressed. Stressed is about what might happen in the future based on the past or the unknown. The uncertainty of not knowing activates psychological and physical tension. In its mildest form, I am unsure and hesitant. I do not feel safe or secure in a way forward. At its extreme, it is paralyzing my abilities. I can be a leader but I will be using terms such as 'I am worried about…' and 'I am paranoid about…' This gives permission for team members to be stressed as well, which detracts from the overall performance. I will not be able to move forward and into a new adventure because I have real or imagined evidence that something might 'go wrong'. This level is disempowering as it puts up a temporary barrier to the proposed change.

Despondent, 10–19

Here, it's hard to get going, to get motivated or to derive real meaning and purpose from the team's activities. The mindset is that whatever I do will be substandard, disappointing or unrecognized, or will not even be listened to, so why bother? There is the domain of being psychologically wounded or hurt and not really recovering from it. Also, it's a lack of motivation connected to not knowing what the purpose of the team is. I can be triggered into feeling like a victim and life can seem like it's unfair. I can be a leader but I am hypersensitive to the trigger that reopens any of my psychological wounds. I could be evasive and will find it hard to look at any areas of personal improvement or to bring to you what your areas of improvement might be. That's too vulnerable a place to be as it's close to my psychological wounds. I might try to play safe and withdraw.

Lifeless, 0–9

This is the most disempowered level. I am losing touch with what I want to succeed. My language is around failure and thoughts of not being good enough or useless are common. It is very hard to get motivated here. There is an underlying pervasive sense of unworthiness and a lot of self-blame can arise. It is very difficult to lead myself, let alone a group or team. The heavy weight of past condemnations pulls me down and I continually find evidence that I am not enough or that others or the team are better off without me.

The Levels of Revelation

Stepping In, 60–69

Here, you are able to assist as a leader by moving past any fear, limitation or pride. You are ready to 'have a go' or move towards an opportunity or new way of doing things. You can have a more positive mindset that is team orientated rather than me/selfish. It can be doing something for the first time. It can be volunteering when no one else will. It can be stepping out of your comfort zone. There may be an unknown or uncertainty about an outcome but that doesn't deter you. You are learning to orientate yourself in a new way and it has a positive, uplifting effect on yourself and others. You are becoming empowered and growing as a person with each stepping in. You are breaking patterns of pleasing or staying small.

Opening, 70–79

After you have stepped in, you are ready to open up. Here, you are feeling an inner enthusiasm and drive to become a better version of yourself. To do this, you just know you are to connect more to the unknown. You are ready to open up to new experiences. You begin to have more awareness by witnessing everything rather than reacting to what you think is happening or what you want to happen. Trust can build as you study the meaning of authenticity and what it takes to be truly authentic. Witnessing is observing without judging. Corrections can now be made and true collaboration occurs.

Transforming, 80–89

Transforming can happen after you have stepped in and opened up. You begin to properly embrace life, especially if you have been able to access your, or your team's, highest callings or purpose. This can generate intense levels of motivation. You would need to look carefully at how to realize your power and qualities and then how to bring them alive so that you maximize your value to the team. Do you know what your realizing value to the team is? Living at this level will lead you towards real, lasting integrity and becoming an inspiring leader in an ongoing way.

Incredible, 90–99

At the other end of the spectrum, if you learn to step in and open and transform yourself and others, the level of Incredible Leadership opens up for you. This happens when you are living daily from above 60. It is a wonderful experience when you feel grateful to be part of a team learning to maximize the potential of the individuals and the collective. Together, you and your team can thrive as dedication drives you. Results are only one part of the dynamics. The heart bursts for other reasons, not just results. We learn to surrender the type of Ego control that caused so much stress. It is replaced by a feeling of being able to achieve the extraordinary. You are like a magnet attracting what is required to you and your team. You are steadfast, compassionate and taking full responsibility for being the best you and your team can be. This responsibility is not a burden, it is a joy.

Limited Awareness issues are deep-rooted, making it very difficult to achieve changes. Many leaders may not recognize that they have Limited Awareness, which means they cannot emerge from the depths of lower awareness or advance through to Empowered Awareness. The challenges are significant and it is important to be able to understand your levels if you are to begin the journey towards your higher calling and become an Incredible Leader.

Beyond Incredible, 100

This is presented as a tile, not a level. Here, you experience the interconnection of all things. Instead of good or bad luck, you have come to realize that you cannot control each and every situation. You will have more involvement and responsibility and, whatever the outcome, you will be an example of persistence, patience, perseverance and goodwill. You sometimes overflow with how the power unleashed at this level can touch the lives of those you have come to be connected to. The bigger picture is always clear, no matter what mini-drama is going on around you.

Understanding How the Map Works

On the 100 table each horizontal level has 10 tiles. Each horizontal level isn't strictly a scale increasing in intensity as you move across the level and a person can move between them according to their issues and beliefs.

Below 60

Within each level the least entrapped tile of that level is found on the far right-hand side of the Code (all tiles ending in '9'). The most extreme version is on the far left of the Code (all tiles ending in '0'). As you move from the right to the left across the table in any one level, you increase the intensity of expression of that level, taking into account that adjacent tiles can reflect significantly different aspects of that level.

Above 60

Within each level the power of the tile increases as you move from the left side of the Code (0s) to the right (9s).

While each tile is unique and has its own 'stand-alone' characteristics, it is related to the adjacent tiles by belonging to that same horizontal line.

Is the Code like a ladder?

No. A ladder is strictly linear and one moves from the bottom rung to the top rung in a strictly vertical, sequential manner. The Awareness Code has both vertical and horizontal movements possible. Fully In (Tile 69) appears to be 'below' Receptive (Tile 70) but can potentially have more power.

The Awareness Code is broken down into two main sections – below 60, there are 60 tiles all relating to some kind of Entrapment. There is the least amount of awareness here and it is called Ego. It has six levels or development lines.

All of the 60–100 tiles are called Revelations as each one reveals a lot about how to live as more powerful leaders. Above 60, awareness is deep and empowered awareness, and there are four levels:

	100	90	80	70	60	50	40	30	20	10	0
Beyond Incredible											
Incredible											
Transforming											
Opening											
Stepping In											
Egotistical											
Controlling											
Wanting											
Stressed											
Despondent											
Lifeless											

Revelations

Entrapments

Higher Awareness ←→ Lower Awareness

Moving throughout the tiles is not as simple as going in numerical order but more in an individual, unpredictable way, depending on many variables. Some people may find themselves challenged in the levels of Despondent and Lifeless, so need to spend more time moving through Stressed, Wanting and Egotistical to get to the empowerment of Stepping In than someone already operating primarily at Egotistical. The phrase 'it is about the journey, not the destination' feels right in talking about moving through the Awareness Code. A leader can have a breakthrough and move into Transforming or Incredible for a week, day or hour before finding themselves returning to a below-70 tile because their Ego has reacted to something. A leader can move through many levels/tiles in one day or begin to stabilize in preferred above-60 tiles, no matter what happens in life.

Each level has a mental and emotional element that can often manifest itself physically. When we look at the below-60 tiles, e.g. the 0s level, we can then see the graduation from the darkest of each level to the lightest of each level, e.g. the 9s. For example, level 50 Egotistical ranges from Narcissistic (50) as the darkest of this level, to Not Buying In (59) as the lightest expression of this level.

Each level is like a miniature world in itself, with repetitive, predictable ways of seeing, behaving, eating, interpreting and basically living life. Each of us will most likely not operate at one level all the time. We operate from multiple tiles and can have several levels operating at any one time. So, someone at Pathetic (2), who is put in a room with Adventurous (66), would not be able to access the perspectives creativity and inner drive that Adventurous would be operating at. Adventurous may have greater capacity to understand the behaviours of Pathetic because intuition and empathy becomes available from 60 and increases in intensity up to 100.

AWARENESS CODE

			United	Doing the Impossible	Breathtaking	Miraculous	Mastery	Superhuman	Profound	100 Beyond Incredible
Incredible	90 Grateful	91 Sincere	92 Heartfelt	93 Devoted	94 Thriving	95 Compassion	96 Altruistic	97 Heart-bursting	98 Extraordinary	99 Revealing Grace
Transforming	80 Highest Callings	81 Realizing Power	82 Realizing Value	83 Fellowship Mindset	84 Embracing	85 Spontaneous	86 Off-the-charts	87 Integrating	88 Integrity	89 Inspiring
Opening	70 Receptive	71 Witnessing	72 Open-minded	73 Trustful	74 Connected	75 Collaboration	76 Emerging	77 Agile	78 Wow	79 Flowing
Stepping in	60 Realizing Truth	61 Ready	62 Preparing	63 Releasing	64 Reorientating	65 Positive	66 Adventurous	67 Conviction	68 Fearless	69 Fully In
Egotistical	50 Narcissistic	51 Arrogant	52 Know-it-all	53 Self-centered	54 Dismissive	55 Defensive	56 Pretentious	57 Ego Confidence	58 Complacent	59 Not Buying In
Controlling	40 Malicious	41 Enraged	42 Bully	43 Confronting	44 Deceiving	45 Resentful	46 Passive-aggressive	47 Annoyed	48 Frustrated	49 Sceptical
Wanting	30 Infatuated	31 Perfectionist	32 Addictive	33 Over-ambitious	34 Scheming	35 Competitive	36 Attached	37 Narrowing Down	38 Identifying	39 Ego-requesting
Stressed	20 Numb	21 Terror	22 Dread	23 Trapped	24 Frightened	25 Worried	26 Anxious	27 Over-pleasing	28 Insecure	29 Hesitant
Despondent	10 Inconsolable	11 Hopeless	12 Unfulfilled	13 Lethargic	14 Wounded	15 Hurt	16 Saddened	17 Disconnected	18 Discontented	19 Disinterested
Lifeless	0 Self-loathing	1 Self-hatred	2 Pathetic	3 Unlovable	4 Burden	5 Embarrassed	6 Wrong	7 Regretful	8 Never Enough	9 Inadequate

There are larger versions of the full Awareness Code at the front and back of this book, which you can refer to throughout your journey.

Activity

- Close your eyes and simply notice the breath enter and leave your body. Spend five minutes doing so.
- It is a simple task. Notice any commentary about this that arrives in your awareness. Do you launch into the activity? Do you wish to skip this part and read on? Do you notice your tiredness? Do you notice the beauty that is your life? Your awareness can take you anywhere according to your consciousness level. This simple activity can alert you to where your mind goes and the type of mind you employ. If you are too agitated, try this activity later.
- As a starting point for opening up the tiles and understanding how they can become alive for you choose a row in the Entrapments part of the Code that catches your eye. For example, you may choose the row Stressed.
- Allow the process to be spontaneous and don't think too much about it.
- Of all the tiles listed in the row you have chosen, select two or three that feel like they are where you might have work to do. For example, these could be Worried and Over-pleasing.
- On a daily basis, do your best to be aware of the tiles and what circumstances take you in and out of each one.
- Do you have any control over how the situation, where the tile is present, unfolds?
- If the tile is below 60, do you know a practical way to get out of the negative pattern?
- Allow someone to give you feedback on their version of you in any one of the three identified tiles.
- Engage a team or family member to share your/their ideas and learn from each other.

Will the Awareness Code Open for Me?

What kind of person is 'ready' to learn from the Awareness Code (AC)? At what stage in our development should we be before we can enter its code? Is there an aliveness and intelligence inside of you waiting for this code to unlock you?

The Awareness Code is more than a list of 100 powerful words laid out to be read and understood in the first reading. A living tapestry of your leadership and life, which shows exactly where you are at any moment, it doesn't contain any 'how to' instructions. There are definitions, explanations and examples provided for each tile, along with 25 keys to help you move out of the Entrapments (0–59) and into Revelations (60–100). Also, those key strategies assist you to move towards increasingly powerful tiles from 60–100.

Every time you contemplate the AC with a view to understanding yourself, your team or someone else, you potentially activate a part of your mind that has the answers to how you are to move forward.

The Code is an instrument waiting for you to play, much like a musical instrument. In the hands of some, the violin will remain a mystery and give forth a cacophony of sound in response to the person who will not approach it with respect and a keenness to practise. It cannot be made to release a symphony without the player learning what it takes to play the virtuoso with the violin.

So, it comes as no surprise that attitude is the key and a person's awareness creates the attitude that is adopted. Every level of the Awareness Code gives forth a different attitude. From the heaviest, darkest most 'lost' place of Self-loathing (0) to the amazingness of Beyond Incredible (100), there are many versions of being human. If you approach the Code from anywhere in the bottom 59 tiles of the Code, called Entrapments, you will be limited in what you can receive from its potential. You will use it to reinforce what you already think you know and how you operate in the world and to judge yourself and others. If you are only able to read the Code from the awareness of one of the Entrapments, no one should judge or condemn you for that.

The last Entrapment before the Code opens up into deeper and more wonderful Revelations is 'Not Buying In' (59). This needs to be at least temporarily transcended for true insight and understanding of the Revelations to emerge.

It is important to give you a heads-up on what can assist you in working through the Code:

The Ego is the home of the 59 Entrapments and cannot feel or experience anything above 59.

When presented with the Code, the Ego's role is to judge and operate 'on its own terms', with what it currently believes. It is resistant to anything that is above 60 and even pretends to be above 60 itself (Pretentious, 56). It operates by being Sceptical (49) because it cannot experience the truth of above 60. It can dismiss (54), thinks it already knows and is above 60 (52) and may even become Frustrated (48) that it's not getting this 'Code thing'! Remember, we build our Ego until we are ready (62) to operate from above 60. The more we operate from above 60, the less useful the Ego becomes. Your Ego will come up with a multitude of reasons for why above 60, the Code doesn't work. But you are much more than your Ego or personality. While the Ego Mind senses a purpose, which we will look at later, it is not the Ego that will unlock the Code – it is an above-60 non-judgemental tile that does that.

The big question is: are you ready for the power that is awaiting you as an Incredible Leader? Are you ready to ask yourself the difficult questions? Are you ready to do the work required to move out of below-60 Entrapments?

Let's address the following 10 fundamental points before you even start working on the Leadership Awareness Code.

1) Are you ready to be challenged around your integrity? Be ready to learn about its value and how it will change your life. Are you prepared for a life of integrity?

2) Are you ready to have your psychological profile investigated? It is important for you to have an understanding of your own psychological patterns, disorders and traits.

3) There is more to wellness than paying attention to the symptoms. Let's create a deep wellness from today onwards that takes into account food/drink intake, exercise, sleep and anything that affects wellbeing. Are you ready to have a daily uplifting practice for the leadership you are looking to find?

4) Your energy levels will be a key to your future as a leader. This is one area almost completely overlooked in preparation for great leadership and leads to burnout and chronic fatigue. Are you ready to receive the techniques that will develop you to recharge, rejuvenate and build a stronger internal energy battery that will provide greater quality and quantity of energy than your current condition?

5) Are you ready to accept that everything changes all the time? Be ready to change when you read the Code.

6) Are you ready to slow things down? The Code is designed for you to read, then contemplate. Read, then meditate. Do this daily from now on. Be ready to meditate on the Code even if you don't know how. Sit with what you have read in silence.

7) Are you ready to change deeply held perceptions of yourself? You are much more than what you believe yourself to be. Be ready to find out more about you and that which is available, through using the Code to help you.

8) Are you ready for a profound connection with yourself and others? Be ready to learn how to do that and move towards love as a way of life.

9) The world needs you well if you are to lead well into the future.

10) You are currently underusing your mind capacity. There are different levels of mind: Ego, Witness and Wisdom. How do we access these deeper minds? We need specialized techniques that are well-tried and tested and known to work. Are you ready to learn them and incorporate them so as to find the Revelation tiles 60 to 100?

If you are ready in most – if not all – of those areas, the Code will open and your Wisdom Mind will answer. Ego will create expectations and demands and not choosing the forcefulness of Ego requires patience, perseverance and the qualities associated with the Revelations of 60 to 100 in the Awareness Code. These qualities are waiting for you to discover and action, they are not in the Code. They are in you and the Code is the technique or key. Read on:

How to apply this chapter

- Choose two lower tiles or Entrapments that stand out for you. Also, choose one higher tile or Revelation that stands out for you.
- Read the notes addressing these specific tiles.
- On a daily basis, do your best to be aware of the tiles and what circumstances take you in and out of each.
- Do you have any control over how the situation, where the tile is present, unfolds?
- If your reaction is below 60, do you know a practical way to get out of the negative pattern?
- Allow someone to give you feedback on their version of you in any one of the three identified tiles.
- Engage a team or family member to share ideas together and learn from each other.

Let's review

- The Code is divided into the Entrapments and the Revelations and the former creates a negative effect while the latter is life-affirming.
- The spine of the Code reveals the six levels of Entrapment and the four levels of Revelation.
- Each level has 10 specific tiles that reveal the degree to which a person is trapped or free.

- The tiles reveal various attitudes or dispositions. Attitude is the key and awareness creates attitude.
- Are you ready for the Code? There are 10 fundamental questions to use to ascertain your readiness.
- We include a description of the lower tiles, with the toughest gateway being 58/59 – the comfort zone.
- The antidote to being entrapped is Stepping In (60) to the Revelations.

CHAPTER TWO

How the Code will be Revealed in the Coming Chapters

In the Egotistical level, the extreme expression is Narcissistic at 50, while the mildest expression, Not Buying In, is at 59. However, for the levels Stepping In through to Incredible, the mildest form is at and the strongest and most powerful expression of the level ends with. So, at level Opening tile Receptive is the beginning of finding your power in this level and by Flowing at 79, a person has mastered the level of Opening.

As you explore each of the levels or rows you may be called to explore various tiles that relate specifically to you. At Wanting, for example, you may be called to look at Perfectionist at Narrowing Down at and Competitive at. You may like to explore every tile in that level to really understand the level deeply. It is recommended that you familiarize yourself with the tiles at each level before exploring the next.

To begin to work with the Code we need to start by exploring one level and the logical, thinking mind says to present the levels from 0 to 100. That is linear, rational and familiar. However, the Awareness Code has a life of its own and the highest potential for your entry, engagement and deep understanding of the Code is to present the development lines in the following way:

Levels:

Wanting	Controlling	Egotistical	Stressed	Despondent	Lifeless	Stepping In	Opening	Transforming	Incredible	Beyond Incredible
3	4	5	2	1	0	6	7	8	9	10

Let's look at this closely. We could start at level 0 Lifeless, but many leaders and potential leaders do not resonate with this so we will begin to unravel the Code by starting at level 3, which every leader can relate to. Instead, most people are able to relate to Wanting as we all started our life using these tiles to varying degrees. We want, desire and crave various things throughout the day so there is the potential for the reader to see how this level works and how the tiles within it may have already been mastered in some areas of life.

What happens if a person does not get what he or she wants? A leader, or any one of us, can go to Controlling at level 4 and try to manipulate the environment to ensure the outcome is realized.

If a leader is successful in getting what he wants by Controlling the situation there is the potential for him to become Egotistical (level 5) and believe all he needs to do is keep Controlling the situation and he will keep getting what he wants regardless of the consequences. Another option for a leader if he does not get what he wants could be to begin to feel Stressed at level 2. If this stress is not addressed, he can become even more Disempowered and Despondent, at level 1, or finally arrive at Lifeless, level 0. The following chapters will describe in detail each of these levels in this order to highlight common erroneous thinking patterns.

These levels do not create good leadership or societies and to move away from these a leader needs to Step In to level 6 through tile 60. This is where a leader lets go of the Ego-thinking Mind and 'feels' intuitively for a more courageous way forward. This is the beginning of integrity and where true leadership begins. As a leader masters staying in Integrity, higher levels of awareness open up. A leader is more Open at level 7 and can, along with the team, become Transformating at level 8. To go any further means a person's heart is asking for Incredible

Leadership at level 9 and the tiles in this level are integrated in a way that deeply inspires those exposed to this level of leadership. Finally, the mastery and amazingness of level 10 – Beyond Incredible – can be revealed.

It is also useful at this point to say that the first three levels – Lifeless, Despondent and Stressed – have access to little energy, with Lifeless at the lowest. To live at these levels means aligning with the victim part of the Thinking Mind, which is explored further in Chapter 15 (*see also* pp. 217–237). Here, a person has negative self-judgement and believes in stories that are unable to grasp positive outcomes. Victim stories are suffering stories. Living in any tile at these levels is to live an unempowered existence accompanied by the feeling of not being able to influence the team in an uplifting and inspiring way.

One way a leader can lift himself out of these three levels of victim is to move to the levels of Wanting, Controlling and Egotistical. These levels avoid the state of suffering and promote the perpetrator state of Thinking Mind. People at these three levels are called perpetrators because the motivation behind any of the tiles is self-promotion, self-interest and self-proclamation. If a perpetrator can get the other person to go down into victim mode, usually that perpetrator can get what he wants. Victims, in turn, will look for a situation in their own lives where they can get out of the suffering and feel the pleasure of being the perpetrator. Like a yo-yo, we can go up and down from perpetrator to victim to perpetrator to victim. Often in the course of one day, this can happen many times, which is dependent on who we associate with and the tiles from which each person operates.

So, let's go back to the level of Wanting. In the following pages you will learn about this level and the 10 tiles that show the progression from mild entrapment towards being fully entrapped in this level. After each tile exploration there is a table of four statements or beliefs that entrap or further embed a person in the perpetrator's way of thinking. These beliefs are a part of a person's story and lock him into that tile. Next to each negative statement there is a corresponding Revelation statement that overrides the negative belief and can help a person move out of the Entrapment. The right-hand column with the recontextualized statements is where the power is. We have also recommended ways to approach the negative trap by offering a tile to study that is 60 or above. Next to this tile recommendation there are also numbers that represent the keys you may like to consider to really let go of the debilitating negative thinking. The 25 keys are explored in detail in Chapter 19 (*see also* pp. 267–295).

The Awareness Code App

We have created an Awareness Code App. The App is designed to allow real-time access to the Awareness Code. Search 'Awareness Code' in the App Store. You can use the app for goal setting, journalling and diarizing activities as well as receiving feedback from your team/fellowship. It can also be used to make shifts when you are below the line to becoming above 60.

In the App, we have identified 10 Entrapment statements that help users identify what has led to a specific tile. For example, if you are Frustrated, 48 – the statement is 'I don't like what just happened', and then you are shown how to be released from the Entrapment. By following the App you are led to an above-60 tile, e.g. Agile, 77. The App also expands on some of the keys in Chapter 19 (*see also* pp. 267–295), showing how you can bring the higher tile into your daily life.

Please be aware as you are working through the book that there can be layers of complexity involved. Moving out of an Entrapment and into a Revelation statement can mean doing some deep exploration. There can be a lot of pain and we highly recommend working with a trained therapist if you find the Code brings out difficult feelings. However, just reading about how to move out of the Entrapment can be of great benefit. Feeling for the truth can move you out of an Entrapment by itself. Contemplate the information provided and allow it to inform you. Being with the statements continuously leads to a more empowering tile. What will it take to stay with the positive statements instead of going back to the familiarity of the old story?

So, here is the Code. Enjoy!

Essential Terminology

Although these terms will be discussed in greater depth in Chapter 15 (*see also* pp. 217–237), it is useful to have a broad understanding of what each of the following terms mean before continuing to read.

Ego-thinking Mind – Below 60

Operates below 60 and is 'I' centred. It is the part of the mind that processes through judging some situations as bad and others as good, related to survival. Often it is that part that will not be silent when an attempt to meditate is made. This chatter can sometimes take up to 20 minutes or more to dissipate before a deeper mind can be accessed. In this mind, duality or opposites exist that are in competition with each other. You will hear about it in the coming chapters described as the victim part of the Ego and transition to a more powerful mind (tiles 0–29) and the perpetrator part of the Ego Mind (tiles 30–59). The Awareness Code shows you how to minimize the use of this mind.

Witness Mind – 60 and above

This part of the mind is 'we' centred, opens up at tile 60 and is solidly in place by tile 79. It is the realm of integrity. Instead of not listening to or shutting down that part of the duality that is not agreed with, the Witness Mind creates gentle enquiry, spaciousness to respond and avoids a right/wrong perspective. There is an inclusiveness that addresses the wellbeing of others, not just one's own personal survival. We can separate this mind out more specifically into two parts.

Liberating Mind – 60–69

This is part of the Witness Mind and is the first appearance of Higher Self. It is capable of exposing, understanding or realizing some below-Ego behaviour in a way that the Ego cannot. It can act upon such realizations and move towards change. Non-judgemental, non-reactive, inclusive, flexible and always seeking more context, it doesn't assume or expect like the Ego but instead wonders at how things might be and how a win-win scenario can occur.

The Discerning Mind

By constant witnessing this mind understands by reason, connecting the dots, accepting others and a willingness to learn and grow. Now that the liberating mind has freed a leader up from a below-60 Ego trait, the leader is open to liaise, arbitrate, guide, mediate, facilitate and generate a 'we' rather than an Ego culture. Impartiality, unprejudiced and unbiased, the Discerning Mind reinforces the win-win scenario.

Wisdom Mind – 80 and above

This part of the mind emerges as a person solidifies in functioning through the Witness Mind. It is the beginning of Transforming at tile 80 and is the gateway to Unity Mind. It grasps the bigger picture, the higher calling and the hidden meaning to much of what it encounters. A much more embracing and attentive mind, the heart is involved and compassion comes naturally. The Wisdom Mind is even more intuitive than the Witness Mind. Both Witness and Wisdom Minds are empowered. This means that they work through to the 60–99 tiles. Creative, innovative, resolving and advocating are features of how it works.

Unity Mind or 'Oneness Mind' – Beyond Incredible 100

This part of the mind is very difficult to describe. Here, the leader feels 'at one' with the team; wonder replaces stress, humility is the foundation of all behaviour, feeling blessed is a daily experience and any chosen endeavour that is actioned intrinsically supports human evolution and the awakening of spiritual oneness.

How to apply this chapter

Finally, before you open up the Awareness Code, consider two things with regards to leadership right now:

1) *What would you like to resolve? What is not working for you?*
   Answer the questions from a space where the answer is about you rather than what other people in the team should or should not be doing.

2) *With regards to your leadership, what is your preferred future? Do you have a vision?*
   After you have read the tile descriptions, come back to what you have identified here in your response. See if you are closer to a resolution and to creating or living that leadership. Now read the entire book and return to what was not resolved and what you have identified as your future. Has anything changed? The Awareness Code is going to give you multiple ways to resolve identified challenges and design your future.

PART 2

TRAPS TO ACCESSING POWERFUL LEADERSHIP – THE PERPETRATORS

CHAPTER THREE

Leaders Who Want Their Way

Opening up the Awareness Code at Wanting

Let's start exploring the Code more deeply by starting with Wanting, which is at the centre of the lower tiles. As mentioned earlier, we start here because it is an intrinsic part of the human condition. Leaders who function from the tiles 30–59 are entrapped in the belief system that the end justifies the means. The outcome is the most important factor and any means available to achieve that outcome is justified. They become the perpetrators, using their Thinking Mind to avoid being a victim.

30–39: The level of Wanting

30	31	32	33	34	35	36	37	38	39
Infatu-ated	Perfec-tionist	Addict-ive	Over-ambitious	Scheming	Com-petitive	Attached	Narrowing Down	Identi-fying	Ego-requesting

Humans look to get what they want: first to survive, then to find pleasure or avoid displeasure to survive. Leaders survive by having a want, or a **don't** want. 'I want more autonomy.' 'I want to be valued.' 'I want to make a difference'. 'I want a more comfortable office chair.' 'I want to be the best.' 'I want the best-performing team.' 'I want to make the most money.' We have a part of our minds that generates non-stop wants so that we have a sense of safety, security, control and wellness. **Wants** generate expectations.

Who doesn't engage in wanting? As a child, I wanted food, attention and toys. The list is endless. The more pain or suffering created by the negative story, the more important it is to generate a want to take me away from the displeasure. Even thinking about getting something can provide relief from uncertainty, loneliness, boredom or any other below-30s malady.

The idea is to move from the 30s through all the tiles 40–60, learning the mechanisms of each one and eventually transitioning into 60 and beyond. And if a person doesn't, then there is a type of developmental delay where that person is acting 'immaturely' and the awareness of a more mature way is not yet available.

How Do I Go from Wanting to Whatever Replaces It?

Before launching into this level, a further clarification is required. Let's look at the mildest version of Wanting at tile 39, called Ego-requesting. What's the problem with requesting? If you don't ask, you won't get what you want, right? It comes down to **how** it is asked and what sits behind the request. Ego thinks of itself and not the other people in the team. It is selfish and there is a different experience for a member when the leader is wanting from Ego-requesting compared to **asking** from above 60. The above-60 leader is interested and motivated by what is actually, really needed or essential rather than what is 'thought' by the Ego to be important or wanted. The Witness Mind is much more capable of intuitively connecting to what they, the team or the situation, specifically needs in order to move on. Above 60, the leader is connected to what's **best** for the relationship of the team. It's not about being self-serving, it's about serving others while creating the best version of yourself. Such requesting feels inclusive and validates the team's requirements. A leader above 60 has access to the Witness Mind that can read the context more than the Thinking Mind can, so the request comes from a space that has taken more things into account. A type of 'knowing' what's required replaces wishing, hoping, guessing or demanding what we think is required. Let's look at each tile in turn. At Ego-requesting (tile 39), the want is not as intense as it is Infatuated (tile 30).

Ego-requesting, 39

All living organisms, including humans, have basic needs such as food, liquid and territory in order to survive. Sustaining life is the basic priority and arises as an innate impulse to continue existing. The need to procreate to maintain survival of the species is another example. But what happens if my basic needs are met and I want more or start believing I should actually have more than what I have?

The answer: I'll compare my situation to others and desire more. I do not even have to think about this, it can just arise by itself, like a wave on the ocean. By simply viewing an external situation/object, the longing to have it arises and the prospect of having/possessing that which is presented releases a pleasurable response.

Hoping to have something is initially an experience of wishing, and daydreaming can occur, which can all be potentially pleasing or pleasurable. Just thinking about it is the start required to activate this tile. The next step is to ask for it, either in my own head or from someone else or the team.

Whether something is actually really required to sustain life (a need) or to stimulate pleasure (e.g. a fantasy) can be very subjective. I can 'talk myself into' anything being essential, so Requesting covers both an objective, measurable need, e.g. hunger, to pleasurable dreaming of something to get me away from the displeasure of Lifeless, Despondent and Stressed. Moving beyond a vague feeling of hoping for something better towards deepening the want leads to the next tile. I do this by Identifying with something.

ENTRAPMENTS: UNHEALTHY SELF-TALK – 39 – Ego-requesting	GUIDANCE TO MOVING FORWARD TO A NEW MINDSET – 39 – Ego-requesting
What's in it for me?	What is the pay-off for me wanting this? Why do I make it about me and not the team or bigger picture? What would it take to do the latter? *Tile 83: Fellowship Mindset – Keys: 1, 2, 3, 4, 5, 14, 19.*
How can I get away from this pain (below 30)?	Can I slow down enough to feel the nature of discomfort or pain of below-30 experiences and the memory or emotion behind it? I will have to get into the 60s to do this. It's best to release it (63) and not keep suppressing it. *Tile 63: Releasing – Keys: 1, 2, 3, 5, 6, 7, 8, 9.*
I can be involved if I can get something from it.	It is easier to be in the 30s than in the 60s. Less effort, concentration, energy. However, it is more rewarding personally if you get to the 60s and don't have to be preoccupied by getting something. *Tile 94: Thriving – Keys: 1, 2, 3, 6, 7, 14, 16, 21.*
I scan life for signs of things that I believe can help me feel good.	What does 'good' mean? Is it deep and ongoing like a constant source of BEING any of the above-60 tiles? *Tile 96: Altruistic – Keys: 1, 2, 3, 5, 6, 7, 16.*

Identifying, 38

This tile arises when the number of things I encounter in daily life is such that requiring or wanting all of them would be problematic. It makes sense to search around my marketplace, home and social life to see what interests me enough so that I can place my energy and time in imagining what it would feel like to acquire that 'thing'. So, I search for meaning and scan the various objects on offer and whether or not the object fits with the self-identity I am constructing as 'me'. The authentic reasons why something appeals, repels, attracts or disgusts may not be available in the awareness at this level. I just feel compelled to act in a way to get what I identify with according to the many programmes and stories I have running below the surface of awareness. I can create any number of 'reasons' why I have a preference with little understanding of how that preference came about and if I am actually bound to it.

At this tile, I go into detective mode, searching for something to stimulate a good feeling or ease a negative feeling. The focus is 'me' rather than 'us' oriented and the objective is not the best outcome for the team, rather how to avoid feeling bad and increase feeling better. Either way, identifying is a means of finding what I believe I have to have or to get in order to have a certain experience. Teenagers can often move from one group to another, identifying with one way of being in friendship and finding out that it does not suit and moving into another identity. This does not need to be a negative process if a person is aware that a particular identity is being explored without identifying with it.

My Ego is made up of different roles, sub-personalities or archetypes. Each of these may have a significantly different identity to the other so that the identity can fluctuate and even radically shift when each part is present. What one part wanted one moment can change dramatically or subtly when another part of us comes to the surface. This can often lead to a feeling of inner conflict or incongruency. Identifying tries to simplify often conflicting internal requirements and then I distinguish a way of focusing to get what I have identified as essential. Variations include associating, linking, labelling and comparing.

ENTRAPMENTS: UNHEALTHY SELF-TALK – 38 – Identifying	GUIDANCE TO MOVING FORWARD TO A NEW MINDSET – 38 – Identifying
To get what I want, I must identify with some external group or person.	I am to find what I am not by experimenting with identifying with others. With each realization of 'Oh, I am not that,' I am getting closer to who I really am. *Tile 76: Emerging – Keys: 1, 2, 3, 4, 6, 7, 8.*
Through identifying, I get something – a belief, belonging or security.	I may have identified very strongly with Mum, Dad, my nuclear family and not developed my true identity. There may be a stuck-ness on how to break out of this identity. The rebel is one way. Above 60 will feel more experimental. At 66, it is adventurous and at 85, there is lightness and openness to do that as it is spontaneous. *Tile 66: Adventurous – Keys: 1, 2, 3, 4, 6, 7, 8, 14.*

I will join in where it seems there is something I will get from it.	I am going to join in where there is something to give. How could not getting anything at all help with my identity? *Tile 90: Grateful – Keys: 1, 2, 3, 4, 6, 7, 14.*
In movies, books and life I identify with that which brings me pleasure or takes me away from displeasure.	This is Ego Mind. Is there anything that neither gives me pleasure nor takes away displeasure? What is the feeling of that? This can be any one of the above-60 tiles. I am to find out what the replacement is. *Tile 95: Compassion – Keys: 1, 2, 3, 4, 6, 7, 14.*

Narrowing Down, 37

Narrowing down the awareness on one thing is now required as the identification process only brings general wants into awareness. As the interest intensifies, a more specific attention is required to increase the likelihood of getting what I feel, or believe I want. Narrowing down is the attitude of eliminating peripheral wants so as to zoom in on something specific. Let's specialize, let's not confuse, but minimize options and simplify. From the many possible options available at Ego-requesting, we identify the general area that will meet the want, then hone in on the specific at this tile, narrowing down. As the want centres on my own self, narrowing down can appear very beneficial in gaining what I want, but it can blur or even miss what the consequences are for other people. It can be so practised and strongly present that it can block unwanted or non-pleasurable consequences for me as the focus is on the pleasant feelings generated in getting and having what is wanted. This is limited awareness as the bigger picture may require feeling uncomfortable for a while until a new skill is learned or the challenge of incongruent attitudes is worked through collaboratively.

Narrowing down can eliminate or discard superfluous requirements or wants that are not a priority. It also means I can miss opportunities because I have blinkers on and am only focusing on what I have narrowed down to. Each Entrapment creates a story that is limiting in some way and narrowing down eliminates options that may have served the person and others. I now have a want that has become more personally important for me to have, so I curtail possibilities, refine choices, categorize, whittle down, downsize and zero in on that which I require, often not seeing what others require as I narrow down. I begin to lose sight of the bigger picture by shrinking the options, reducing possibilities and scaling back from the unknown.

ENTRAPMENTS: UNHEALTHY SELF-TALK – 37 – Narrowing Down	GUIDANCE TO MOVING FORWARD TO A NEW MINDSET – 37 – Narrowing Down
That one thing is becoming increasingly important for me to own, possess and have.	How much energy is this taking that I could place elsewhere? Why this? What positive outcome could happen if I didn't have this? *Tile 63: Releasing – Keys: 1, 2, 3, 4, 6, 7, 8, 14.*
Something new has taken my attention and it can feel good if I focus on having it or doing it.	What areas of my life remain under-developed due to little attention? Can I redirect this attitude to the Awareness Code? *Tile 66: Adventurous – Keys: 1, 2, 3, 4, 6, 7, 14.*
The more I focus on this, the more I can understand it. But I exclude other potentially important things and people.	I am going into a dot. I can get lost in a dot. How do I go back towards the circle? (*See also* pp. 239–241.) *Tile 84: Embracing – Keys: 1, 2, 3, 4, 6, 7, 14.*
I don't want to let go of this.	Where is the balance? Is this healthy? Is it making me a better person? *Tile 77: Agile – Keys: 1, 2, 3, 4, 6, 7, 8, 14.*

Attached, 36

Attachment arises because I narrow down and become focused on what I want, investing time and energy in some ongoing capacity. I constantly remind myself of the importance of staying connected to and eventual possession of the desired object, person or outcome. This focus is to ensure I get what I want. I can physically attach in many ways, such as not being able to start the day without a coffee. A person can symbolically attach, such as signing an agreement to lead a new project. A person can also emotionally or mentally attach, such as I believe I must have the final say.

The greater the perceived requirement, the more potential for attachment and more narrowing down can occur so that my desired person, object or outcome becomes attainable. The 'want' becomes more of my identity and I become more needy. Wanting grows through placing more time and energy in this way at these Entrapments. It seems like greater security or safety as attachment grows but it may be at the expense of independence or a sense of a strong self or autonomy. Dependency can arise. Ego identity is very much defined by what the individual can collect around himself, hence the importance of not just wanting but getting what is wanted.

Attachment then anchors or eventually cements into place all the parts of the identity that Ego has collected in order to be itself. Without them, what is Ego? Its existence is based on what it gathers around itself. The 'other' person can feel tethered or unhealthily bound to me if attachment prohibits freedom. Attachment can set up expectations of other people in unhealthy ways. We become bound up, cemented in, tethered, chained and tied to some idea or ideal.

ENTRAPMENTS: UNHEALTHY SELF-TALK – 36 – Attached	GUIDANCE TO MOVING FORWARD TO A NEW MINDSET – 36 – Attached
I have finally found a friend, an ally. I am not letting go easily.	My job, position, partner, they are available for me to enjoy while they are there – a day, a lifetime. Attachment tries to hold on when it may be time to let go. *Tile 77: Agile – Keys: 1, 2, 3, 4, 6, 7, 8, 14.*
I have found something pleasurable, I must hang on to it.	I never own anything. It is all passing through my hands, on loan to me. The ground beneath me is not truly mine, even if I have a piece of paper that says so. *Tile 77: Agile – Keys: 1, 2, 3, 4, 6, 7, 8, 14.*

If I keep expecting something from the person or object then that will keep me connected to it/them.	This puts pressure on the other person. I'll make the transition from 'I' to 'we' focus. *Tile 77: Agile – Keys: 1, 2, 3, 4, 6, 7, 8, 14.*
Daydreaming and fantasizing keeps me thinking about it or them when I haven't got them physically.	This can be advantageous if healthy and above-60 qualities are being exchanged. It can also be draining and a distraction if it's just pleasure seeking. *Tile 64: Reorientating – Keys: 1, 2, 3, 4, 6, 7, 8, 14.*

Competitive, 35

Competition arises when there is an external opponent or opposition to acquiring what I want. There is someone to beat or compete against that energizes the Wanting. This intensifies the effort required to get what I want and more energy moves to the competitive behaviours in order to achieve success. The beliefs embedded in the story that action the Wanting drive the behaviour, which then creates emotional charge, which then fuels the original story and so on. This can play out in many different ways. For example, there can be an inner competition with an internal opponent called the saboteur or judge. This inner voice can be insisting that I will not have what I want, so I go into competitive mode to combat or suppress that inner critic to achieve the desired outcome.

Competitive ups the ante, provides more focus and more narrowing down. The urge to get what I want replaces the urge to survive or live and can become all-consuming to the detriment of others and self as I can neglect other areas of responsibility in order to win the competition.

Competition evokes a win/lose scenario, with rival egos competing against me. This can put time pressure on me as it turns into a race. Vying is pressure, rivalling is pressure. The prospect of losing is pressure. Competition among team members works against the cohesiveness of the fellowship. Variations of this energy are: ruthless, win at all costs, merciless, cut-throat and dog-eat-dog. Vying for position, pushy and combative also exist here.

ENTRAPMENTS: UNHEALTHY SELF-TALK – 35 – Competitive	GUIDANCE TO MOVING FORWARD TO A NEW MINDSET – 35 – Competitive
I want the success I see others having. What will it take for me to get that success?	How can I feel good when I am not winning? Striving can be the way I learn and measure success. *Tile 94: Thriving – Keys: 1, 2, 3, 4, 6, 7, 12, 14.*
It will feel amazing when I have success.	I am setting up my own suffering if I can only feel good when I am winning. *Tile 94: Thriving – Keys: 1, 2, 3, 4, 6, 7, 14.*
I compare myself constantly and see she/he is more than I am. I want to be more than others.	I will be myself and strive for my best rather than being better than others. Being better today than I was yesterday replaces being better than others. *Tile 95: Compassion – Keys: 1, 2, 3, 4, 6, 7, 8, 14.*
Winning is the ultimate goal.	Ask others for their perspective on who I am in relation to success. Feeling amazing no matter what I am is the ultimate goal. *Tile 94: Thriving – Keys: 1, 2, 3, 4, 6, 7, 14.*

Scheming, 34

Scheming can now open up because being competitive may not be enough to get what I want. Plans and agenda abound in this space. From simple to elaborate, this attitude has a real determination to get what it wants and because it is limited to a personal win alignment, the scheme can be detrimental to friends, family and colleagues. Cause-and-effect principles apply in order to control contributing variables. If I do this then I can have that, but the scheme may not ever realize others are also going to be affected. There is one change I am after and I need to devise a way or plan for that to happen. There may be a time pressure or competitors are involved so even less consideration for others and the bigger picture occurs. As the nature of the agenda is personal or for someone else who can then provide me with something, it is an Entrapment as it is not done with integrity.

Anything not done with integrity has a tendency to denature, decay or rot so there is a perpetual requirement to keep feeding the scheme.

This requires ongoing attention and is an energy drain. Eventually I will have to weigh up if it's costing a lot more (in friendships, being upset, time) than the getting of the desired outcome or object is worth. I might be described as cunning, crafty, calculating, devious, shifty, deceitful, double dealing, 'yes but no', controlling, seductive or manipulative.

ENTRAPMENTS: UNHEALTHY SELF-TALK – 34 – Scheming	GUIDANCE TO MOVING FORWARD TO A NEW MINDSET – 34 – Scheming
They are not going to know anyway.	But I will know. Above 60, power is internal and full of integrity and authenticity. I need to study these, I will study these. *Tile 88: Integrity – Keys: 1, 2, 3, 4, 6, 7, 8.*
No one will know what my agenda secretly is.	Withholding to get my own way is deceitful and deep down, doesn't feel good. I will own up and release the tension of the situation. *Tile 88: Integrity – Keys: 1, 2, 3, 4, 6, 7, 8, 21.*
What does it matter to them if they don't really know why?	I would like to have as much context around each situation as I can so as to maximize my input and understanding. *Tile 89: Inspiring – Keys: 1, 2, 3, 4, 6, 7, 8, 21.*
I have a secret plan and no one else needs to know.	Isn't it about who I become, not what I get? Look carefully at the plan to see if it will benefit others. That's required to enter above 60. *Tile 88: Integrity – Keys: 1, 2, 3, 4, 6, 8, 14.*

Over-ambitious, 33

Over-ambitious is a flow on from scheming and requires even more time investment. Ambition is like a solid scheme, a rigid agenda that grows and accumulates ideas until the story is built around big expectations and requirements from myself and others. Ambition itself is a type of maturation story to establish myself on a path of what I want. It becomes over-ambitious when I invest more of my time and energy into the story at the expense of my other stories and other people's stories. There can be real hunger and striving for personal gain. Satisfaction is not derived until the story gives the required outcome.

This can be observed by others as excessive or exaggerated and it can interfere with relationships. I can be open to judgements like 'he is overdoing it' and 'she is over-enthusiastic'. At its peak there can be an overzealousness and the results are driving the behaviour more than the journey. Others cannot relax or trust me or trust that I have the team or other best interests in mind. I can be seen as greedy, acting from non-integrity, 'only in it for myself' and not to be trusted. Behaviours can tend towards extravagant and flamboyant. Showy, over-the-top, flashy, greedy and artificial sneak in. Overtly, we might see demanding attention through a delirious state where a frantic, ostentatious display occurs. Subtly, a one-goal orientation or an uncompromising attitude can prevail.

ENTRAPMENTS: UNHEALTHY SELF-TALK – 33 – Over-ambitious	GUIDANCE TO MOVING FORWARD TO A NEW MINDSET – 33 – Over-ambitious
'I know. Let me show you.'	How do I feel for the impact my actions and drive have on others? Why do I have to 'know'? Can I be shown and if not, why not? *Tile 75: Collaboration – Keys: 1, 2, 3, 4, 6, 7, 8, 16.*
I will flatten anything that gets in my way. I am a steamroller.	What are the consequences of this amount of focus? Who am I trying to impress? What is the story that gets me to do this? *Tile 70: Receptive – Keys: 1, 2, 3, 4, 6, 8, 14.*
I want this so badly I will step on other people to get there.	Can I be more aware of what I inflict on others? That's empathy, isn't it? How I treat others is how I will end up being treated. *Tile 96: Altruistic – Keys: 1, 2, 3, 4, 6, 8, 16.*
Everybody else around here is just looking after themselves.	This is a story with selective evidence. People are more important than positions or things. Maybe others don't know that I can be the one to change, take the initiative? *Tile 96: Altruistic – Keys: 1, 2, 3, 4, 6, 7, 8.*

Addictive, 32

Addictive arises when the desired outcome, person or object that I am attached to becomes seemingly indispensable and required to fulfil me or ease me in some way. Dependence has arisen from continually engaging with the story of what I want and how to get it. The effects that arise from the consequences that have built up within me grow to the point where if I do not have the focus or the end result of the addiction, I will 'suffer' withdrawal symptoms.

Regardless of whether the addiction is work, a chemical substance, another person, a physical activity, without it I feel incomplete and stressed in some way so I feed the addiction by having more. A person's system can habituate or get used to a certain level of that which is sustaining the addiction so I need more and more to ward off the withdrawal symptoms or to gain the 'high' pleasure that getting what I want provides. 'Just having one more' seems innocuous and reasonable. 'I will change tomorrow' is the deflection that doesn't seem to happen. The absence of what has now become an essential requirement results in a deeper urge or craving. Hooked, dependent, reliant, fixated and tunnel vision are all applicable in this Entrapment.

ENTRAPMENTS: UNHEALTHY SELF-TALK – 32 – Addictive	GUIDANCE TO MOVING FORWARD TO A NEW MINDSET – 32 – Addictive
I can't get enough. I need to fill up on this constantly and I need my fill now!	It is my internal lack that seeks the external fill. What do I lack? What can I do about that? *Tile 74: Connected – Keys: 1, 2, 3, 4, 6, 8, 14.*
Just one more…	I can face the withdrawal symptoms knowing I will not die from them. Just one more is a trap, a lure. What other, above-60 feeling can replace this craving? *Tile 74: Connected – Keys: 1, 2, 3, 4, 6, 8, 14.*
I can't let go of it now but I will stop tomorrow.	The addiction presents as a strong wave and I can ride it out, knowing it will pass. It's just built-up charge from getting what I want. In time it will dissolve as I redirect my mind and energy. *Tile 74: Connected – Keys: 1, 2, 3, 4, 6, 8, 14.*

I can fix things by having what I want over and over and over.	It's not that I will live without that which I am addicted to, but that I will live with something new that will be healthier for me. Then I can have that over and over, promoting wellness. *Tile 67: Conviction – Keys: 1, 2, 3, 4, 6, 8, 16.*

Perfectionist, 31

Perfectionism is a special type of intense addiction. The perfectionist really narrows down on the detail required to get what is wanted. Happiness or satisfaction is evasive until the story is satisfied and when the story is satisfied, there may be more of a sense of relief than happiness. The narrowing down can be mild to extreme. An example of the latter is becoming so meticulous that every detail is accounted. Criticism of self or others for the lack of achievement of the details can arise. Accuracy can become overly important. Painstaking measures may be required and rigorous procedures may need putting into place. Punctuality, methodical, fastidiousness and precision can all play their part in attempting to achieve what is believed within the story to be required to move forward.

I may even create a story of a utopian situation and stop at nothing to achieve that. It may be rigorous and painstaking but the perfectionist remains on task, motivated deeply by the external event or outcome that will bring happiness or relief from unhappiness. A perfectionist is driven to be meticulous, pedantic, finicky and nitpicking. There are negative consequences for others in the team, such as delays and getting lost down a rabbit burrow. We can celebrate rigorous exactness and precision but overcritical, dogmatic fault finding can move a team away from its best performance.

ENTRAPMENTS: UNHEALTHY SELF-TALK – 31 – Perfectionist	GUIDANCE TO MOVING FORWARD TO A NEW MINDSET – 31 – Perfectionist
I have to get it right.	'Burnout' is not what I choose. Right is subjective. I can scale the Entrapment. *Tile 79: Flowing – Keys: 1, 2, 3, 4, 5, 6, 8, 11.*

If the outside world is in 'order', I can feel better and more in control on the inside.	Let's order the inside aspects of the mental, emotional and physical worlds and systematically deal with them. The relationship to the external world will then be more flowing and less controlling. *Tile 79: Flowing – Keys: 1, 2, 3, 6, 19, 20.*
If I can't do something perfectly, I won't do it at all.	I may have a fear of not being in control or not being good enough. Which tile is that? Where did 'perfect' start? Who did I need to be perfect for initially? *Tile 79: Flowing – Keys: 1, 2, 3, 4, 6, 14, 19.*
I have to prove myself to myself and others.	A minimum viable product that can be delivered and built upon is best. Proving myself never ends. Perfection is pressure. I am to be myself, find myself on the Awareness Code. *Tile 95: Compassion – Keys: 1, 2, 3, 4, 6, 11, 14.*

Infatuated, 30

Infatuation is the extreme end of an addiction where time, effort and life itself is being handed over to the story that has now built to such an extent that it controls the person. The story is running the show and I am along for the ride. I have little choice and the story sweeps me up so that I am in my own very narrow 'reality'. A type of fixation or obsessiveness has overtaken this part of my life in a way that is not healthy long term. Fanaticism for a narrowed-down result blocks the bigger picture. If the centre of attention is a person, I will idolize that person. I can put them on a pedestal and expect or demand them to fulfil the expectations that accompany infatuation.

I can deeply believe that the object of my infatuation is going to 'solve all my problems', 'release me from my torment', or will be the 'project of a lifetime'. I can learn to give 'everything' to this idol, team, company or child, but when the idol does not believe or provide the expected outcome I can start to feel the below-30 Entrapments. There may be a correlation between how much entrapment I feel below 30 and the level of the 'escapism' that is required. The more pain, the more I can use infatuation to get away from it.

This extreme narrowing down, without Wisdom or Intuitive Mind involved, can lead a person into becoming fixated on the perceived 'here is everything I ever needed', which is an Entrapment as it is an object outside of the person. This can be the mania part of manic depressive. It requires a lot of energy to run this tile and exhaustion can occur, which brings you close to the below-30 tiles or the depression tiles.

ENTRAPMENTS: UNHEALTHY SELF-TALK – 30 – Infatuated	GUIDANCE TO MOVING FORWARD TO A NEW MINDSET – 30 – Infatuated
That's the answer to my prayers, so it becomes everything.	The meaning of an object, person or situation is dependent on the observer, me, so I can shift my attitude. I can scale the want and adjust the dependence, attachment (36). *Tile 82: Realizing Value – Keys: 1, 2, 3, 5, 11, 15.*
I must hold on to this because losing it would mean losing all sense of happiness and meaning.	What is lacking in my life that I am using this to fill me? Where else can I find 'meaning' and 'happiness'? How do I generate that without relying on external conditions? *Tile 60: Realizing Truth – Keys: 1, 2, 3, 13, 15, 19.*
Losing this would mean sliding down into stress, so I must do all that I can to hold on to it.	What would cause me stress if I lost this? What am I afraid of? Is this a distraction away from the core issues that I really need to look at? I'll look at the attachment (36). How Agile (77) and flexible can I be? *Tile 77: Agile – Keys: 1, 2, 3, 6, 15, 19.*
It feels so good to give deep meaning and value to something external as it lifts me out of myself.	This will create an endless wanting so I need to find help to look at myself and change myself. Where am I not seeing my own value (82)? *Tile 82: Realizing Value – Keys: 1, 2, 3, 7, 8, 11, 13.*

Let's review

- This chapter goes to the core of an incredible survival mechanism that we all inherit as part of being human: Wanting.
- From the mildest form of Wanting at Ego-requesting 39 to the most pronounced version of this level at Infatuated, 39, the common thread for the leader positioned here is serving the self as the key motivator.
- This self-interest negatively affects the potential that is possible in relationships. How a person seeks to attain something, the motivation behind the seeking and the effects of the seeking all have particular consequences on working teams and relationships.
- This is a difficult level to transcend as the by-product, if the Wanting is attained, is often a good feeling that reinforces the negative behavioural pattern.

Coming Up Next

What happens when a leader does not get what he wants? What is the difference between being persistent and being controlling? What are the sensations felt in the body that alert a person to being stuck in a forceful way of interacting? Are you using force or power to affect the direction in which your company, team or family is heading? The next chapter looks at attitudes that identify a forceful leader who aims to control outcomes at all costs.

CHAPTER FOUR

Leaders Who Force Their Way

40–49: The Level of Controlling

40	41	42	43	44	45	46	47	48	49
Malicious	Enraged	Bully	Con-fronting	Deceiv-ing	Resentful	Passive-Aggressive	Annoyed	Frus-trated	Sceptical

If I do not get what I want or what I don't want, I then move into an outlook of life that increases my efforts to retain the desired outcome by controlling the situation or others. There can be a compulsion to repeat controlling behaviours that I learned in my past because these have worked somewhere with somebody and are now an essential part of my controlling toolkit. An impulse to get something from 'out there' can make someone or something in the outside world seem like it's the answer 'worth fighting for' and the story can be that control and force are essential to getting.

Some leadership positions are incredibly difficult for individuals to successfully perform. In these instances, leaders are, in effect, set up to fail. Others have impossible tasks trying to lead corrupt, incompetent organizations that resist Incredible Leadership. These are situations where as a leader I could easily default to controlling.

I start judging other people and projects based on whether I get the results I want. Judgement is a type of control. Failed leadership can often be traced back to poor, inappropriate, over-demanding judgement. So, what do I do when something goes wrong? The team's ability is stretched, endurance and stamina are tested. Your team is underachieving. Do I derail or try to control everything? Micromanage and not delegate? A leader's relentless drive to achieve more and more with fewer and fewer resources can lead to controlling tiles being activated. This old style of leadership results in exhaustion, lack of motivation and burnout.

Old-style leaders are unable to produce exceptional results. They feel overcome by pressure and tend to run away from their problems and the stressful situation often by judging other people or projects. This scapegoating behaviour can create a very politicized organization torn by rivalry, bullying and competitiveness. In research published by the Trades Union Congress (TUC) on 12 November 2015 on bullying at work, it was documented that 29 per cent of employees have been bullied at work. In 72 per cent of cases the bullying was carried out by a manager.

The traits of a controlling destructive leader cause distress and Stress (20–29) and hostility as they are Controlling (40–49). These leaders are prone to negative emotions and are likely to be callous, antagonistic, fearful of subordinate initiatives and prone to exhibit exhaustion. Such leaders are unwilling to communicate effectively with subordinates and are likely to collapse into controlling behaviours when dealing with minor day-to-day problems. This disruptive behaviour can result in corruption, hypocrisy, sabotage and manipulation. Behaving in this controlling way as a leader gives permission subconsciously to other subordinates to behave in this way if they in turn have subordinates.

Many leaders who do not outwardly use controlling behaviours can turn inwards. This can lead to the level of Lifeless (0–9), depression, Despondent (10–19) or Stressed (20–29). In order not to feel the heaviness of these levels a leader may become Addicted (32) to alcohol or drugs and even contemplate self-harm. What differentiates those who 'crash' (fall victim to alcohol, drug abuse, alcoholism) from those who don't (change toxic behaviours) is the latter's ability to stay in touch with reality and take these psychological forces in their stride.

Sceptical, 49

Why am I not getting what I want? What is being offered here? What am I being sold? Is there anything here I want? What do they want from me? Do they have what I want? What am I getting myself into here?

This is a place of disbelieving. It is a negative holding pattern until I get more information, whereas Witnessing (71) is a positive holding pattern until more context is acquired. Sceptical is negative as it perceives the other person as an enemy rather than a person to understand. It is better to be suspicious than gullible is one storyline. I have probably been tricked, conned or manipulated into something before, so I am trying to work out if someone has an agenda or scheme. I might believe you do have an agenda at this tile so I look for any evidence to support that. If I borrow this approach many times, I may even become cynical, finding a way to feel dubious about anything new. There can be a lot of questioning and to stay at this level, it is required that I remain unconvinced. I am not getting what I want, but I'm not falling for any trap either. It is a place where I 'put on hold' any agreement to get what I want as it is unclear exactly what is being offered and the person is compelled to try harder to convince me otherwise.

Here, team members are kept at arm's length by doubting, disbelieving and distrusting them. A person is stuck in 'unsure' and indecisive as to how to proceed to ensure the desired outcome is achieved.

ENTRAPMENTS: UNHEALTHY SELF-TALK – 49 – Sceptical	GUIDANCE TO MOVING FORWARD TO A NEW MINDSET – 49 – Sceptical
My view is not the same as yours. I don't believe your view has as much merit as mine.	This blocks my growth and progress. How would I feel if this was done to me when I tried to explain myself to others? *Tile 75: Collaboration – Keys: 1, 2, 3, 4, 8, 14.*

I stay convinced your perspective is flawed and I do this in silence.	It's best to share what I am feeling about but can I do it without judgement? Do I feel vulnerable? How can I be okay with a difference of opinion and not build a wall? *Tile 72: Open-minded – Keys: 1, 2, 3, 4, 12, 14, 21.*
I am not going along with you.	What is it that I object to? Can I stay open when I feel this? Am I afraid of something? *Tile 73: Trustful – Keys: 1, 2, 3, 4, 8, 21.*
I assume based on my past.	This is Ego Mind. Assumptions limit the potentials. The past is an indicator only and limits opportunities. What do I do to get to Witness and Wisdom Mind? *Tile 85: Spontaneous – Keys: 1, 2, 3, 4, 6, 8, 10.*

Frustrated, 48

Frustration arises when I feel the pangs of not getting what I want. I may have been thwarted, deceived or unheard and a disgruntled feeling arises. It is a mild heat and activates a stronger sense of having to have the required object or outcome.

I am dissatisfied and can use this energy to try to motivate myself or others by increasing the sense of urgency of having to have the required objects or outcome. Me being displeased can send someone else towards being stressed at my reaction or they may want to please me more. However, if they are sensitive it can also send them to despondency or depression.

At this type of trying to control I might experience disgruntled, irritated, disillusioned or hindered. They are all expressions of a mild form of controlling others or myself through frustration. The accompanying irritation makes me 'hot under the collar' or like a 'cat on a hot tin roof' and I start to mildly blame myself or others for not getting what I want. There can be some perceived shortcoming like forgetfulness or lack of respect or being treated in some way that is deemed inappropriate or not what the person wants.

An expectation has been set up at Wanting and it's not quite come to fruition yet. The meeting running overtime or not starting on time can be good triggers.

ENTRAPMENTS: UNHEALTHY SELF-TALK – 48 – Frustrated	GUIDANCE TO MOVING FORWARD TO A NEW MINDSET – 48 – Frustrated
I don't like what just happened.	What do I not like about it? When did that start to be important to me? Can I let go of the requirement or expectation if I can't control it? *Tile 77: Agile – Keys: 1, 2, 3, 4, 8, 16.*
I don't like how this is going.	I will put my energies into finding that better way than being lost in the drama of the moment. What am I doing that might interfere with the result? Is it meant to be going in another direction I don't want it to? *Tile 78: Wow – Keys: 1, 2, 3, 4, 7, 16.*
I am starting to see I am not getting what I want.	Let's pause here. Recalibrate. Reorientate. What is really happening here? Can I let go of Wanting? *Tile 64: Reorientating – Keys: 1, 2, 3, 6, 8, 16.*
I can feel an agitation with what is happening now.	How much does it mean to me? Am I able to change that or the way I react? Agitation means powerlessness so what will it take to let go of the agitation and speak from a place of calm? *Tile 68: Fearless – Keys: 1, 2, 3, 8, 12, 14, 15.*

Annoyed, 47

If frustration has not acquired the outcome, annoyed may arise as a bigger expectation or demand presents itself. Perhaps the outcome has not been delivered quickly enough or exactly enough or something else enough. I have been mistreated in some way and it is not the first time. Annoyed can range from quite unhappy to rough, riled or cross. It is a deeper expression of discontent. I am not pleased by the unfolding events and I can be easily insulted or really disillusioned by lack of success.

An antagonistic attitude may lead me to becoming the perpetrator in a scenario where the other person is going to become a victim if I do not get my way. Although annoyed can be justified away through statements like 'Well, wouldn't you have?' or even 'Everyone gets annoyed sometimes,' this is only true of those who still get angry and those who don't have another way of dealing with the perceived unfairness. It would be laziness that is present in a person who activates the tile of annoyed. If annoyance continues unabated as a way of dealing with life's issues, a person can learn to 'bottle it up' so that he seems passive but aggression is never far away.

Here can exist feelings of being provoked, hassled or aggravated. Frustration has been exacerbated and feelings of 'fed up' or riled arise.

ENTRAPMENTS: UNHEALTHY SELF-TALK – 47 – Annoyed	GUIDANCE TO MOVING FORWARD TO A NEW MINDSET - 47 – Annoyed
How many times do I have to tell you, go without or not get what I want?	Really, is it that important? What is patience? There are many examples in my own life where I needed multiple practices or reminders so that I could 'get it'. We all learn at a different pace. *Tile 79: Flowing – Keys: 1, 2, 3, 4, 8, 9, 12.*
This is going in the wrong direction for me.	Patience is a virtue. I'll go in deeper to see if I am able to steer this in a different direction without force. What is Acceptance? *Tile 84: Embracing – Keys: 1, 2, 3, 4, 8, 12.*
Wait a minute! Can't anyone see I'm not getting what I want?	What is so important to me that I need others to see? What do I get from that that I can't provide for myself? What is going on for me to have to rely on others seeing me? *Tile 60: Realizing Truth – Keys: 1, 2, 3, 6, 8, 14, 16, 21.*
Hello? Is anyone noticing that I'm missing out?	How can I assist others with perceived inabilities? *Tile 67: Conviction – Keys: 1, 2, 3, 6, 8, 14, 16, 21.*

Passive-aggressive, 46
When a person becomes passive-aggressive, there is an attempt to lock in the feelings of frustration or annoyance but the pressure builds and is either released elsewhere, where it is perhaps not so problematic as it would be if I were to release it at the point where it was initially experienced. Or I release it in the moment but it is not in proportion to that scenario because the gate has been opened to the pushed-down

frustration or annoyance of previous occasions and that is now released alongside the current occurrence.

Behaving calmly satisfies some learnt conditioning regarding proper and respectfully responding to events but if feelings of frustration are being generated without understanding what causes them by employing the Wisdom Mind then the tension and heat energy of frustration and annoyed build up. The charge has to go somewhere. This can be the tantrum of the toddler, where it just becomes too much in the moment to accept that he can't have what he wants. Snarling comments or putting someone down can occur in the aggressive phase and the 'silent treatment' can occur with the passive phase. Waiting and patience haven't been developed perhaps and the urge to 'have' is just too strong. Some teenagers use this orientation and some adults are still throwing tantrums with little to no awareness. During the release, there can be accusations as a part has finally found expression or there may just be a loud, long scream if the person knows how to release without the venom being directed anywhere.

ENTRAPMENTS: UNHEALTHY SELF-TALK – 46 – Passive-aggressive	GUIDANCE TO MOVING FORWARD TO A NEW MINDSET – 46 – Passive-aggressive
I don't know how to respond, but I will not forgive or forget this.	I will begin to set boundaries. Let's start small with 'safe' people and have achievable targets. I'll watch out for hidden expectations and assumptions. *Tile 71: Witnessing – Keys: 1, 2, 3, 4, 7, 16.*
I am feeling powerless right now. I will take this away with me and build anger around it, but not express it.	I will have a courageous conversation with someone about how annoyed I am and release the tension through exposing it without blaming the person. *Tile 63: Releasing – Keys: 1, 2, 3, 4, 7, 10.*
I will not get angry but will show them my disapproval another way.	I will scream or punch the anger into sport, a pillow, a run, a swim or write it out in a journal. I will find out why the anger builds and what triggers it. *Tile 63: Releasing – Keys: 1, 2, 3, 4, 7, 16.*

I find it hard to set boundaries.	Suppression of feelings doesn't work. What will it take to find someone to make a gentle boundary to start with? Who can I speak to about what I need to stay well? Do I know? Tell myself first? *Tile 69: Fully In – Keys: 1, 2, 3, 4, 7, 16.*

Resentful, 45

Resentful can be felt as a simmering, prolonged heat arising from the bitterness of being denied something that Ego wants. A hostility is building that feels like a type of pain from not getting what is desired, so instead of just a burst of frustration or aggression in between moments of passiveness, a 'here, you feel what it's like!' or 'now you miss out' arises. The dynamic of being told 'I can't have it' is packaged with a grudge and it sits in my energy field. I can push it down, or fantasize with it to build all sorts of ways at 'getting back' at the perceived antagonist.

The triggers are endless – betrayal, being stolen from, someone backstabbing me, missing out on a funding opportunity, etc. So, I start to feel jealousy or envy. This is a mild form of hate and it may not even be acted upon. Here, at this approach to life, the 'other' deserves punishment and I deserve retribution and the energy percolates and builds. In its milder form, it creates sulking, a type of withdrawal of love, attention or presence. At a deeper level, it creates 'bad blood' in relationships. At its darkest, it can feel venomous and toxic, full of animosity and feelings of separation and seeking revenge.

ENTRAPMENTS: UNHEALTHY SELF-TALK – 45 – Resentful	GUIDANCE TO MOVING FORWARD TO A NEW MINDSET – 45 – Resentful
It's all right for all of you, you don't know how this affects me.	How do I start to share how I feel without becoming a victim? I need to learn how to own my feelings. Where can I find an AC Mentor to help me? *Tile 60: Realizing Truth – Keys: 1, 2, 3, 6, 8, 10, 15.*

If only I had what you had, I would be okay and I wouldn't have to be reacting in this way.	I am deflecting, taking the responsibility away from myself. I own I am not okay and strive to work through this. What help can I get from an Awareness Code therapist or coach? *Tile 60: Realizing Truth – Keys: 1, 2, 3, 6, 8.*
This feeling I have against you is building.	I will ask for a courageous conversation so we have the opportunity to express what we value. *Tile 65: Positive – Keys: 1, 2, 3, 10, 11, 12, 14.*
Whatever you are, represent or remind me of, I am starting to react against it.	I will explore what you do that triggers me so I can understand the reasons behind it. I need to witness these and express them calmly. *Tile 71: Witnessing – Keys: 1, 2, 3, 6, 8, 10.*

Deceiving, 44

Resentful energy can build up and this puts more pressure on a person. A person can either be passive-aggressive or overtly aggressive to relieve that pressure but what happens if the aggressive part is not allowed out for fear of getting into more trouble? A person can then become deceptive so that his ability to control things to get what he wants isn't compromised. I distort the truth. I exaggerate the story. I manipulate the facts. I believe in my distortions until perhaps my illusion of what happened becomes a delusion.

I pretend something did or did not happen. I fake emotions to get what I want. I become underhanded to succeed or short-change others so I can have more. There are lots of ways Ego can play this game: trick, con and fraud my way through the day, falsify testimony, fudge the evidence, hoodwink when I can and use treachery to really stir things up and get what I want.

I'll try being cunning and sly so no one will catch on. I fool them into believing me or outright cheat if I have to, but cover my tracks and don't get caught. I'll mislead, send them down the wrong path, fake it, be insincere or take it to the extreme and be corrupt. I easily double-cross my friends or team members. I can be wily, misinforming or create a scam. Being shady, shrewd and sly will help me deceive.

ENTRAPMENTS: UNHEALTHY SELF-TALK – 44 – Deceiving	GUIDANCE TO MOVING FORWARD TO A NEW MINDSET – 44 – Deceiving
I'm going to do something about my resentment and you won't know about it.	How I am with other people will come back to me eventually in some way. It will stay on my conscience and I need this to be clear from now on. *Tile 61: Ready – Keys: 1, 2, 3, 15, 16.*
There is no problem with misleading others. False information is everywhere.	I will start to treat others how I would like to be treated. I cannot justify my behaviour because others do it. I will set the example. *Tile 88: Integrity – Keys: 1, 2, 3, 5, 6, 8.*
Everybody lies. I have to cover my tracks.	I will have to live with the lie or secret for the rest of my life. Everybody is a generalization. Deceit causes illness. *Tile 67: Conviction – Keys: 1, 2, 3, 6, 8, 10.*
Avoid confrontation. Avoid problems. Avoid blame. Do whatever it takes to avoid.	Confession is the way out. I will own it and free myself of the burden of carrying the lie. Disclosing the truth will set myself free and I can start anew. *Tile 68: Fearless – Keys: 1, 2, 3, 7, 13, 15.*

Confronting, 43

Being confronting is where I step up my aggression rather than hiding it and I confront the situation/person directly and impose some force to get what I want. This is a more acutely directed reaction to the situation/person and doesn't leave much room for misinterpretation like a temper tantrum (passive-aggressive) can. Being exact in what is required can be advantageous for me and confronting for the other person. It creates a challenge and may be experienced as too hard, rough or awkward. If the other person joins me in becoming demanding too, then a back-and-forth accusation trap ensues, where neither person is really listening to the other. It can seem like a contest at times. There may be a daring element to the confrontation, presenting unwanted consequences if demands are not met. If things are complex, the situation can become arduous and confusing. There can be no time for explaining or niceties, especially if the demanding is severe. It can go out of control into a full-blown dispute, provoking each other with bravado.

ENTRAPMENTS: UNHEALTHY SELF-TALK – 43 – Confronting	GUIDANCE TO MOVING FORWARD TO A NEW MINDSET – 43 – Confronting
I have been pushed too far and unfairly.	What is it about their behaviour that really pushes my buttons? What would be a more mature above-60 way of dealing with it? *Tile 77: Agile – Keys: 1, 2, 3, 10, 11, 15.*
Because of unfairness, I am fighting back.	What am I not owning within myself that makes me need to resort to confronting someone with aggression? What do I need to change to have more fairness? Am I being unfair anywhere? *Tile 68: Fearless – Keys: 1, 2, 3, 4, 6, 7, 8.*
I have a right to force my boundaries on to you without consideration of consequences for you or the team.	Is the one I am confronting acting like a mirror for me to see something about me? How can I deliver empowered boundaries? *Tile 83: Fellowship Mindset – Keys: 1, 2, 3, 8, 10, 15.*
You'd better have a damn good look at your behaviour and do something about it.	Maybe I should also have a good look at myself and why I need to resort to forcing another person to be different. How do I do that? I am to stop forcing others to stop doing something. *Tile 72: Open-minded – Keys: 1, 2, 3, 8, 10, 15.*

Bully, 42

Little regard is given to the other person's feeling or self-opinion as the bully targets an aspect of the person's character to attack. Intimidation is a usual ingredient, where the other person is deliberately made to feel small, useless, excluded, upset or belittled in some way. The bully is harassing someone on the basis of their education, gender, age, skin colour, country of origin, intelligence or anything else he/she can find. What does the bully get from this threatening behaviour? I feel superior, satisfied through retribution, in control and the pleasure of controlling someone keeps me distracted from the lack I feel at a core level.

Persistent unwanted attention is one way of bullying or a short burst of abusive browbeating. Other forms are bulldozing, hounding, domineering and intense heckling. Just being in someone's face with aggression or using scare tactics is bullying control. The bully can be admonishing, either in public or in private, in their mistreatment of the other person. The bullying can feel justified as warranted. It can be a very deep learned behaviour and modelled during early stage development, or it may be a carry-over from when I was bullied and now there is an opportunity to not just feel the perceived injustice and resentment but to put someone else down and extract revenge, or to bully myself with inner dialogue.

ENTRAPMENTS: UNHEALTHY SELF-TALK – 42 – Bully	GUIDANCE TO MOVING FORWARD TO A NEW MINDSET – 42 – Bully
I am better than you are and I am going to let you know.	I am behaving immaturely here. A younger part of me is still in developmental delay and believing I can get away with this. *Tile 88: Integrity – Keys: 1, 2, 3, 8, 10, 15, 16.*
I don't care about your feelings, I need to express mine.	Your feelings are important too. I need to ask others to provide me with feedback when I am doing it and be open to their constructive feedback. *Tile 69: Fully In – Keys: 1, 2, 3, 4, 10, 15, 16.*
You are either with me or against me. If you are against me, you're fair game.	We're all in this together. Instead of taking sides, can we be one team? How does Fellowship Mindset (83) really work? *Tile 83: Fellowship Mindset – Keys: 1, 2, 3, 14, 16, 17.*
I get a buzz out of treating you as a subordinate, an object, a transaction or somehow less than.	How would I feel on the receiving end of this energy? The buzz is egotistical and always comes at a price to the other person first and eventually me. *Tile 64: Reorientating – Keys: 1, 2, 3, 5, 8, 10, 16.*

Enraged, 41

Enraged is Controlling that is out of control. Not getting what I want has resulted in me losing sight of the bigger picture or 'losing the plot'. Being livid is being unable to understand or cope with the pressure of the situation anymore and 'all hell breaks loose'. There can be a burst of furiousness that includes the bully but there is less constraint and organization so the attack is more unpredictable. Incensed and maddened are good terms for the nature of this 'out-of-control' state. It's a different type of tantrum to the passive-aggressive. Here, a wrathful undercurrent of possible violence, either physically or psychologically, may pervade the atmosphere. A seethingness has been unleashed and the exchange can be quite savage.

A person has perhaps lost touch momentarily with their humanness and returns to acting within animal instinct, which gives rise to fighting to survive. The wind-up may have been obvious or have gone unnoticed. It doesn't matter as the fury is unleashed with little or no regard for the consequences. It's like I am overtaken and need to vent as the build-up of pressure is too great to contain in any way, e.g. news of a big stock market loss.

ENTRAPMENTS: UNHEALTHY SELF-TALK – 41 – Enraged	GUIDANCE TO MOVING FORWARD TO A NEW MINDSET – 41 – Enraged
How dare you!	Can I see it's *all* about me? I want something and I am using other people to get it. What do I need to change so I do it myself? What is in the way of me realizing the outcome with integrity? *Tile 88: Integrity – Keys: 1, 2, 3, 4, 10, 15, 16.*
I DEMAND respect.	My Ego is upset. Why am I so desperate for superiority? Can I allow myself the time to explore what is behind this toxic attitude? *Tile 72: Open-minded – Keys: 1, 2, 3, 4, 10, 15, 19.*
You WILL obey me.	Realizing I am expressing my needs while excluding the 'other'. What do I need to do to be more tolerant? How can it be a win-win for all? *Tile 70: Receptive – Keys: 1, 2, 3, 4, 10, 15, 16.*
I am entitled to this authority.	This is how I have been programmed, conditioned to be. I deliberately place myself in situations where I am not entitled to have multiple opportunities to explore this. How can I begin to explore beyond my comfort zone? *Tile 66: Adventurous – Keys: 1, 2, 3, 4, 8, 12, 15.*

Malicious, 40

Maliciousness is a type of calculated rage. It is the bully with a big sting – vicious, tyrannical, hostile, brutal. Nastiness creeps into the delivery of the Controlling energy and the delivery is hostile. There can be an undercurrent of spite as the thing that was wanted is not being given or forthcoming. The idea is to 'take it out' on the one considered responsible for the crime. I am so far away from experiencing my own pain that the only way to deal with the uncomfortableness of not getting what I want is to act out with vengeance what is hidden or suppressed from my own awareness. Malevolence, meanness and cruelty are examples of a malicious attitude. Hate is present and being projected on to the accused. There can be sinister, even wicked or vile expletives, descriptions and accusations. Vindictiveness prevails and often an excuse of being a victim to some perceived deprivation will accompany the attack.

Poisonous words, expressions and delivery make for a foul exchange. Acrimonious, bitter, caustic, sarcastic, cutting condemnation can be present as the intention is often to hurt the other person into submission so as to get what is wanted.

ENTRAPMENTS: UNHEALTHY SELF-TALK – 40 – Malicious	GUIDANCE TO MOVING FORWARD TO A NEW MINDSET – 40 – Malicious
When your back is turned, I will 'stitch you up', get you back.	Doing this feels toxic. It is not integrous, it creates disharmony in the team and me. *Tile 88: Integrity – Keys: 1, 2, 3, 4, 6, 7, 8.*
My resentment has built up and now it's my turn to get you to feel what it's like.	This is eating me up. I need help to release this. The past is done, it's over. I must stop polluting the team and myself with this. Exceptional leaders do not do this. I must find a way to Release (63) this. *Tile 63: Releasing – Keys: 1, 2, 3, 4, 6, 7, 8, 11.*
I will show you what happens when you take from me, challenge me.	I don't want to seek revenge. It sets up a toxic internal environment that can lead to un-realness and illness. *Tile 64: Reorientating – Keys: 1, 2, 3, 4, 6, 7, 8, 10.*

I will deliberately seek revenge and retribution.	I must learn to recontextualize the event. What do I react most to? Is there a theme to my reacting? How do I get out of this dot (*see also* pp. 239–241) and back into the bigger picture? What is forgiveness? *Tile 60: Realizing Truth – Keys: 1, 2, 3, 4, 6, 7, 8, 10, 15.*

Let's review

- A person who has a particular outcome in mind can fall into the trap of seeking the outcome at the expense of valuing the relationship and the process. The end doesn't justify the means at this level and in the long run creates negative consequences for all involved.

- From the mildest form of Controlling at Sceptical, 49 to the most pronounced version of this level at Malicious, 40, the common thread is perceiving the other as a threat to attaining a particular outcome and this sets up the survival instinct, which is about competition rather than collaboration. This can be very unconscious in how it plays out.

- At this level, the body experiences the sensations of wanting to control or not being able to control as heat pumping through the body and an outlet for release is sought. Adrenaline is activated to prepare for fight or flight. Passive-aggressive, Annoyed, Confronting, Bully and Enraged, for example, all inspire the rising up of heat that needs releasing and the process is one where the self feels better by dumping the charge on another.

- This can be a difficult level to transcend as the instant gratification felt at releasing the charge and Controlling others can reinforce the negative behavioural pattern.

- Stepping out of the beliefs that keep people trapped in the level of Controlling others begins with the Revelations outlined in this chapter. Start with tile 71, Witnessing. Watch and take note of when you are being the perpetrator by wanting something and how you go about accessing it, when you try to control others or situations and when your desires may blind you to the bigger picture.

Coming Up Next

What happens when the pattern of wanting a particular outcome and attaining it through Controlling others becomes really ingrained in a person? What is the toughest gateway to be mastered in order to attain a more powerful way of interacting that does not use force? The next chapter looks at how to identify egotistical dispositions that keep people trapped and unable to relate with others in co-operative and collaborative teamwork.

CHAPTER FIVE

Leaders Stuck in Their Way

50–59: The Level of Egotistical

50 Narcissistic	51 Arrogant	52 Know-it-all	53 Self-Centred	54 Dismissive	55 Defensive	56 Pretentious	57 Ego Confident	58 Complacent	59 Not Buying In

When I am able to use the level of Controlling to get what I want, a type of self-esteem or Ego Confidence (57) arises. It feels like I only have to repeat the Controlling behaviour or suggest to others that I may have to repeat that behaviour and I can get what I want. I start to inflate myself with my ability to get what I want. This is the domain of the peak of Ego awareness: Egotistical.

Ego leaders lack self-awareness and distort the degree or level of skills that they possess. They can rely on fiscal reports and shareholder returns to justify themselves. Egotistical leaders strive for recognition and are likely to self-promote rather than self-nominate. Also, they employ the skills of deception, manipulation and intimidation to remain in positions of authority or at the level of Controlling. I resist advisors' suggestions, take more credit for successes than are due and blame others for my own failings or shortcomings. I am prone to lapses in my professional judgement and personal conduct and I am distrusting, rejecting and destroying of loyal supporters. I can possess narcissistic arrogance, which is associated with difficulties in interpersonal relationships. This arrogance has also been blamed for lack of reality testing, which in turn can lead to failures based on complacency, inflexibility and short-sightedness.

I will ignore important input from third parties such as the wise counsel of external consultancies, or fellow peers. This level ignores environmental changes (macroeconomic factors) and the challenges from competitors through being too slow to act or failing to predict competitors' moves.

I constantly self-aggrandize in an attempt to defend against feelings of emptiness or hurt. Even when idealized by flattering sycophants and imbued with unquestionable authority, I do not have the ability to sustain positive feelings about myself. Because of this, the slightest mishap or misstep by a follower can provoke dangerously exaggerated reactions.

I have a lack of empathy. Empathy is considered a key aspect of emotional intelligence – a leadership trait that is just as important as other traits. Empathy is a precursor to other emotional abilities but also cognitive leadership abilities such as perspective taking and pattern recognition, which in turn creates positive leadership outcomes. As empathy starts at 60 and above, I miss out on this vitally important ingredient.

I am inflexible in my thinking and behaviour, which promotes short-termism and short-sightedness. I have inner feelings of having to prove myself and a lack of insight about myself. However, egocentric leaders who are Ready (61) to step in, or adapt their thinking and behaviour, are able to surpass 59 into 60 and beyond.

It can be suggested that every leader needs an element of egocentrism in order to function 'effectively'. Interestingly, some of the greatest leaders have had narcissistic tendencies. However, these leaders experience common fallacies. These include a belief that their interests are paramount, a belief that they know everything, a belief that they will get away with everything. As a consequence, leaders with excessive or out-of-balance Egotistical tendencies can miscalculate risks when making key decisions. By their nature, above-60 leaders are in a position of trust, and can marshal resources without supervision. Consequently, all of their decisions have moral consequences.

58/59 – The toughest gateway

Complacent (58) and Not Buying In (59) get a special mention because they stand at the gate of Realizing Truth (60). They are the last protection of Ego (0–59) and are full of Entrapment perspectives designed to not break through into the Witness Mind (above 60). There is an attitude of having made it, being able to get what is wanted in life, and so life is great. In fact, these levels will borrow all the 60–100 words to convince itself and others that there is no need to look further, get counselling, ask those who might know more or delegate to another.

Here lives Ego Self-esteem (based endlessly on an 'I' statement that promotes itself and Ego Confidence, which are distinctly different to Conviction (67) and Agile (77). Below 60 focuses on what it can get from the world. There is no team mindset. 58/59 is Ego Proud, which places a type of pressure on the person (self, or other) to repeat the behaviour to get the desired results in order for 58/59 to stay Ego Proud.

Witness Mind just feels great (60–100) for another person's success. How great the feeling is depends on how close to 100 a person is. 58/59 says 'I did this for you' but there is a 'want' lurking and a hidden agenda (Scheming, 34). Compare this to 60 and above, which may say 'I did this for you,' because they actually did.

It's the truth.

Not Buying In, 59

Not Buying In is a space where I probably do not know that I am resistant as I cannot see that something separates me from understanding something or some trait at a deeper level. The last bastion of my Ego Mind, it appears to have the capacity to block me from hearing, seeing or understanding another way of living. This is the last step before the Witness Mind takes over, which is an entirely new way of seeing life, so Ego puts up a wall between itself and another type of mind. Ego, which is tiles below 60, looks after itself first, whereas above 60, others are served. The deeper truth of another way is shrouded or obscured here. Above 60, behaviour can appear cryptic and unavailable to Not Buying In as Ego envelopes itself for protection. Watch someone trying to be convinced of a new way of approaching a situation and he can appear screened, enveloped and unable to comprehend. Not Buying In can be like a type of shutdown, hanging on to a private world. Why would I want to change? I don't need to – I'm doing fine already.

Here, it's easy to suggest and even believe that what is being proposed has no credibility. It is not believable or outside the scope of understanding so is not needed, required or even worth thinking about. It's all 'too hard' or justified away in preference for what the Ego thinks. Attempting to enthuse someone who is listening from this tile can be difficult. Attempting to convince someone living from this tile can be even more difficult. I believe I have it all worked out and to entertain an idea that falls outside the scope of my own comprehension is not possible.

ENTRAPMENTS: UNHEALTHY SELF-TALK – 59 – Not Buying In	GUIDANCE TO MOVING FORWARD TO A NEW MINDSET – 59 – Not Buying In
Why do I have to change? I'm okay!	Can I change why I do something so it is more for others than me, or at least it is about the other as well as me? *Tile 94: Thriving – Keys: 1, 2, 3, 4, 6, 8, 9, 10.*
I don't have to look at any of my below-60 tiles. Leave me out of this!	I do have to look at my below-60 tiles until I'm living well above 60 to inspire others. *Tile 72: Open-minded – Keys: 1, 2, 3, 4, 5, 6, 8, 10.*
You agree with me so I like you. That feels good.	Real Trust is where I must align until that is my natural state, to trust my intuition. *Tile 72: Open-minded – Keys: 1, 2, 3, 4, 6, 8, 10.*
I hear you, but I'm stubborn.	Stubborn is a learned behaviour. I can unlearn it and be humble. Teams achieve much more and reach higher levels when gifted with humility. *Tile 72: Open-minded – Keys: 1, 2, 3, 4, 6, 8, 10, 12.*

Complacent, 58

Having established how I can get what I want, I can afford to become comfortable. Here, I am feeling satisfied and pleased with myself. It's as close to fulfilled as Ego can get. I have what I want and believe that's all I have to do to stay feeling good. I might even say I am content, but it is dependent on keeping what I want, so it is very conditional. If that changes, I lose the feeling and have to drop back down into Controlling level. Here, I rely on Controlling to get what I want.

Change doesn't make sense as I can get what I want by doing what I am already doing. Leave me alone. Go bother someone else. I can relax without the stress of trying to improve or being way better than I already am. In this way of being, the ever-evolving nature of relationships and the loving presence that is required to maintain them are not accessible. Here, people need to stay as they are to fulfil Ego requirements for safety and comfort. I am indifferent to anyone offering me a better way or feedback on my performance if it is challenging. This is a good defence mechanism against having to look at myself.

I have a handle on things. I will work it out. I will stop/start when I am ready. I don't have a lot of drive for doing anything other than what I already am. Isn't what I have achieved enough? It will suffice. I think I am successful. I am self-satisfied and pleased with myself. There is a sense of security here but it's all based on continuing to get what I think I want.

ENTRAPMENTS: UNHEALTHY SELF-TALK – 58 – Complacent	GUIDANCE TO MOVING FORWARD TO A NEW MINDSET – 58 – Complacent
I am comfortable here, leave me alone.	It might have become nagging or complaining because I didn't listen when it was gentle. Did I listen and didn't do anything about it because I didn't want to, or know how to? *Tile 60: Realizing Truth – Keys: 1, 2, 3, 4, 6, 8, 10.*

How good is this? How easy is it to get what I want?	No matter how good it currently is, change is life and it is essential. How can I embed that so it stays in my brain? Time to have a change in mindset. *Tile 77: Agile – Keys: 1, 2, 3, 4, 6, 8, 10, 11.*
I don't need to look at consequences. Nothing will happen to me.	This is a false belief. What I do to others comes back to me in some similar way, shape or form. It is inevitable and only ignorance denies this. *Tile 60: Realizing Truth – Keys: 1, 2, 3, 4, 6, 8, 10.*
Karma? Isn't that just a belief, an idea? Can't see it having any relevance to me.	This is because I haven't studied or learned about it. There is so much more to life than what I can physically see. *Tile 60: Realizing Truth – Keys: 1, 2, 3, 4, 6, 8, 9, 10.*

Ego Confidence, 57

At this level a person needs to resist considering doing something someone else's way, or differently, to what seems to be already working well. This limited awareness settles into the feeling of Ego self-esteem that is Ego confidence. It believes it can repeat what it has been doing ad infinitum. Change doesn't make sense as I can get what I want by doing what I am already doing. This is actually a ramped-up version of Complacent.

I don't realize that a belief is a narrowed-down version of myself. The belief around what makes me happy is attached to whatever means I used at the level of Controlling or Wanting to get what I required. I just repeat that and feel like I can keep doing that and I may not want to hear that this is affecting other people in a negative way.

So, I develop an Ego self-esteem, confidence or belief in myself from which I can operate to get what I want. I develop a sense of self based on the story version I have created about myself and repeatedly refer to the times I have succeeded by Controlling others. This is what a belief is. Repeatedly referring to the past when I have succeeded by Controlling and projecting that into the future. This gives Ego a platform on which to operate 'in the world' and is required to back itself in times of doubt, feel adequate when others doubt it, believe in itself when others don't and predict a future outcome with some confidence. I might seem a bit 'stuck-up' but that's a good thing, isn't it? And why refer to mistakes or errors? They are to be avoided or hidden in order to stay at Ego Confidence. I am propped up by constant referral to my successes. This builds pride but also pressure to keep achieving particular outcomes deemed successful or at the very least there is a hope that referring back to past 'accomplishments' will still give me status.

ENTRAPMENTS: UNHEALTHY SELF-TALK – 57 – Ego Confidence	GUIDANCE TO MOVING FORWARD TO A NEW MINDSET – 57 – Ego Confidence
I now know how to get what I want. I will just keep repeating that pattern over and over.	Is winning everything? Is fulfilling my own wishes more important than helping others? This will affect the team negatively. *Tile 79: Flowing – Keys: 1, 2, 3, 4, 6, 8, 10.*
It feels good to win, better than losing. Everyone else is trying to win.	Is it possible to lose and feel good? It is! How do I do that? What is the shift required? *Tile 66: Adventurous – Keys: 1, 2, 3, 4, 5, 6, 8, 10.*
I can't put myself in other people's shoes. When they lose, I might lose.	What would be the win-win here? I am to move away from win-lose or lose-lose. *Tile 74: Connected – Keys: 1, 2, 3, 4, 6, 7, 8, 10.*
My self-esteem is based on continuing to get what I want.	Could I feel good for someone else if they receive what they wanted and I miss out? This is what endears team members to me. *Tile 94: Thriving – Keys: 1, 2, 3, 4, 5, 6, 8, 14.*

Pretentious, 56

Now that I have Ego Confidence (57) and am feeling okay about myself, I can exaggerate it and pretend I am even better than I am and that feels even better. More important, it means more attention, which is a good thing, right? More success, more money … as long as it is always more and not less. The more I pretend to be important, the more I get away from below-30 emotions that I do not want to feel. I am exaggerating my Ego Confidence.

I do not want to recognize that this tile is actually a lot to do with insecurity. No point in focusing on that. Artificial is not what I want to recognize. Fake and unnatural is what others may be able to see but I encase myself in the feeling of pretending so deeply that I convince myself the story is who I actually am.

I might try to impress or educate others with my wisdom. I can start to live a fantasy by behaving and dressing in a way that elevates me. I create a mask in public, but who am I when I am alone?

At this level, superficial seems normal, especially if others around the person join in and participate in the charade together. I assume you are buying into this usually inflated caricature of myself because I am. I imitate what I feel will attract your attention and I might easily drop out of my charade into being offended. If you challenge me in some way, I can avoid that by becoming more defensive. Variations include lacking genuineness, being pseudo kind and living a sham.

ENTRAPMENTS: UNHEALTHY SELF-TALK – 56 – Pretentious	GUIDANCE TO MOVING FORWARD TO A NEW MINDSET – 56 – Pretentious
Bend the truth or exaggerate the description. What matters the most is what they think of me and that I am important.	Can I learn to approve of myself? What they think of me will be based on a lie, not the truth. Liars can't be trusted. *Tile 89: Inspiring – Keys: 1, 2, 3, 4, 6, 8, 10.*
When I imagine I am better than I actually am it feels good. If I inflate my deeds, that feels good too.	Can I get above 60 to experience the true value of others? I will be known as an exaggerator and lose the power of my word. *Tile 60: Realizing Truth – Keys: 1, 2, 3, 4, 5, 6, 8, 10.*
I'm doing really well – great, in fact. No problems here.	What is humble and humility? How can that feel great? How do I own that if I was really honest, I have problems? I am not perfect, no one is. *Tile 64: Reorientating – Keys: 1, 2, 3, 6, 7, 8.*
My life is an example of how to do things properly.	Team members are uncomfortable with excessive displays of Ego Pride. Humility is to recognize the positive qualities in others too. *Tile 87: Integrating – Keys: 1, 2, 3, 9, 14, 21.*

Defensive, 55

This tile includes a type of 'fighting back' so the Ego can re-establish itself. Ego is protecting itself from a real or perceived threat to its authority, importance or otherwise. It needs to prevent the accusation or suggestion for improvement from penetrating. It doesn't need to know what awareness the challenge is coming from, only that it needs to stay protected, otherwise its self-belief may momentarily collapse and below-30 feelings of lack and disempowerment will be present so there are conscious and subconscious defence mechanisms such as:

- Deflection – make someone else the blame;
- Justification – explain in any way I can why I am not to blame;
- Denial – deliberately forget or not agree;
- Projection – make it about someone else. Those thoughts and feelings that would interfere with having a good self-belief can be projected on to others and talked about endlessly and I can see it within them but not me.

There are more defence mechanisms and essentially, they are employed to conserve the best sense of self the Ego can have through believing in the ways it can get what it wants. Ego is guarding its set of self-beliefs, preserving them without knowing what it is like to have awareness above 60.

Here, we set up a screen, avert from the truth, shield ourselves, oppose whatever confronts us and generally safeguard our Ego reputation.

ENTRAPMENTS: UNHEALTHY SELF-TALK – 55 – Defensive	GUIDANCE TO MOVING FORWARD TO A NEW MINDSET – 55 – Defensive
I didn't do it, it wasn't me. I deny it.	Taking responsibility is being integrous, which feels a lot better than hiding, although I may have to look at my fear. What am I afraid of being responsible for? *Tile 88: Integrity – Keys: 1, 2, 3, 4, 6, 8, 14.*

I don't know.	This is a surface reaction and it's my responsibility to know why I do certain things. I will stay with it until I have a possibility. I will get past the fear of getting it wrong. *Tile 68: Fearless – Keys: 1, 2, 3, 4, 6, 8, 10, 12.*
Why me? Ask or pick on someone else.	I am trying to pass the buck or get out of it. Being honest and truthful will mean I gain the respect and trust of the team. This feels much better longer term. *Tile 68: Fearless – Keys: 1, 2, 3, 4, 6, 8, 10.*
I can create as many reasons as I like to help you understand I am not to blame.	While this seems to work short term, the other team member(s) will feel the lack of honesty and it will become a part of my story and legacy. I will stop doing this, I will listen and be honest. *Tile 68: Fearless – Keys: 1, 2, 3, 4, 6, 7, 8, 10.*

Dismissive, 54

To be dismissive is a form of protecting a set of self-beliefs. Rejecting another's opinions, ideas, support or accusations gives me internal space to manage my own self-beliefs and hang on to them. There is time to collect evidence so as to stay with my opinions in the face of change. Even if the perceived 'opposition' coming from Awareness (above 60) is offering me a deeper truth than my current belief system, I'm not buying in so I dismiss it. Ego Mind is not Intuitive Mind so it utilizes probability, educated guesses and references to the past in order to predict the future so its defence mechanism is to use flippancy in its mild form of dismissive and a more extreme version is smug and indifference to others. At this level of Ego, the attitude is not derogatory, just disrespectful of another point of view. Disapproving of another's set of opinions or self-beliefs can be easy here as I don't have time for anything too far away from what I have acquired as a way of operating in the world. A cursory glance is enough to assume there is nothing there for me. Disregarding saves energy and time. Fleeting connections, unenthusiastic encounters and underestimating others all live here. Variations include contempt, denial, disinterest, unenthusiastic and being offhand when offered something.

ENTRAPMENTS: UNHEALTHY SELF-TALK – 54 – Dismissive	GUIDANCE TO MOVING FORWARD TO A NEW MINDSET – 54 – Dismissive
I am not interested in your analysis.	Everyone has something to contribute for team growth if they can be shown how to offer constructive feedback from above 60. I need to lead the way. *Tile 74: Connected – Keys: 1, 2, 3, 4, 6, 8, 14.*
It feels good to be talking about what others are not good at and dismiss what I am not good at.	Relationships are an opportunity to learn about how I can be a better person. People trust others who can reciprocate feeling good about each other. *Tile 83: Fellowship Mindset – Keys: 1, 2, 3, 4, 6, 8, 14.*
Who do you think you are when you think you know more than me?	How I value another person is a reflection of how I value myself. Let go of superior/inferior relationships and find humbleness. What is humbleness? *Tile 75: Collaboration – Keys: 1, 2, 3, 4, 6, 8, 14.*
I don't want to talk about anyone else, just me. I am the important one here. Look what I've done for the team.	To be more considerate and kind is a higher calling and part of the best me I can create. There is no need to complain and I have the capacity to look at challenges. How do I step into being okay with what is being brought into my awareness? *Tile 83: Fellowship Mindset – Keys: 1, 2, 3, 4, 6, 8, 14.*

Self-centred, 53

Being self-centred is taking the feeling of being proud to another level, where opinions matter very much and having them heard is very important. It is like the opinions and history of the person's accomplishments define the person and help draw attention to him. Attention feels good. Here, I am not defined by what I truly am, as happens at above-60 tiles, but instead by what I think, what my opinions are and how to get what I want. If someone is at a higher status or rank than me then I might listen. But if they are not, I establish myself as the provider of the information and sit at the 'head of the table', constantly seeking credibility through expressing my Ego. It can appear selfish and self-indulgent.

My self-centredness can be greedy and neglectful of other people and their requirements. Self-interest can extend to include others if it is seen to enhance the Ego by being with or associated with others. Others then become part of the self-identity. If the other person provides Ego with something that is wanted then the other will very conditionally be included. Self-centred can be experienced as 'hard-hearted' or pretentious. Self-centred can get lost in giving attention to itself and eventually can turn into believing Ego knows everything. Self-absorbed, selfish, inconsiderate, uncaring, uncharitable, self-seeking all live at this tile.

ENTRAPMENTS: UNHEALTHY SELF-TALK – 53 – Self-centred	GUIDANCE TO MOVING FORWARD TO A NEW MINDSET – 53 – Self-centred
You owe me something.	We all have receiving and giving qualities. Let's not make it all about what I can get, but what I can give for the betterment of the team. *Tile 75: Collaboration – Keys: 1, 2, 3, 4, 6, 7, 8.*
I did so much for you and this company.	Do I need to be wiser with my giving? I can prioritize and delegate. *Tile 75: Collaboration – Keys: 1, 2, 3, 4, 6, 8, 21.*
I am going to blame you for any pain I feel.	It's not your fault I feel this way. Things happen and I have a choice as to how to react but I need to study the Awareness Code to fully realize this. At tiles 0–30, I may not have a choice as I react from Entrapment charge. *Tile 60: Realizing Truth – Keys: 1, 2, 3, 4, 6, 20, 21.*
Why should I do it your way when I know I am right?	Am I asking why to prove my point, or am I really interested in the answer? I strive to be inclusive and let go of having to be 'right'. *Tile 70: Receptive – Keys: 1, 2, 3, 4, 6, 8, 14.*

Know-it-all, 52

This tile is more than just dismissing others although this element is also present. At this tile I promote myself, often at the expense of others. A person at this level is often referred to as a 'smarty pants', 'wise guy', 'smart Alec' or even a 'smartass'. The Know-it-all feels comfortable in believing that his way is the best, or perhaps only, way. There is no problem letting anyone who will listen understand that 'I know what's best, even for others, not just me'. Sentences that start with 'Listen', 'look' and 'I don't want to dominate here, but...' There is a conceited attitude where the Know-it-all can be experienced as overbearing in his approach. 'Bighead' is at it again, pointing out how his opinions are all that matter. Know-it-all comes across as overly opinionated and sensitive people can withdraw their input and creative energies as the Know-it-all hasn't got room to accommodate other people's opinions. It is like opinions are being forced on to the other person. In this tile the Ego identity is established by how big or persistent its opinions, beliefs and concepts are about anything that is up for discussion.

People at this level can listen to stories, but do so with a view to getting their own story heard and so they can be formulating something bigger, better or somehow more impressive while the speaker is delivering his story. The Know-it-all can appear 'cocky' and full of themselves. He may even boast to emphasize that he does indeed know it all and be seen as a braggart. The Know-it-all may not be aware he is presenting in this way and become Wounded (14) when told. The bigger the wound, the bigger the Know-it-all. This is the 'wind bag', 'braggart', 'big mouth' and 'show-off' tile.

ENTRAPMENTS: UNHEALTHY SELF-TALK – 52 – Know-it-all	GUIDANCE TO MOVING FORWARD TO A NEW MINDSET – 52 – Know-it-all
I don't have to wait until they have finished speaking.	I will learn to listen with patience. What have they got to say? What can I learn from them? What is their contribution? Can I thank them for sharing? Being yin is fine. *Tile 70: Receptive – Keys: 1, 2, 3, 4, 6, 7, 8.*

As they are speaking, I am working out what I want to say.	Can I be a part of a whole conversation without speaking? Can I ask others how it feels to have a conversation with me? *Tile 70: Receptive – Keys: 1, 2, 3, 4, 6, 7, 8.*
It's my way or the highway.	Can I converse without offering an opinion? Can I ask my team members what it's like to work with me? I wonder if they will be honest with me, or if they may feel intimidated? *Tile 70: Receptive – Keys: 1, 2, 3, 4, 6, 7, 8.*
I have to press on with my ideas and thoughts. They feel essential.	This is the way I get attention. I feel valued when others are listening to me. I need to find another way of feeling good about myself. *Tile 72: Open-minded – Keys: 1, 2, 3, 4, 6, 7, 8.*

Arrogant, 51

Being arrogant takes Know-it-all to a new level by adding a type of put-down to perceived inferiority. A person at this level is seen by others as being 'too big for their boots'. If I am arrogant, I feel totally justified that my position, knowledge and socio-economic status is all superior. There is a vanity in arrogance where it is not only all about me, but there is also a disdain or dislike of anything less than me. At its extreme form it can be pompous and snobbish, not having much or anything to do with perceived 'lower' intelligence or 'lesser than' people. Hierarchy is important. Hub and spoke leadership style promote arrogance, which in turn discredits equality in fellowship. A 'stuck-up' approach to life places Ego near or on top of any hierarchy and it feels arrogance has a right to display its superiority at any time. A person can drop back down into Controlling level by being outraged at any trivial challenge to his superior authority. A 'high and mighty' or even 'lordly' attitude is an attempt to create power through privileged money or position. There is a dominant attitude and it is obvious who has the final say. Aloof, overbearing and haughtiness lives here.

Patronizing and condescending are central to the repertoire of activities Arrogant uses to establish its superiority. Bombastic is an extreme form.

ENTRAPMENTS: UNHEALTHY SELF-TALK – 51 – Arrogant	GUIDANCE TO MOVING FORWARD TO A NEW MINDSET – 51 – Arrogant
I know what's best for you.	I don't know what's best for you, I only know what's best for me. *Tile 72: Open-minded – Keys: 1, 2, 3, 4, 6, 7, 8.*
I can cut you off mid-sentence because I have been thinking about what I can say rather than listening to what you're saying.	I will practise waiting until you have finished speaking. Can I be more aware of the unspoken messages I am sending to my team? *Tile 74: Connected – Keys: 1, 2, 3, 4, 5, 6, 7, 8.*
Unless what you are saying is in alignment with my argument, I can dispense with you.	I'm going to be more open to differing views of team members. Diversity is powerful. *Tile 60: Realizing Truth – Keys: 1, 2, 3, 4, 6, 7, 8.*
I will quickly appraise what and who you are based on what I and the team can get from you and what it would cost me and us.	Instead of being transactional with my team members, I will create team relationships that are meaningful and caring. *Tile 75: Collaboration – Keys: 1, 2, 3, 4, 6, 7, 8.*

Narcissistic, 50

Tile 50 is the extreme end of feeling good about myself because 'I am going to get what I want, no matter what the cost'. I am losing touch with the value of others and it is all about me. I collect evidence daily that I am someone others need to admire, look up to or be aware of in some way and I distort reality towards this story. Self-involved to the point of self-obsessed is possible and a lot of interest and energy is directed towards the version of the Ego I have created that feels amazing. Being concerned only with myself, there is a preoccupation to fine-tune the Controlling mechanisms and Egotistical dynamics that can sustain this all-consuming pattern.

The narcissist may have been conditioned externally by repeatedly being told they are amazing, incredible or similar without attention being directed at other behaviours that have or are being pointed out, which need improvement. It may have even been the narcissist's own making by fantasizing about being incredible, amazing or similar without that being grounded into actioning out and living those very high tiles.

I am self-congratulatory and have a swollen head; I as the narcissist presume all others are interested in what I am interested in. Stepping into another person's shoes doesn't occur to me. It appears the child is still very much present in me as the narcissist, as I am intensely focused on who I am and what I can get.

Pompous, vainglorious and insolent live here.

ENTRAPMENTS: UNHEALTHY SELF-TALK – 50 – Narcissistic	GUIDANCE TO MOVING FORWARD TO A NEW MINDSET – 50 – Narcissistic
I am the only one that knows what to do.	I will role-play and act out with exaggeration what narcissism looks and sounds like. Expose it. *Tile 60: Realizing Truth – Keys: 1, 2, 3, 4, 6, 7, 8.*
Regardless of what everyone says or does, we will be doing it my way.	What stops me from reaching out? I am restricted by the past. Where did I learn to be one-dimensional? *Tile 60: Realizing Truth – Keys: 1, 2, 3, 4, 6, 7, 8.*
I am unable to find self-love. I don't know what love is.	I have been thinking, using my Ego Mind. I will look at the above-60 tiles and learn to make a real connection through the Witness and Wisdom Mind. *Tile 90: Grateful – Keys: 1, 2, 3, 4, 6, 7, 8.*
Don't you know who I am?	Do I really know who I am? Have I taken the time to tell them who I am? *Tile 83: Fellowship Mindset – Keys: 1, 2, 3, 4, 6, 7, 8.*

Let's review

- Part of being human is acknowledging the propensity for wanting as a means to achieve happiness. It is a limited form of awareness and does not create good leadership as outcome often becomes more important than process.
- Wanting can lead to Controlling events in order to achieve the object of desire.
- Being rewarded for achieving success in this manner can lead to Egotistical dispositions.
- Stepping out of the beliefs that keep people trapped in Wanting begins with the Revelations outlined in this chapter.
- Read over the moving-out statements as often as you need to reset how you respond.

Coming Up Next

What happens when a person is addicted to pleasing authority figures, or when anger controls a person's reactions? What are the consequences when a person is so egotistical, he alienates his team? The following case studies demonstrate the capacity of limited awareness, at Wanting, Controlling and Egotistical, to sabotage relationships and working together in harmony.

CHAPTER SIX

Case Studies

Based on Real-life Case Studies of the Perpetrators and Their Victims

The following case studies show people trapped in being the perpetrator and the behaviour that keeps them there. These Entrapments can feel better as their role is to avoid the heavy victim energy of tiles 0–29 and for this reason can be difficult to break. Seeking therapy is a positive step forward and highly recommended for more embedded behavioural patterns of 30, 40 or 50. The case studies all show various tiles from 30–59 in particular and some of the attitudes that assist with moving out of the Entrapments. The case studies are based on real-life experiences but some events and names have been changed in order to maintain confidentiality.

Harry – Wanting

Harry was in his early twenties and had just completed his first two years as a graduate trainee. A Perfectionist (31), who took great pride (50s) in his work, he would deliver every project on budget and on time. He was motivated to do well and felt a real high when he impressed his boss and senior management. He would work extra-long hours and made sure he outshone his peers at every opportunity (35). He rubbed some people up the wrong way (33), but he didn't care as long as he was considered the best by his boss.

At last his efforts were rewarded and he was offered a promotion to team leader. Harry was ecstatic and jumped at this fantastic opportunity. All went well for the first few months, a couple of the guys weren't pulling their weight but he shrugged this off. Then critical deadlines were missed and his team projects started to get management's attention for all the wrong reasons. Harry started Narrowing Down (37) on his team, focusing only on giving them strict, tight deadlines to ensure a timely delivery. On one particular day he saw that certain team members were leaving before they had completed their work and he felt the anger (47) rise in him: 'What is wrong with them? Don't they WANT to stay? Don't they WANT to deliver this project on time?' Before he knew it, the anger took him over and he started to berate (43, 44) those leaving. They looked at him astonished, shook their heads and left. Harry stayed on and tried to finish their work so that the deadline could be met. He worked late into the night (26, 27), ending up exhausted and defeated.

At home, he reviewed the day but he could not shake his anger. His colleague and close friend called him that night and let Harry know how he felt and that the behaviour was workplace harassment. His friend mentioned there must be something that Harry needed to address within him and that he knew a good therapist. Harry agreed because as he turned his focus inwards to feel the physical and emotional effects the anger was having on his body, he realized the deep tension and Anxiety within him (26).

With therapy, Harry came to understand that he felt an urgency, a Wanting (30s) underneath his anger. He realized that this feeling of Wanting was a strong desire to please the management team and not let them down. He identified so strongly with this desire that it had become an Addiction (32) for him. As team leader, this addiction consumed him so much that he had not been able to hear or see the needs of his team. He also realized that he was attached (36) to delivering to deadlines and would try to meet them at all costs.

As Harry stepped up (60s) and started Realizing Truth (60), the Wanting was released to reveal what was fuelling his desire to succeed – his core belief that he was Never Enough (8). This was a familiar feeling for him. This was how he felt in the eyes of his father and his reaction to his team mirrored how his father would control him. With these realizations he developed a new sense of self-awareness and was able to review projects with Open-mindedness (72) and no attachment. This allowed him to work closely with his team (74, 75) to set new deadlines based on a realistic view of the project's objectives and constraints. This in turn motivated his team as they felt heard and valued.

Kala – Controlling

Kala arrived home after a busy day at her boutique public relations firm. As she sat down to dinner with her partner Chan, he asked, 'How was your day?' Kala responded that she had been very Hurt (15) by one of her clients. She went on to explain that she had met with one of her top five clients only to be told he was going with another PR firm and wanted to terminate their contract in 30 days.

As the story unfolded, Kala expressed her feelings to Chan: 'Internally, I felt a bubbling hot anger start to rise from my stomach to my throat. It wanted to explode but I kept it in [Passive-aggressive, 46]. When I spoke, it all came out in quite an abusive way [Bully 42, Confronting 43].' With all these emotions and feelings swirling around inside, Kala felt Trapped (23). She knew to take herself away for a walk before bringing this inner rage home her partner. Chan felt it was time to be very frank with Kala as this was a pattern he knew well. He let her know that responding in the way she did was not at all productive and people were being Bullied (42) by her.

Kala knew that the triggers that prompted such responses were related to memories of a troubled childhood but she had not done anything about it as she felt she had it under control (Passive-aggressive, 46). She was aware that if she took responsibility for how she responded and consciously slowed everything down that the strong feelings would pass and potentially she could find a place of courage (Stepping In, 60s) to explore and learn about herself from this seemingly disappointing news and her unhelpful response to it. Up until now, however, she had been Complacent (58) about changing her behaviour and seeking help. The next day, she rang a highly recommended therapist and began her journey towards healing her Wounded (14) self (Preparing, 62).

A month later, Kala felt Ready (61) to face her client and asked to meet him to resolve the conflict and make amends. She was (Ready, 61) and able to ask the client for more context (Preparing, 62) around the decision to end their business relationship. The client looked surprised and relieved and went on to share that his team felt she was too Controlling and dominating in her responses (40s) to their creative input. It felt like it was always 'Her way or the highway' (Know-it-all, 52) and some of their team no longer wanted to deal with her because they felt invisible, unheard, not valued and steam-rolled (Stressed, 20s). She noticed how neutral she had become (Witnessing, 71) and how she was able to receive the client's honesty.

Kala softened her gaze and relaxed her body language. She had shifted from being Defensive (55) to being open to receiving information (70). Kala thanked her client for the feedback and instead of going back to the office, she went to the park where she could be alone to review and process what had just unfolded. Kala sat for an hour while she explored where else in her life she was being controlling. The therapy and the meeting had helped her to see (Realizing Truth, 60) that she was making other people feel the very things she herself had felt by being controlled by others – for example, feeling small, invisible and unheard.

Kala reflected that although she was aware of her need to control and had come a long way, there was still work to do around Releasing emotions (63) and Reorientating (64), learned behaviour that kept her safe from feeling abandonment and disappointment. Being in control of her life and the lives of those around her was just a way she recognized to keep order and to make sure everyone didn't step out of line and then they wouldn't leave her. Kala recognized it did just the opposite – it pushed people away. Also, being Controlling is exhausting, which had taken its toll on her, mentally and emotionally.

'It's okay to be told no. It's okay for people to choose another way. It's okay not to have all the answers.' Kala also realized she was not responsible for making everything 'nice' or 'perfect'. She made a Conviction (67) that she would do all she could to be aware of when the old patterns started to arise again and to replace them with being patient, inclusive, consultative and tolerant.

Felipe – Egotistical

Felipe always wanted to play football. At the age of 16, he was approached by a scout and eventually drafted. He was a brilliant footballer with wonderful skills (Realizing Power, 81) and was of great value to his team (82). But something else was rapidly developing alongside his football ability: pride-fullness and Arrogance (51) crept in.

He didn't seem to care what others thought of him. Felipe would Dismiss (54) people's feedback. He continued playing great football and earning many accolades and this seemed to feed his Arrogance (51). When he played football, his team and club seemed to cope with his arrogance because he could contribute and be of value. Others outside the club knew he was a great player but seemed to focus on his narcissism instead. Felipe displayed some leadership qualities and after a decorated playing career, he took up coaching. This is where his Egotistical ways finally caught up with him.

As a player, he didn't care what anyone thought of him. He was in control on the football ground and he could control his personal skills to win acknowledgement. But now, as a coach, he could not control his players as they did not warm to his arrogance. Felipe quickly lost the respect of his players and failed to earn their admiration. Disconnect (17) and Resentment (45) grew among the playing group and they weren't performing. This continued for a few years until the spotlight came upon him in a whole club review. Player morale was very low. The club president asked players to provide honest feedback (Stepping In, 60s).

Player after player, club staff members and assistant coaches provided feedback on his personality and leadership style. His Ego took a massive hit as the truth of who he had been finally crept in (Realizing Truth, 60).

Felipe took two weeks away to consider his position (Preparing, 62). To his credit, he took all of the feedback on board and decided to work extremely hard on changing his attitude. He invited more players to share their experiences of how they experienced his coaching (Witnessing, 71 and Open-minded, 72). He took responsibility for his past behaviours and made a pledge to the players, the club and the fans to change.

Within 12 months, Felipe had transformed into a more transparent and open (70s) version of himself. He had gratitude for the efforts of his players (90) and they responded in kind. The players began warming to the new version of Felipe and began playing for him. They started to enjoy the game more and Felipe and his team went to a whole new level of performance (Embracing, 84).

Let's review

- In the course of our lives we will experience many challenges and we are sometimes not equipped to deal with them because parts within us are underdeveloped and these parts respond through limited awareness.
- Perpetrator dispositions often hide a deep hurt or pain and dealing with the source of the pain can alleviate the negative energy at the heart of the perpetrator.

Coming Up Next

What happens when a leader or person consistently is unable to get what he or she wants? Feelings of 'not good enough' can arise and this heralds in the energy of victimhood. Have you ever felt like a victim of circumstances? What happened for you? Perhaps you will recognize yourself in some of the following tiles. If so, know there is a way out of this limited way of looking at the world!

PART 3

TRAPS TO ACCESSING POWERFUL LEADERSHIP – THE VICTIMS

CHAPTER SEVEN

Leaders Unable to Avoid Stress

The Victims

When leaders continue to aim for a particular outcome by any means possible and the outcome is not attainable, they can tip into the victim part of the Code. Tiles 0–29 show the Entrapments and belief systems of disempowered and spiritless leaders. At these levels there is a sense of being a victim of circumstances as environments cannot be controlled and wants are not attainable. Let's begin at the level of Stressed, which is where most leaders live when outcomes cannot be controlled and a more empowered way is not accessible.

20–29: The Level of Stressed

20	21	22	23	24	25	26	27	28	29
Numb	Terror	Dread	Trapped	Frightened	Worried	Anxious	Over-pleasing	Insecure	Hesitant

On the surface the pain is often described as 'just being there' and it hasn't really been closely looked at. When we do, it often has a physical dimension or description to it – it feels like tension, tightness, a stabbing pain, a throbbing; a huge hole that is empty and horrible. It can also feel like a disappearing, shrinking or a drying-up. It is inside these painful experiences that the original situation lives on, but the core can be so deep and painful that we have learnt to avoid it by engaging in tiles 30–59 to escape it.

When a therapist is trying to help someone out of the 20s to above 60, they are asking them to talk about stress in order to uncover what may lay inside of it. If it is not uncovered, it can keep opening up like a scab that is hit over and over without a chance to heal.

If the stress is pushed down and not dealt with, it builds up. It may take weeks, months, years or decades, but eventually your whole system will have some kind of 'crisis'. The body is telling you it needs to release the accumulated charge. A trigger can reopen the wound that was supposedly 'dealt with' and the original charge is still there. One small incident can tip the person over the edge.

The Centre of Creative Leadership created a research white paper on the stress of leadership in April 2015. The results showed that 88 per cent of leaders found work to be a primary source of stress in their lives. In addition, more than 60 per cent of leaders cite their organization as failing to provide them with the techniques they need to manage stress.

The pace of changes, the expectations of consumers and shareholders are also higher than they were five years ago, compounded by a leader's lack of self-awareness. The survey also shows that 85 per cent of leaders believe they are actually managing their stress levels effectively when this is not the case. Leaders seem to lack insight into the fact that they are actually extremely stressed and burnout is perhaps the first time they acknowledge that the stress is not being managed appropriately.

Anxiety can have acute psychological repercussions, which may include hypersensitivity, chronic worrying, decreased capacity for concentration, poor levels of perception, loss of memory, appetite and sleep. A leader may even lose touch with what is required as the anxiety increases.

Isolation can be common in the top leadership position in an organization where there is a separation from other executives who report directly to the leader, leaving him without peers, confidantes, support or reassurance. The leader may not be seeking external help, therefore not getting that help, despite 79 per cent of leaders stating they would benefit from a coach to help deal with the stresses of leadership. Unrealistic employees, not being what the leaders expect because the employees might imagine their leaders to be infallible and even gifted to some degree with magical power. There is little or no security in some instances, so stressed leaders may become fearful that it may not last, hence they unconsciously cause themselves to fail – self-fulfilling prophecies that are compounded by negative self-talk.

Stressed leaders can panic about the lack of time they have to execute strategic ideas that will make a difference for shareholder returns. These feelings of detachment manifest in leaders' work and personal life – resulting in a distancing from colleagues and from family and friends.

From the survey, the main complaints of stressors under old leadership included: developing others in the organization, establishing and maintaining executive relationships, collaboration across teams, differing communication/work styles and personal insecurity/self-doubt. Is the leader able to understand their challenging stressors and reach out to learn about how to operate from above-60 tiles? Under new leadership, it is the responsibility of the leader to work with the organization, not compete with all the people within it. Competing with others will fuel the Ego (50s) and perpetuate the stress cycle.

Hesitant, 29

Being hesitant is a pause button without answers. It's a space where a person is not getting what he wants and is not sure why, or what can be done about it. Even if I or someone else has a plan, because of the perceived problem, difficulty or lack of ease that I have regarding getting what I want, I take a step backwards or away from the situation. My default pattern is 'hang on a moment'. Doubt enters as to whether I can achieve the goal/aim/want. Thoughts I have can include: 'Maybe I am not meant to have the promotion, others have been here longer than me', or 'Maybe I don't deserve it?' or even 'Maybe others deserve it more than me'. *Maybe* is the key phrase here. A person at this level does not know so guesses using past experiences but that doesn't provide a clear, solid enough plan to galvanize the person into further action to acquire the want.

Uncertainty and apprehensiveness surface and infect the project, performance and people. Others feel it and those susceptible to its impact can join in, especially if the hesitant leader is using words like reluctant, dubious, tentative, averse or ambivalent. These words trigger hesitancy in others and undermine as well as disempower the team.

ENTRAPMENTS: UNHEALTHY SELF-TALK 29 – Hesitant	GUIDANCE TO MOVING FORWARD TO A NEW MINDSET 29 – Hesitant
I am a little dinghy amid big ships.	I am a one-off like everybody else. What is my Realizing Power (81) and Realizing Value (82)? Small and large cogs each play their part in the turning of the wheel. If the tiniest cog fails, that wheel stops turning. Such is its value. *Tile 82: Realizing Value – Keys: 1, 2, 3, 4, 6, 7, 8.*
I am not as confident as others.	What is Ego Confidence (57)? I need to be willing to do trial and error and not be so hard on myself with the error part. Confidence is valued by the below-60 Ego. Above 60, the humility of not knowing leads to Opening (70s) and Transforming (80s). *Tile 61: Ready – Keys: 1, 2, 3, 4, 6, 7, 10.*
I am not certain of what is required. Who really knows anything anyway?	What can I do to know more? Where do I go for more context? What questions can I ask? Who can I ask? I will learn how to let go of having to be 'certain' and replace it with a goal that's less pressure. *Tile 68: Fearless – Keys: 1, 2, 3, 4, 6, 7, 8.*
This is just out of my comfort zone.	I can be just outside of my comfort zone. This grows me, I can enjoy a challenge. *Tile 86: Off-the-charts – Keys: 1, 2, 3, 4, 6, 7, 8.*

Insecure, 28

A leader may feel unsafe in a particular situation or environment because he is not getting what he wants. These feelings may stem from not being heard or seen or perhaps the leader feels he does not have a voice or presence and so feels uncomfortable with what is happening. Precarious predicaments arise when I am not able to communicate what my needs are, or I do and those needs are being ignored, overlooked or forgotten. Here, I can feel vulnerable as the surroundings are not stable enough or are too confusing to provide me with what I need.

Things may be risky, and while experiencing insecurity, the ability to be a risk-taker is not available. Instead, I can feel exposed as someone unable to establish what it takes to make things work or generate desired outcomes. At this level I am starting to feel passive and disempowered in my ability to cope with what I see might be a problem. I can feel unprotected here because I have stated what I think I need but I cannot find a place to land. If there is an antagonist, lack of Ego Confidence (57) sneaks in and I can feel undermined or a little fragile. Without the energy of the want being met, I am left waiting, unclear and unsettled.

ENTRAPMENTS: UNHEALTHY SELF-TALK – 28 – Insecure	GUIDANCE TO MOVING FORWARD TO A NEW MINDSET – 28 – Insecure
I don't know my place here. What are the rules?	What does safe really mean for me? Can I be more for myself? *Tile 70: Receptive – Keys: 1, 2, 3, 4, 6, 7, 8, 13.*
I think in terms of safe and unsafe and try to create my version of safe and when I cannot, I feel unsafe.	How can I meet all unfolding events as a challenge to grow rather than with avoidance? What if unsafe is actually an opportunity to reach into above-60 qualities? The Ego (below 60) is focused on being safe while above 60 sees things in terms of growth, awareness and opportunity. *Tile 66: Adventurous – Keys: 1, 2, 3, 4, 6, 8, 10.*

I don't know what you're going to do next, or what's coming next.	What does it take to be resourceful in the face of change? No one really knows what's next, so how do I go to Stepping In' (60s) and Opening (70s)? *Tile 69: Fully In – Keys: 1, 2, 3, 4, 6, 10, 15.*
I don't know what's coming or what the future holds.	Change is inevitable, so how does one learn to go with it rather than be afraid of it? I will train myself to prepare for anything and have the outlook that I'll always be doing my best. *Tile 69: Fully In – Keys: 1, 2, 3, 4, 6, 8, 10, 15.*

Over-pleasing, 27

To avoid the feeling of insecurity a person may act from the belief or story that he is to please others. This is not pleasing the other for the other's sake. It is pleasing because it stems from insecurity and the avoidance of the consequences that are perceived to be unfavourable. Pleasing becomes a learned pattern to not feel something negative. However, that something negative is still there, waiting to be triggered. For example, staying back at work to be liked or win brownie points or to avoid getting into trouble, or perhaps doing whatever senior colleagues want so they do not make life at work challenging.

There is a nervousness around the energy of being over-pleasing. A constant background fear of 'Have I done enough?' A second-guessing of what others might want but the person never really intuitively knows at this level of awareness because of the unpredictability of the other or the situation, so the person is trapped in a tight, tense place and hopes that what is being done is enough to please the other.

It is sometimes not even in the awareness of the person who is over-pleasing because the pattern is so old and the story so deep. Perhaps even as far back as the first family dynamics, where to over-please was normal and encouraged by the family, or what the person resorted to in order to avoid insecurity.

At this level I can say 'yes' when I really mean 'no'. Initially, any friction can be avoided, but this is never a solution as the 'yes' can cause complications and difficulties as more demands or requests are made. Niceness can be very stressful as who a person really is, isn't able to shine through. Do I even know who I really am when the focus is pleasing others?

ENTRAPMENTS: UNHEALTHY SELF-TALK – 27 – Over-pleasing	GUIDANCE TO MOVING FORWARD TO A NEW MINDSET – 27 – Over-pleasing
I walk on eggshells for you. What will it take to keep the peace? I am uncomfortable with confrontation.	Realizing what it is that is being avoided or desired. Rejection, attack, aggression, not being accepted. What is the pay-off for walking on eggshells? *Tile 60: Realizing Truth – Keys: 1, 2, 3, 4, 6, 10, 18.*
I can become whatever is required to stay friends and I will 'belong' if you stay happy.	This is not my truth. I need to find out what makes me happy. We can be friends but not at the expense of depriving me. Belonging is a Heartfelt (92) experience when we value each other's Realizing Power (81) and support each other to transcend or transform our below-60 traits. *Tile 92: Heartfelt and 81 Realizing Power – Keys: 1, 2, 3, 4, 6, 10, 13.*
What will happen if I don't please you?	What boundaries might I consider? How Controlling (40–49) or understanding (60+) will the other person become? Can I help them to above 60? Whatever the outcome of displeasing them, I will be able to respond in an above-60 manner. When I please someone from below 60, I am supporting them in remaining below 60. If I challenge that energy, we all have a chance to grow. *Tile 92: Heartfelt – Keys: 1, 2, 3, 4, 6, 10, 13.*
If I don't please you, I will lose everything so I will comply, no matter what.	What's the worst that can happen if they are not pleased? What stops me overcoming that? What above-60 tiles would change that? How can I learn to value myself and my Realizing Power (81)? *Tile 81: Realizing Power – Keys: 1, 2, 3, 4, 6, 10, 13.*

Anxious, 26

Anxiety arises because the problem of not getting what I want has not been resolved and being Over-pleasing (27) hasn't taken away the feelings of insecurity or hesitancy. In fact, the required result may be getting further away from being achieved and this creates a deeper feeling of insecurity and doubt that cannot be eradicated by being over-pleasing. A deep tension sets in, accompanied by a troubled mental or emotional state. A direction in which to move in order to feel secure is not forthcoming and an underlying apprehension to make a decision grows.

Anxiousness is often expressed here as concern and its accompanying biochemistry affects the body, especially the nerves. I can feel 'on tenterhooks' at the uncertainty of what is coming. The unpredictability of attaining security and safety is taking its toll and I can feel pressed to make a decision but unable to know the way forward. This is experienced as 'ill at ease'. 'What if' can be the dominant thought form and usually ends with a negative interpretation. A positive interpretation can either not be found from memories or cannot arise because I do not trust myself, those around me, or the situation. Wariness abounds and relationships are strained. The fear and anxiety at this level can show up as being disturbed, perplexed, fretful, on edge, overly sensitive or being 'on tenterhooks'.

ENTRAPMENTS: UNHEALTHY SELF-TALK – 26 – Anxious	GUIDANCE TO MOVING FORWARD TO A NEW MINDSET – 26 – Anxious
I just don't know.	I will look to find calm in nature. Whatever decision I make does it have to be set in concrete or can I change my mind? *Tile 70: Receptive – Keys: 1, 2, 3, 4, 10, 16, 18, 19.*
I am not practised at following my higher intuition.	Re-read tiles above 60. This engages Intuitive Witnessing Mind. I will learn the Awareness Code Mastery Techniques. *Tile 71: Witnessing – Keys: 1, 2, 3, 4, 6, 7, 10.*

I am pulling back and the walls are starting to come up as I feel a spiked nervous response to this situation.	There are always higher and lower potentials. Anxiety closes down higher potentials. What is the story activating? *Tile 60: Realizing Truth – Keys: 1, 2, 3, 4, 6, 8, 19.*
Things are starting to speed up and scramble.	I aim to speak my truth. Breathe. Take time out. Move. Go to nature. *Tile 87: Integrating – Keys: 1, 2, 3, 4, 10, 15, 16, 19, 20.*

Worried, 25

Being worried is a step closer into fear. The anxiety has built to a point where the person is now troubled by an outcome or unresolved situation. That which is not opening up for the person to create feelings of safety is experienced as increasing apprehension. Thoughts are repeating themselves and looping without resolution. I am building up the charge of negative and repetitive thoughts and the story is becoming more limiting as time goes on. A growing distress can be felt and my positive patterns and behaviour can be disturbed by the growing negative story.

I am increasingly perturbed by the situation and reading it as a problem rather than a challenge. I can tend to become over-preoccupied with the problem, weakening myself and the resolve of others. I can even become anguished, twisting and turning inside a story that is not coming up with answers. Combined with sleeplessness, this state plays havoc with my immune system and hormonal balance. My nerves can feel jittery and I can begin to fret that it will not improve, or that a solution will not be forthcoming. Feelings of being 'strung out', bothered and edgy all live in this level of Entrapment.

ENTRAPMENTS: UNHEALTHY SELF-TALK – 25 – Worried	GUIDANCE TO MOVING FORWARD TO A NEW MINDSET – 25 – Worried
How is this going to work? What if it doesn't ever work?	I am not a fortune teller who constantly predicts negativity into my future. What if it does work? Let's go with that for now. *Tile 73: Trustful – Keys: 1, 2, 3, 4, 5, 7, 11, 14.*

How is this possible?	I am to make it possible. Instead of closing it down, I am to open it up. *Tile 84: Embracing – Keys: 1, 2, 3, 4, 5, 7, 14, 19.*
It's not clear how I'm going to break this.	How have I found solutions in the past? If I just sit in 'not clear', it will never be clear. I have to release that and choose an optimistic above-60 tile. *Tile 63: Releasing – Keys: 1, 2, 3, 4, 5, 7, 8, 13.*
I can only find questions, not answers.	Questions are excellent, just ask to find the answers. More context is great. *Tile 70: Receptive – Keys: 1, 2, 3, 4, 6, 10, 15.*

Frightened, 24

Being frightened is another layer deeper in. It can become quite scary to be worried either for an extended time, or intensely over a short duration. Groundhog Day can wear me down. Being frightened really can take a lot of energy and the story that keeps fear alive can be quite compelling. There is no foreseeable future or resolution. My worrying intensifies to a state of contraction called fright. This can set off an internal alarm, where fear of fear itself may arise. A panicky feeling is accompanied by a building pressure and tension.

The story looks for evidence that something bad is looming and inevitable. Sudden news can shock me into being frightened or it can be a gradual build-up through experiencing the less intense stress Entrapments. There can be a predisposition towards feeling frightened about events that are similar or like the original event that caused fear.

If there is an external antagonist or persecutor, a person may feel browbeaten at this stage and the wants can get lost in tiredness. A person may feel haunted by a person or situation and find real or imagined evidence to support and justify the waves of fright that can well up from inside.

Being shaken, intimidated or being 'a bundle of nerves' can all live in this level of Entrapment.

ENTRAPMENTS: UNHEALTHY SELF-TALK – 24 – Frightened	GUIDANCE TO MOVING FORWARD TO A NEW MINDSET – 24 – Frightened
I am about to be exposed.	Breathe deeply. It's all conjecture. It's a story. What does 'exposed' mean here? How can I be stronger? *Tile 76: Emerging – Keys: 1, 2, 3, 6, 8, 16.*
People are looking at me.	Is this really happening, or am I in a memory? Is there a problem with them looking at me? Do I look at others? *Tile 84: Embracing – Keys: 1, 2, 3, 6, 8, 11.*
I am hearing 'I want to have a word with you'.	Find the thread to the bigger picture ASAP. What is the problem with having a word? I am willing to consider whatever anyone brings to me with awareness of how they bring it to me. *Tile 83: Fellowship Mindset – Keys: 1, 2, 3, 6, 8, 16.*
I will be criticized.	How much truth is there in what they are saying? Can I change criticism to 'positive, constructive feedback'? Are they seeing me and speaking to me from a place above 60? *Tile 72: Open-minded – Keys: 1, 2, 3, 4, 6, 8, 16.*

Trapped, 23

The experience of feeling trapped has a real stuckness about it, where the person cannot seem to find a way out of or away from a situation or person. The person is caught in some disempowering entanglement, perhaps even feeling captured in someone else's world of lies, deceit, blame, arrogance or whatever the story may be. The story that's unfolding has sucked me into being cornered with no way out, confined without the key, ensnared without being able to find or untie the knot. My Ego wants to believe it can control the outside world, get the results it wants. When it realizes it cannot always do that, it can collapse into this state of feeling trapped.

This can be very scary and daunting. I may be jammed into a compromising no-win scenario with someone about to ambush me. Or the perpetrator already has me and I am in a type of prison. This can be because of a physical external presence or internal real or imagined chain of events. I can feel like prey to the predator, shut down to the aggressor, enmeshed in someone's control game, or a prisoner to some jail sentence for something the person may not even know about. I can become too frightened to escape. Feelings of being 'cut off', isolated, cornered, closed in or imprisoned all live at this level of Entrapment.

ENTRAPMENTS: UNHEALTHY SELF-TALK – 23 – Trapped	GUIDANCE TO MOVING FORWARD TO A NEW MINDSET – 23 – Trapped
What is the other person going to think or do?	How do I not be as attached to what the other person thinks or does? Why am I worrying about what the other person is doing? That is using up my energy that could be put into finding solutions. What does it take to be more solid? Which tile above 60 can help me? *Tile 64: Reorientating – Keys: 1, 2, 3, 4, 6, 7, 19.*
There is no way of doing this differently.	Just do one small thing differently. It doesn't have to be big. I'll do something new to break away, break the pattern. Or a different above-60 tile, e.g. *Tile 85: Spontaneous – Keys: 1, 2, 3, 4, 6, 8, 19.*
I hear that as an ultimatum.	I'm probably projecting a belief given to me from my caretakers or a teacher. I will change my programming. *Tile 88: Integrity – Keys: 1, 2, 3, 4, 5, 15, 19, 20.*
I have no say here.	I don't have to sit and listen to this from the inside or the outside. I know I am better than this, I just have to get moving. What would it feel like to collaborate (75)? *Tile 75: Collaboration – Keys: 1, 2, 3, 4, 14, 16, 20.*

Dread, 22

Feeling trapped or trepidation for an extended period of time can lead to feelings of dread. At this level of entrapment, a person does not know how, where, when or why. It can feel like torture being this disempowered, especially if no known event or person seems to be causing it. A deep, unconscious story can be operating outside of my awareness and unfathomable dire consequences seem about to manifest without evidence, but it seems so real. There can be an external circumstance that is present that seems to perpetuate the state of dread in me, but Controlling it is too far away so I sink into an abyss of fear.

Other terms are distraught, aghast or terrified as things overtake my decreasing ability to hold on. Terrible, horrible and appalling are descriptors for what seems to be going on. The story is getting darker and darker. What else is there? Feelings of foreboding, alarm and being stricken with fear can live at this level of Entrapment.

ENTRAPMENTS: UNHEALTHY SELF-TALK – 22 – Dread	GUIDANCE TO MOVING FORWARD TO A NEW MINDSET – 22 – Dread
There is no way out of this.	Okay, I see the worst-case scenario, now what are the other possibilities? If I can imagine alternative outcomes, the feeling of doom will lift. *Tile 60: Realizing Truth – Keys: 1, 2, 3, 4, 6, 8, 9, 11.*
I can see only black/white, all/nothing, yes/no. No other option.	A small shift is neither 'all' or 'nothing' yet can make a big difference. Any action in the spirit of helping makes a contribution. *Tile 64: Reorientating – Keys: 1, 2, 3, 4, 6, 10, 11.*
What is the worst-case scenario?	What is the best-case scenario? I will go for that. *Tile 65: Positive – Keys: 1, 2, 3, 4, 6, 8, 9, 10, 11.*
I feel overwhelmed at what is being asked of me and what lies ahead.	Which part is overwhelming? I'll ask for help, map it out. *Tile 61: Ready – Keys: 1, 2, 3, 4, 6, 10, 15.*

Terror, 21

Terror is an extreme contraction and withdrawal away from abusive physical or psychological situations. Ongoing Dread (22) or Trapped (23) can lead to a hypersensitivity to any stimulus that is similar or might be similar to the initial impacting abuse. A 'panic attack' can ensue, where the person feels like there is nowhere to turn, no answer forthcoming, and there may be no rational explanation for the intensity of the terror. There is a feeling of 'nowhere' to hide.

This can be a fear of fear itself and it builds with repetition of the stimulus or thought of the impending confrontation, doom or unknown. If phobias persist or grow in intensity, terror can arise with the presentation of the perceived or real threat. Terror can involve being at the receiving end of a lot of intimidation, nightmarish scenarios, Malicious (40), Enraged (41) or Bully (42) behaviour from colleagues of other team members. The workplace can feel menacing, even horrifying. I can recoil and start to close down as a protective mechanism. I may even go into shock, which is moving towards being Numb (20).

ENTRAPMENTS: UNHEALTHY SELF-TALK – 21 – Terror	GUIDANCE TO MOVING FORWARD TO A NEW MINDSET – 21 – Terror
It's all closing in on me.	Where can I get help to recontextualize the story? It will take courage to own it and require help to shift it and I will find that courage (Stepping In). *Tile 60: Realizing Truth – Keys: 1, 2, 3, 5, 6, 8, 9.*
There is no solution.	There is a solution, it's just that I am unaware of it at the moment. *Tile 63: Releasing – Keys: 1, 2, 3, 5, 6, 8, 9.*
There is nowhere to go.	I will learn, no matter what happens. Can I do one thing differently? Change just one thing to start moving towards above 60? What will it be? *Tile 62: Preparing – Keys: 1, 2, 3, 5, 6, 8, 9.*
There is no end to this.	Maybe not right now. What tile above 60 do I need to see this through to its conclusion? When did I first start to believe there is no end to this? What is the pay-off for holding on to this belief? *Tile 60: Realizing Truth – Keys: 1, 2, 3, 6, 8, 9, 11.*

Numb, 20

Numbness can occur when all other options have failed to work. Close down, anaesthetize, don't feel, forget, suppress, repress, any *-press* to get away from the stress. Deaden expression, be blunt, desensitize, be heartless, so I don't feel anything. Be indifferent and detached from the other or situation, either consciously or not. I have reached overload. I freeze, harden, become thick-skinned or whatever it takes to stay numb, and I may not even be consciously thinking to do this. It's done for me in this state as the programme plays out. It is a type of protection or exhaustion. Emotionless, inert, tuned out, blocked out and listless are part of this realm. Numb is a defence mechanism that isn't satisfactory or pleasing but suffices in a time where nothing else is attainable. This is emotional flat-lining.

ENTRAPMENTS: UNHEALTHY SELF-TALK – 20 – Numb	GUIDANCE TO MOVING FORWARD TO A NEW MINDSET – 20 – Numb
I cannot do anything as it has repercussions.	I will just ride out this shutdown, let it pass. Am I able to find a tile above 30 so the repercussions of my behaviours do not become such a negative focus? *Tile 63: Releasing – Keys: 1, 2, 3, 8, 9, 16, 18.*
I don't want to feel or remember any of this emotionally.	Communication of some sort is required to get me out of this. I could talk to someone or keep a journal. I need to get to the bottom of the repressed emotions. *Tile 68: Fearless – Keys: 1, 2, 3, 8, 10, 15.*
I must protect myself at all costs.	For a start, I need some kind of nourishment, a hot drink, a good friend, an uplifting movie. I will connect to warmth. What is it that is in me that needs protecting? *Tile 73: Trustful – Keys: 1, 2, 3, 8, 10, 15.*
I am to close down, close off, disappear, vacate and see you later.	Body work, like massage, reflexology or shiatsu, will help me to unwind inner tension. It has been built over time and needs to be released. I will give that to myself. *Tile 63 – Releasing – Keys: 1, 2, 3, 10, 13.*

Let's review

- In this chapter you became familiar with where feelings of 'not good enough' can originate. A person who consistently fails to get what is wanted or is unable to control people or events can fall into the trap of becoming a victim of circumstances.
- A victim is unable to find the motivation, solutions or energy required to meet challenges appropriately and so there can be a build-up of stress.
- From the mildest form of Stressed at Hesitant, 29 to the most pronounced version of this level at Numb, 20, the common thread is a reluctance to meet challenging situations that hold the potential for growth by developing skills of competence through a 'can-do' or 'will try' attitude.
- Stepping out of the beliefs that keep people trapped in the level of Stressed begins with the Revelations outlined in this chapter. Begin with Fearless, 68 and try something new. Endeavour to fail at many new activities and focus on the new skill you are developing.

Coming Up Next

If a person is unable to find a mentor or assistance in dealing with stress and the attitudes that promote stress, before too long a sense of despondency can arise. Have you ever been in a situation where the overriding feeling has been 'What's the point?' If so, the next chapter can assist you in mapping how negative attitudes breed negative attitudes. This self-perpetuating negativity eats up your energy reserves, leaving you with even fewer resources to find your way out of the negativity.

CHAPTER EIGHT

Leaders Losing Their Way

What happens when leaders slip past Stressed (20–29) to a place further away from getting what they want?

10–19: The Level of Despondent

10 Inconsolable	11 Hopeless	12 Unfulfilled	13 Lethargic	14 Wounded	15 Hurt	16 Saddened	17 Disconnected	18 Discontented	19 Disinterested

A person at this level starts to blame himself and feels 'What's the point?' and lives as if he is missing out. This is the realm of despondency.

Disinterested, 19

Disinterested is the mildest form of despondency. If my energy has become very low from being stressed out and not getting what I want, this state can creep up on me without me choosing or realizing it. Or I can consciously decide 'I have had enough of wanting and stressing and it's not working for me,' so I will slide into disinterested. It's easy and maybe even familiar. Why be interested when people are not interested in me? Why set myself up to be stressed again? It's easier to pull back. I am 'over' others promising and not delivering. Here, I do not have to be concerned or stressed. I can be aloof and distant, uninvolved while I attend to my own needs. I don't have to rely on the outside world to provide me with anything. It's like Wanting has slipped away out of reach and I am heading into a long, slippery slope of being withdrawn and this is the starting point of the way down.

It's hard to find any motivation or willpower to get involved. I may be a bit 'battle-weary' or 'change fatigued'. This can arise as a series of small events showing me that I am not capable of getting what I want, or that someone else is not capable of giving me what I want. Sometimes it is one big event that leads a person to feeling disconnected.

ENTRAPMENTS: UNHEALTHY SELF-TALK – 19 – Disinterested	GUIDANCE TO MOVING FORWARD TO A NEW MINDSET – 19 – Disinterested
I close down to any situation that might hurt me.	What does it take to stay in the conversation exchange when I can feel the pull to leave? What would that look like? *Tile 72: Open-minded – Keys: 1, 2, 3, 6, 8, 19.*
What would I really like to be doing instead of this?	How can I contribute here before moving on to something I am passionate about? *Tile 80: Highest Callings – Keys: 1, 2, 3, 4, 5, 14.*
What am I really meant to be doing instead of this?	Closing down prematurely means I may miss something valuable. *Tile 79: Flowing – Keys: 1, 2, 3, 4, 6, 10.*
This is not my expertise so I am not putting myself out there.	*What is 'curiosity' anyway? How would that feel? Can I do something, anything, that would help another person so it's not all about me? Tile 88: Integrity – Keys: 1, 2, 3, 6, 14, 16.*

Discontented, 18

If a person stays Disinterested (19) for an extended period, it becomes easier to slide into being discontented. A person at this level has decided that there is no way to acquire what is wanted by being with friends, work or family, and they seem further and further away due to the disinterest. Becoming discontented is a state that arises as relationships disintegrate.

Exactly why a person feels discontented may be too unconscious to know. The story can be too deep. The person does not have access to why he is dissatisfied and the tile of Complacent (58) is unavailable to create a feeling of ease or comfort and so discontented becomes the pervading inner experience. I am disgruntled and uneasy and in mild discomfort and I may not be able to tell you why. I am not getting something I believe I want, but I may not be able to tell you what that is – 'I don't know, all I know is that something is not right with me or the world or something'. This can be a confusing place. Displeasure, unrest, disillusionment are all experiences at this level of Entrapment. A lot of the time, it is what I haven't got or can't find any more such as pleasure, satisfaction, a smile or feeling 'happiness', whatever that was, that results in the persistence of this level. It could be boredom, which is the lack of something that stimulates me into Complacent (58). It might be loneliness. Where is the comfort? Things are somewhat dreary, uninspiring, dim or dull. What happened to my inner drive when I was ready to take things on? If this keeps going, the experience of disconnection can arise.

ENTRAPMENTS: UNHEALTHY SELF-TALK – 18 – Discontented	GUIDANCE TO MOVING FORWARD TO A NEW MINDSET – 18 – Discontented
Right now, there is no reason to be happy, so I am unhappy.	This too will pass. I can read the statements of truth that help people get into above 60. I only need one of them to focus on. *Tile 64: Reorientating – Keys: 1, 2, 3, 4, 5, 16.*
I am not satisfied with what I am focusing on. If I keep going, it will be all of life.	It's all about where I focus. I don't have to know why I was here. Let's make a movement towards getting out of here. *Tile 65: Positive – Keys: 1, 2, 3, 4, 5, 11.*
I am uneasy about who I am. Do I know who I am?	I know some of my stories, preferences, dislikes and mistakes. I need to focus on my strengths, my value and abilities. I'll ask others. *Tile 64: Reorientating – Keys: 1, 2, 3, 4, 5, 11, 13.*
I don't feel pleased with things, I feel the absence of being pleased.	Do I know what I want? Do I know how to strive for what I want? Do I know what to do when I get what I want? *Tile 75: Collaboration – Keys: 1, 2, 3, 4, 11, 12, 13.*

Disconnected, 17

Being disconnected is a type of abdication, a pulling away, not through fear but a type of giving up. I separate away from the real or imagined source of pain, which is either not getting what I want or getting what I do not want. There is a disentanglement from the energetic flow or relationship as it used to be. Unplugging from some inappropriate conditions can create space but may give rise to a type of loneliness. This shutting down can be automatic or thought through and at this level the effects are negative.

Switching off gets me away from the persecution or failure but leaves me feeling incomplete and perhaps victimized. Taking a break can feel like a good idea but the charge of this Despondent level does not feel good. Something is lacking and I am left with that after the split, separating out, alienation or parting. The inner critic can make it my fault – 'they will be better off without me' or 'I am only an imposter anyway'.

ENTRAPMENTS: UNHEALTHY SELF-TALK – 17 – Disconnected	GUIDANCE TO MOVING FORWARD TO A NEW MINDSET – 17 – Disconnected
There is nowhere to go.	The outside world is a playground. There is everywhere to go but I have been holding myself back. *Tile 66: Adventurous – Keys: 1, 2, 3, 4, 8, 9, 15, 16.*
I do not feel heard or seen.	I have been looking in places for connections that don't serve me. I have been asking to be heard or seen from people who may not know how to or even want to. I'll let that go and do it myself. *Tile 74: Connected – Keys: 1, 2, 3, 4, 5, 6, 8, 10.*
I am not important.	I am a magnet for experiences and that magnet is my attitude. What tiles will help me attract more meaningful connections? *Tile 67: Conviction – Keys: 1, 2, 3, 5, 6, 8, 10.*
I am not required here.	Where am I required to be then? When can I be useful? Where can I find myself? *Tile 80: Highest Callings – Keys: 1, 2, 3, 4, 5, 8, 10, 21.*

Saddened, 16

Saddened is a light version of hurt. Something has happened that triggers a person into feeling let down or in an unhappy state. It feels like I have missed out on something, have been wronged or disturbed in some way. It starts with some disappointment, which is my first reaction, then I sink into feeling saddened. Perhaps I have been offended, persecuted, mistreated, provoked or affronted by an external source or from the inner critic or judge. Experiencing these provocations from the level of Controlling (40s) and judgement (50s) can trigger the victim and the feelings of being sad about it. Saddened or disappointed is the initial reaction to an event that challenges a person's Attachment (36) to something. With the perceived 'loss' or predicted loss, a sense of incompleteness or 'less than I was before' arises. Whatever I was using on which to base my sense of self has just been judged and it's off-putting and creates upset that can leave me teary and missing the previous uplifted feeling provided by that which has now been taken away.

The feelings of downcast, melancholy, cheerless, glum, mournful, disconsolate, dejected, down-hearted, doleful and sorry for myself all belong at this level of Entrapment.

ENTRAPMENTS: UNHEALTHY SELF-TALK – 16 – Saddened	GUIDANCE TO MOVING FORWARD TO A NEW MINDSET – 16 – Saddened
How can they do that to me? I am sad.	Why does it mean that much to me? What part of me places that much value on it? *Tile 70: Receptive – Keys: 1, 2, 3, 6, 7, 11, 14, 15.*
Why am I always missing out? Things seem unfair.	*Always* in an exaggeration. My suffering is due to setting up an attachment to something I want and believing I have to have it. *Tile 60: Realizing Truth – Keys: 1, 2, 3, 6, 7, 11, 14, 15.*
That's NOT what I was expecting or wanted.	Share the issue with someone who can genuinely listen. How do I learn to let go of that much expecting and Wanting? *Tile 64: Reorientating – Keys: 1, 2, 3, 4, 6, 11.*

I am fed up with how things don't always turn out right – I missed out again.	I cannot control *all* the variables in the mix. I am holding on to past let-downs and carrying them around inside of me. Enough! *Tile 64: Reorientating – Keys: 1, 2, 3, 6, 7, 14, 16, 19.*

Hurt, 15

Hurt is a place people visit when they feel any one or more of the following: abused, neglected, abandoned, left out, cheated on, attacked, harmed, forgotten, invalidated, overlooked, misunderstood, taken for granted, injured, blamed, disturbed, wronged, wounded, slighted, backstabbed. Obviously, this is not a complete list but there are many triggers that send people into feeling hurt. All of them stem from either not getting what I want, or getting what I don't want.

If people are relying on an external source to like, respect, love or want them then they set themselves up to being hurt, as many people are so preoccupied with their own wants that they are unable to, don't know how to, or are disinterested in giving warmth, respect or love.

In this space I am in pain as my story, fantasy, daydream or very reasonable expectation is not being realized. It feels like a psychological injury and can be described as an ache, a sharp, knife-like cut, a squeezing around the heart, a burning or stinging. An even deeper despondency is when the hurt turns into a wound.

ENTRAPMENTS: UNHEALTHY SELF-TALK – 15 – Hurt	GUIDANCE TO MOVING FORWARD TO A NEW MINDSET – 15 – Hurt
I am taking it personally and it is painful.	Where did all of this start? Which younger part of me set up this pattern? Can I recontextualize the pain? *Tile 71: Witnessing – Keys: 1, 2, 3, 6, 8, 9.*
I take to heart any criticism.	Is there any truth in what others are saying or doing that leads to experiencing this pain? Are they hurting me or am I using what they are doing/saying to repeatedly hurt myself because I haven't got to the core of the hurt and discharged it? *Tile 70: Receptive – Keys: 1, 2, 3, 6, 8, 9, 10, 16, 21.*

I am hypersensitive to any comments that are seen or experienced as negative in any way.	I have been conditioned this way. Instead of being victimized and giving into this, I am going to learn a new way. An above-60 way. I'll start by rereading tiles 60–63. *Tile 60: Realizing Truth – Keys: 1, 2, 3, 4, 6, 8, 10.*
I suffer when others disapprove of me.	I have a story that is sensitive to what others think of me. This is my suffering. How can I let them be themselves and have their opinions? I need to like myself and be solid in who I am. *Tile 67: Conviction – Keys: 1, 2, 3, 6, 8, 9, 16, 21.*

Wounded, 14

To be wounded is more intense than being hurt. This is more like a psychological injury that feels like being damaged in some way. Hurt is painful but wounded can be agonizing. It can be experienced as a deep cut, an open sore, a broken heart, 'completely gutted', 'write-off', mutilated, scarred, a 'tortured soul' or the 'walking wounded'. Severely ill-treated or abused is the perception of what has happened and this story keeps a person in being a victim. I have been harmed and perhaps my story is that I have been irreversibly harmed. I have been battered, mistreated, scandalized, back-stabbed or totally misrepresented. The hurt is ramped up and I can feel raw and hypersensitive, bitten, violated or marred. I may not be the same again. I may not recover. This can leave me unsound of mind, crippled or legless, with limited to no options as the pain intensifies. If I don't know how to get out of here, I might use up so much energy that I head into lethargy or apathy.

ENTRAPMENTS: UNHEALTHY SELF-TALK – 14 – Wounded	GUIDANCE TO MOVING FORWARD TO A NEW MINDSET – 14 – Wounded
I feel violated.	All things that happen to us have the potential for victimhood or empowerment. How is it humanly possible to be empowered by this? *Tile 78: Wow – Keys: 1, 2, 3, 6, 7, 8, 12.*

I have been severely mistreated.	What would above 60 do in this situation? How can I empower myself rather than be overcome by this challenge? *Tile 69: Fully In – Keys: 1, 2, 3, 12, 13, 16.*
I am extremely sensitive to judgement, both internally on myself and externally from others.	Judgement occurs when I have no empathy and little context about the situation or person. I will help others understand me by understanding myself first. *Tile 70: Receptive – Keys: 1, 2, 3, 5, 6, 8, 9.*
I am in disbelief at what has happened. This feels traumatic.	Is the insult/abuse real or perceived? Am I perceiving it the way it actually happened or is my story twisting it against myself? *Tile 60: Realizing Truth – Keys: 1, 2, 5, 6, 8, 9.*

Lethargic, 13

Lethargy is a feeling of sluggishness that arrives from the unwillingness to keep using up the amount of energy it takes to maintain living in a prolonged state of despondency. As no answer lives down here, it is bleak and lifeless so lethargy is a place to rest but it contains a lot of negative charge. Listlessness sees a person dragging his feet and being in this space they are less inclined to initiate. Longer term, a person can start to feel he is lazy and a 'good for nothing' story emerges. Apathy settles in and that can be judged as a 'cop out' and 'faced into'. My energy reserves are compromised 'Just leave me alone' is a common statement. Slothful is a rather extreme version, along with dormant, whereas passive and feeling dense are at the lighter end of lethargy. Life or the situation can be experienced as an uphill battle with little chance of resolution. The evidence is piling up that life is against me or I am plagued by 'bad luck'.

Stagnancy sets in and it's hard to move in any direction as positivity and aliveness to solve the situation is like a candle in the distance. Unresponsiveness is easier than being vulnerable again.

ENTRAPMENTS: UNHEALTHY SELF-TALK – 13 – Lethargic	GUIDANCE TO MOVING FORWARD TO A NEW MINDSET – 13 – Lethargic
I am emotionally fatigued.	Nothing is permanent. Rest and come back with a fresh approach. Which emotion or tile would be useful? What is it about that? *Tile 64: Reorientating – Keys: 1, 2, 3, 10, 16, 18, 19.*
I'm so physically tired.	There is a time to do nothing, which is not lethargy. It is deep yin, time to rest, absorb, sleep, meditate. Then there is a time to get moving again, yang action. My body is letting me know to rest and be in a yin state. *Tile 70: Receptive – Keys: 1, 2, 3, 10, 18, 19.*
Someone else can do it for a change.	I will participate in some group activity to feel some connection and aliveness within the team. *Tile 72: Open-minded – Keys: 1, 2, 3, 10, 18, 19, 20.*
What's the point?	The point hasn't arrived yet, or I dismissed it. Did I ever have a point? What is so important about having a point? I chose to cultivate patience and learn the Awareness Code Mastery Techniques. *Tile 92: Heartfelt – Keys: 1, 2, 3, 10, 14, 16, 19.*

Unfulfilled, 12

At the level of unfulfilled, life is demoralizing. Unrealized potentials or dreams on a larger scale can feel gut-wrenching. What I want has not been achievable so a feeling of not being enough can seep into my existence. Internal judgement of myself can begin to take over. I am not able to overcome the internal voice that uses words like 'never', 'always' and 'forever' when talking about how things will not work out for me. This space has been described as a hole, a blank canvas, a missing piece of the jigsaw puzzle. Even if I have attained what I think I want, an empty, all-pervasive feeling can still be there. I might even be surrounded by all the things I thought would make me happy, all that money can buy, but it doesn't fill the inner-longing ache or sense of missing something.

Sometimes it's like I have fulfilled all external requirements and expectations but inside the achievements have not given me an uplifted feeling. Something is missing or is unaccomplished. An inner disillusionment descends and failure takes hold. The negative Entrapment story can come up with all sorts of possibilities as to why I am incomplete and less than.

ENTRAPMENTS: UNHEALTHY SELF-TALK – 12 – Unfulfilled	GUIDANCE TO MOVING FORWARD TO A NEW MINDSET – 12 – Unfulfilled
I have no purpose like others.	Focus in the moment on something simple like asking for context. Anything that demands my full attention and can be achieved. *Tile 60: Realizing Truth – Keys: 1, 2, 3, 6, 7, 8.*
Everybody else knows what they want to do with their life.	Breathe into the feeling, sit in it until it passes. 'Everybody' is a generalization. Can I share my perspective? Life purpose doesn't open up until tile 80. Contemplate what it takes to get there. *Tile 80: Highest Callings – Keys: 1, 2, 3, 6, 7, 8.*
I have put another person on a pedestal and they turned out to be human.	Can I learn to be of service to someone or something? We all have to learn about idols and experience let-down. *Tile 89: Inspiring – Keys: 1, 2, 3, 6, 7, 8, 10.*
I imagined this job to be far more rewarding/exciting/creative than it really is.	We all expect (level of Wanting) until we learn not to. Let's not expect as much. The job is what it is. Do I want to stay or go? *Tile 94: Thriving – Keys: 1, 2, 3, 6, 7, 8, 10.*

Hopeless, 11

To feel hopeless is a dark existence. The light is just going out and a forlorn dejection arises. Pessimism is everywhere as the positive perspective is behind a sky of dark clouds. A person feels useless. The situation is useless. Trying is useless. Misery can creep in and the state feels incurable. Others with their positive attitude when trying to help me can seem to interfere rather than assist. Things are not quite impossible but close to it.

Feeling dejected seems the only response to have considering the evidence the story has accumulated. There appears to be so much evidence on the negative side of the story to focus on that the person might even lose sight of the positive lessons the situation presents. Being hopeless is much more than being unfortunate. It is very bad luck, even disastrous bad luck, and it is easy to blame myself. There are so many ways to put myself down. Desolation is close. I am feeling like a desperado. Opportunities and chances appear to close down – 'What's the point of doing or trying anything? It's hopeless even believing there is a way out of this'. If I keep going, it turns into inconsolable (10).

ENTRAPMENTS: UNHEALTHY SELF-TALK – 11 – Hopeless	GUIDANCE TO MOVING FORWARD TO A NEW MINDSET – 11 – Hopeless
It will turn out to be nothing.	Nothing is okay. Empty is okay. What is the problem? This is a chance to practise the releasing of emotions with my meditation. *Tile 70: Receptive – Keys: 1, 2, 3, 8, 10, 15.*
I am stuck and I won't or cannot be rescued.	If I hold on to this for any longer it will make me sick. I will own my pretending and ask for help. Let's not stay an imposter. Focus on what I am good at. *Tile 67: Conviction – Keys: 1, 2, 3, 8, 10, 16, 19, 20.*
I am overlooked, unseen, unwanted and rejected.	Do they really know the real me? Do I know the real me? How do I start to know? I can persist with a new project or hobby to show myself I can. *Tile 64: Reorientating – Keys: 1, 2, 3, 8, 10, 12.*
I'm not the person I'm made out to be. I am an imposter, a charlatan.	Okay, so I have fabricated, distorted or pretended. I will move on and agree not to do that to the best of my ability. Let's have a break from the lifestyle that created the tile. *Tile 63: Releasing – Keys: 1, 2, 3, 8, 10, 20.*

Inconsolable, 10

Inconsolable is arrived at through perceiving the situation or myself as irredeemable, irreversible or irretrievable. There appears to be no way back and it starts to feel like torture. Life with no hope is one of deep anguish and repeated thoughts of such despair that the story grows heavier and heavier. Descriptions such as 'lost cause', no-win situation, tragic and disastrous can further cement the heaviness and gravity of being inconsolable. Perception is clouded and an ineptness is my constant bedfellow. Everywhere I look, my perceived deficiency renders me valueless. A wretched landscape as far as I can see.

Others have described this as a type of torment and torture that is very hard to get on top of because it is invisible. It's inside of me and I can feel like no one else knows this space or what I'm going through because there doesn't seem to be anyone in it with me. No one knows how to talk about it or they are perhaps too embarrassed to talk about it.

ENTRAPMENTS: UNHEALTHY SELF-TALK – 10 – Inconsolable	GUIDANCE TO MOVING FORWARD TO A NEW MINDSET – 10 – Inconsolable
I will never get over this.	All things pass. There is a wave in nature where it hits a peak and discharges unless you feed it. What do I do to help this pass? *Tile 69: Fully In – Keys: 1, 2, 3, 8, 13, 15, 16.*
It's devastating and way too much for one person to deal with.	How can I delegate? Can I ask for help? Can I reschedule? There is a way through this. *Tile 75: Collaboration – Keys: 1, 2, 3, 16, 19, 20.*
You can never know how much you love someone/something until they are/it is gone.	Am I able to find that love and refocus on that? The powerful feeling of having had them in my life. What does that feel like? *Tile 90: Grateful – Keys: 1, 2, 3, 8, 15, 18.*
I am immersed/consumed in over my head with thoughts and feelings.	I will look for the crack of possibility or potential. I will volunteer my services with an organization I choose. How do I find a glimmer of hope? How in the past have I found hope? *Tile 64: Reorientating – Keys: 1, 2, 3, 7, 8, 15, 16, 19.*

Let's review

- Stress chews up energy and so it becomes easier to feel despondent about situations and one's capacity to deal with challenges.
- At this level it becomes a coping mechanism to pull away from life and to conserve energy. Any gains that are made in building energy are lost through the negative self-talk that arises at this level. It becomes difficult to motivate yourself out of sadness or hopelessness and lethargy dulls all joy.
- Finding a mentor or some type of assistance at these levels becomes crucial.
- From the mildest form of despondency at Disinterested, 19 to the most pronounced version of this level at Inconsolable, 10, the common thread is a decreased connection with the energy at the centre of the life force. Negativity is becoming more pronounced and a person's spirit dulled to the point where the spark of life is not felt.
- Stepping out of the beliefs that keep people trapped in the level of Despondent begins with the Revelations outlined in this chapter. Begin with Releasing, 63 and do so with a trusted friend, therapist or work colleague.

Coming Up Next

What happens when thoughts become more negative, heavier or darker and the energy to release them is simply not available? What are the common thinking errors that keep people trapped in this level of seeing the world? How can you identify a person at this level and how do you help someone feeling completely alienated from life? The following chapter explicitly shows you the attitudes at the level of Lifeless and how to transcend this spiritless place.

CHAPTER NINE

Leaders Who Have Lost Their Way

What happens when thoughts or feelings become heavier, darker or more isolating?

0–9: The Level of Lifeless

0	1	2	3	4	5	6	7	8	9
Self-loathing	Self-hatred	Pathetic	Unlovable	Burden	Embar-rassed	Wrong	Regretful	Never Enough	Inad-equate

What happens when you don't get what you want, or get what you don't want? You can move up into Controlling (40–49) or you can slip into Stressed (20s) or even slide further into Despondent (10s) or now down to the lowest level, Lifeless. This is the part of being human that is experienced as a victim, disempowered, in lack, unable to 'read' the situation without personalizing it, full of old negative stories, self-condemning, unsafe and lack of control. There is no solid ground to hang on to and a lack of centredness exists. Here, I can't tell the difference between what is truth and non-truth, or what is real and not real. Emotionally and mentally (and eventually physically), it is painful.

The lowest 10 ways of existing now open up. The mildest version is at 9 and the heaviest is at 0.

Inadequate, 9

Being in this realm is a very personal space, where all thoughts and feelings are about me and these thoughts and feelings are somehow all against me in some way. This detrimental perspective of oneself begins with some deficiency or 'not quite good enough' feeling. Any unsatisfactory outcome is used to reinforce the story that fundamentally there is a flaw of some kind or something about me that is deemed inappropriate by myself. The self put-down can be felt as being unsuitable, lacking or faulty in some minor way. I will be left with an edge of inadequacy that can penetrate relationships and work ethic and infect the team so they start to notice it or even feel it too. The imposter syndrome (IS) can live here and dwells as an undercurrent of not being quite up to the required expectations, standards or expertise. Egotistical (50s) with its Ego Confidence (57) feels just out of reach. There can be guilt that leads to not being enough.

ENTRAPMENTS: UNHEALTHY SELF-TALK – 9 – Inadequate	GUIDANCE TO MOVING FORWARD TO A NEW MINDSET – 9 – Inadequate
I feel so awkward.	I am different. How can I see my difference kindly? I am in transition and always learning. *Tile 76: Emerging – Keys: 1, 2, 3, 4, 6, 8.*
I have two left feet.	Each of us has our unique qualities. What might mine be? It takes time to learn so why am I putting myself down? *Tile 87: Integrating – Keys: 1, 2, 3, 10, 12, 14, 15.*
I have nothing for you.	If I stop focusing on inadequacies I can have an opportunity to keep improving. Learning is empowering. I have something for you, even if I don't know what it is yet. *Tile 85: Spontaneous – Keys: 1, 2, 3, 4, 7, 8, 15.*
I'm not really skilled for this.	I will start a course, any course. A new sport. A new activity. I'll start small and achieve in steps. *Tile 61: Ready – Keys: 1, 2, 3, 6, 8, 10, 13.*

Never Enough, 8

Feelings of never being enough underlie the belief that I am being ineffective and do not have enough of whatever it takes to be free of the feeling. It is deeper than Inadequate (9) in that inadequate can be somewhat temporary but never enough is where the feeling is, staying around and undermining all activity.

It can be associated with feeling constantly small, substandard, incapable and a failure at having what it takes for completion.

There are constant reminders available in anything that is attempted to suggest not being what is required. Only one thing has to be too challenging or deemed a mistake or failure and the story opens up and the past seems to swallow up the actual achievements and successes. The one thing that wasn't present as an ability or foresight or whatever was required means that I will never be enough. It is a generalization of inadequacy that makes it very hard to enjoy a task as the story is just waiting to judge me. Here, I can receive mostly compliments from my colleagues but the one criticism is what I focus on exclusively and I use that criticism not to learn something but to bring myself down. Where did all the compliments go? They do not 'fit in' or register with the story that is 'never enough'.

ENTRAPMENTS: UNHEALTHY SELF-TALK – 8 – Never enough	GUIDANCE TO MOVING FORWARD TO A NEW MINDSET – 8 – Never enough
I am a waste of space.	The bigger picture is here somewhere. What is it? I just don't know what it is yet. Then I will know I am to be valuable in this space. *Tile 79: Flowing – Keys: 1, 2, 3, 15, 18, 19.*
I don't belong here, I am not good enough.	This situation provides me with a space to find a new skill and to practise it. I'm good at something, what is it? *Tile 70: Receptive – Keys: 1, 2, 3, 4, 7, 8, 10.*

I cause people grief.	Lots of people experience despondency. I might trigger that and will look at my role in that with a view to having more empathy. *Tile 91: Sincere – Keys: 1, 2, 3, 6, 8, 13, 15.*
No one asks for my help.	When I wasn't heard, what did I learn to do as a child? How do I offer help? With empowerment or otherwise? *Tile 74: Connected – Keys: 1, 2, 3, 6, 8, 15.*

Regretful, 7

Being regretful arises because I believe more and more the story that I am inadequate or not enough. 'Sorry' is a common phrase to excuse myself for the oversight or lack that is perceived or real. Remorse is the reaction to what just went 'wrong', requiring an apologetic attitude. I can lament that which didn't give rise to success or whatever I wanted, and I can ruminate on how I could have done it differently, better, smarter or some other way that would ease this dejected feeling. Rehashing the inadequacy builds regret. At this level there is no ability to learn new things as regret takes up all the energy.

A self-reproaching, guilt-ridden reaction is toxic and detrimental to a person's biochemistry, but in this outlook on life there is no choice. My inadequacy has once again shown to be who I am and regret seems to be a place I go, more as a default than as a way of working through it. Due to its disempowering nature, working through it is not possible here. It was once considered appropriate for someone to be remorseful as if it was a good thing and that it would lead someone to be a better person than who they were before. It is a type of stuck internal existence that brings a person down instead of motivating them to springboard over 60 and be that improved version of themselves. However, time spent here can help me to realize not to do this to myself but find a way above 60 to help myself out of here and help other people in my life.

ENTRAPMENTS: UNHEALTHY SELF-TALK – 7 – Regretful	GUIDANCE TO MOVING FORWARD TO A NEW MINDSET – 7 – Regretful
I should know better than that.	I am judging others and myself instead of guiding them. How do I learn to guide and support? What can I do differently? *Tile 89: Inspiring – Keys: 1, 2, 3, 4, 5, 6, 7, 9.*
I make bad decisions.	How bad? What criteria am I using? What is 'that bad'? These so-called 'bad decisions' are stepping stones to a smarter me. I will review and learn the lessons. I can also help others to review them. *Tile 77: Agile – Keys: 1, 2, 3, 5, 9, 12.*
I have poor judgement.	What can I do to be more 'solid' in who I am in the face of 'self-criticism'? Who can show me another way? *Tile 72: Open-minded – Keys: 1, 2, 3, 4, 7, 8, 16.*
How could I not see that coming?	I am allowed to have numerous attempts before I am expected to learn. Intuition starts at 60. Let's get above 60 now. *Tile 70: Receptive – Keys: 1, 2, 3, 4, 7, 8, 10.*

Wrong, 6

At this level I have interpreted or been told that the situation is one where I am in the wrong, or I am at fault by being me. This can lead to feeling like I am personally a mistake. Someone may have been referring to an aspect of my behaviour but the trap is that I experience it as 'I am all wrong' or 'They think that's what I am, wrong, that's me'. Wrong starts to define me and the story grows. I can feel that I am always incorrect, problematic, an error, the one to blame, bad, not right or unsuitable. This is the place I go to realize my imperfections and lack of anything – intelligence, beauty, ideas, etc. But it's not a freeing, above-60 realization of the truth. Instead, a victim mentality arises, reinforcing the negative story that weighs a person down with 'Yeah, that's me, another mistake'.

Feeling wrong starts to make me feel sluggish and apathetic and to avoid that my mind can focus on how unfair this wrongness is – 'Why do I always have to get it wrong; be wrong; be the one who's blamed?' Comparison happens a lot here and it's always unfavourable. Looking into the future, I know I will be unsuitable, unfit and inappropriate for the job because I have either told myself that so many times or others have told me that. I am convinced that this is me, my identity – I am flawed, weird, different.

ENTRAPMENTS: UNHEALTHY SELF-TALK – 6 – Wrong	GUIDANCE TO MOVING FORWARD TO A NEW MINDSET – 6 – Wrong
I am one big mistake.	No one is perfect. This story is an exaggeration. I can begin to change myself by letting go of this negative interpretation. *Tile 63: Releasing – Keys: 1, 2, 3, 5, 7, 8, 12.*
It's my fault, my mistake.	So-called mistakes or errors are how I learn. How can I know accepting mistakes leads to humility? *Tile 64: Reorientating – Keys: 1, 2, 3, 4, 6, 7, 8.*
They or I am displeased or disapprove of me or what I did, do, represent.	What can I learn from that which has been perceived to be wrong? I can be a better person from it if I study it. *Tile 65: Positive – Keys: 1, 2, 3, 5, 7, 8, 10, 12.*
You are more likely to be correct if I see you as an authority figure.	I may default to an adult/child relationship, where I am the child. What is that about? What is the situation that promotes that? What would it take to remain the adult? *Tile 64: Reorientating – Keys: 1, 2, 3, 5, 9, 10, 15.*

Embarrassed, 5

Being embarrassed follows on from feeling wrong in some way. The wrong is embarrassing and something I want to avoid or hide away from and keep secret. While Inadequate (9) and Never Enough (8) were perhaps mildly uncontrollable and I felt ill at ease and awkward, here I can feel humiliated and disgraced. I want to shrink up and disappear at the apparent lack of something like wisdom, understanding or the right thing to say or do. Or I want to shrink up and disappear at the apparent presence of something like another 'bad' choice, a 'useless' comment, another 'mistake' assumption, etc. It seems to be all about getting it 'wrong' according to my or someone else's set of rules, doctrine or expectations. I didn't give them what they wanted or I didn't manage to give myself what I want so I took a deep dive down into dishonouring myself or my team. I can feel indebted to the other for personally being so 'wrong'. Showing the other person or team I feel bad can be a learned subconscious pattern, like saying 'I'm sorry' without having to say anything.

ENTRAPMENTS: UNHEALTHY SELF-TALK – 5 – Embarrassed	GUIDANCE TO MOVING FORWARD TO A NEW MINDSET – 5 – Embarrassed
How could I do such a thing?	What's done is done, it's history. How can I now become a better version of myself from this experience? *Tile 63: Releasing – Keys: 1, 2, 3, 5, 8.*
What will they think of me? What they think of me is very important.	How do I begin to become more solid in my own uniqueness? Hold on to my positive rather than let negative get a hold of me? *Tile 73: Trusting – Keys: 1, 2, 3, 5, 19.*
Can I take that back?	I cannot change what just happened but I can definitely change the story or tile that interprets the event. *Tile 69: Fully In – Keys: 1, 2, 3, 16.*
If only it were different. If only I were different.	The past cannot be different. Who I become from what my story is can definitely be different and I can start by choosing a higher tile that interprets the situation in a positive way. Which tile is it? *Tile 65: Positive – Keys: 1, 2, 3, 5, 10, 12.*

Burden, 4

Feeling like a burden is a more intense experience of guilt, where not only is there a personal, internal attack on my character or performance but the 'other' person or team is taken into account and I feel guilty that I am affecting them detrimentally. I can feel like I am a heavy weight for others and that they would be better off without me. I may leave and not even tell anyone why as it is 'better for everyone' without me 'interfering'. It feels like me being present is a strain on others and that I will encumber the progress. I feel myself to be a liability and a 'best outcome' will not be achievable if I am involved. In some way, the team project is hampered, even handicapped, by me being part of it.

The story has really grown substantially for me to perceive that I am overloading the unfolding with whatever negative quality I have or absence of some positive quality that I should have. I am a millstone around someone's neck and adding to the hardship of workload for the others in some way. Maybe I am dead wood or an albatross and it is best I am not part of it. It is easier to abdicate into this story and leave than put myself back in the 'firing line'. I feel I am creating more work for my team, therefore slowing them down – a hindrance.

ENTRAPMENTS: UNHEALTHY SELF-TALK – 4 – Burden	GUIDANCE TO MOVING FORWARD TO A NEW MINDSET – 4 – Burden
I am just in the way.	What am I afraid of if I were to contribute or join in? Was there ever a time when I contributed or joined in and it was wonderful? If so, how do I remember that constantly and motivate myself with that feeling? *Tile 64: Reorientating – Keys: 1, 2, 3, 6, 7, 8.*
They would be better off without me.	I could ask others who appear above 60 what value I am, what I have contributed in the past or what Realizing Power (81) I have. *Tile 64: Reorientating – Keys: 1, 2, 3, 4, 6, 7, 8.*
I am a dead weight in this relationship/position/ project.	What makes me believe I am a dead weight? How do I get past the victim and find a role model or mentor for myself? Who can I ask for guidance? In the meantime, what can I contribute? *Tile 64: Reorientating – Keys: 1, 2, 3, 4, 6, 7, 8.*

| I can't change, even if I want to. | I made it up some time ago. It's not me, it's a negative story. How do I change it? Apparent failures are a doorway to learning what not to do for as many times as it takes.
Tile 64: Reorientating – Keys: 1, 2, 3, 4, 6, 7, 8. |

Unlovable, 3

This tile appears as a deep sense of unworthiness. It is like somewhere, sometime, someone forgot to help me understand I am lovable by not showing me or telling me. Maybe my parents or caretakers were unable to or too busy, or simply didn't know how to truly love me when I was younger. I looked for a sense of self by listening and watching others to see if I was lovable. What feedback did I get? I was like a sponge, just soaking it all up, and it may not have been the message that I was loved. And that still sits deep inside of me, at my core.

This can feel very empty, like a hole. I may not have learned how to like myself. Without being loved from the outside means there is a place that remains waiting for the validation that being loved brings. Having a sense of being unwanted, outcast, rejected, discarded or someone to be avoided can be gut-wrenching. This is when someone 'out there' is not loving me because I am unlovable. I might use any addictive substance or situation to get away from this part of myself. I might even create a big Ego (50s) and pretend I am lovable or become Addicted (32) or Attached (36) to anyone who says they love me, even if the person is manipulating or Controlling (40s) me to get what they want.

ENTRAPMENTS: UNHEALTHY SELF-TALK – 3 – Unlovable	GUIDANCE TO MOVING FORWARD TO A NEW MINDSET – 3 – Unlovable
Nobody wants to hang with me or be my friend.	I need to like myself. What can I do that inspires me and would help me to feel good about myself? To be my own best friend, what could I do differently? *Tile 64: Reorientating – Keys: 1, 2, 3, 6, 7, 8.*

Good things happen to others.	This is because they hold good beliefs about themselves. What good beliefs do I hold about myself? What am I scared of, if good things were to happen to me? *Tile 64: Reorientating – Keys: 1, 2, 3, 6, 7, 8.*
I am a bad person.	I listen to a story that comes from not being good enough for someone who needed me to be a certain way. Where is the story that promotes me in a good way? *Tile 64: Reorientating – Keys: 1, 2, 3, 6, 7, 8.*
I don't get picked/invited because of what I am.	How do I let people decide who they want on the team? How can that happen? What am I in my story that leads to not being picked/invited? Do I do that to others? *Tile 64: Reorientating – Keys: 1, 2, 3, 6, 7, 8.*

Pathetic, 2

It is one thing to be unlovable because I am not seen or understood, but what if I am seen and understood and judged very harshly? I may be told externally or internally that I am obnoxious, a waste of space or unwished for. It can be that somehow, I am very low on the ladder of achievement or hierarchy. Whatever it is, I am doomed to a soul-crushing feeling of being just plain lousy. I may be a shadow of my former self or someone who simply hasn't lived up to any potential and so I am condemned for that, according to the story that lives at this level of Entrapment.

I might even be considered to be plain bad or irredeemable as a friend, colleague or employee. This can be accompanied by a feeling of being cast out, castigated or excommunicated on account of being pathetic as in some way I am undeserving of staying. Perhaps I am deemed tainted in some way or inferior to the point where I am unable to be around. The story has really deepened as certain things about my nature are highlighted. Anything that seems to make me different can and will be used against me down here by my internal story, the inner judge in me.

ENTRAPMENTS: UNHEALTHY SELF-TALK – 2 – Pathetic	GUIDANCE TO MOVING FORWARD TO A NEW MINDSET – 2 – Pathetic
I will never get past this habit/addiction/way of living.	I either give up or get going. I choose to get going. How do I get going? What's first? What feelings lead me to this way of living? What can I do to begin a new way of living? *Tile 64: Reorientating – Keys: 1, 2, 3, 6, 7, 8.*
How did I miss that?	Remember times when I didn't miss it? Remember how good that felt? If I have felt it once and acted from it, then I can do it again. Next time I will hold on to it a little bit longer. *Tile 64: Reorientating – Keys: 1, 2, 3, 6, 7, 8.*
I am an embarrassment to myself and to my team.	I am using a small percentage of my mind's capacity. I need a role model to show me how to become more. I am more than my past feelings. I am more than my personality. I am more than what 'they' say I am. I am more than what I think I am. What am I? *Tile 64: Reorientating – Keys: 1, 2, 3, 6, 7, 8.*
What do I have to contribute to this? I can't see it.	Ask someone I admire what they perceive I have contributed in the past and now do everything to connect with that quality or skill again. *Tile 64: Reorientating – Keys: 1, 2, 3, 4, 6, 7, 8, 16.*

Self-hatred, I

Self-hatred follows on from feeling or being told I am Pathetic (2). All the words like self-loathing, self-deprecating, self-contempt and self-disgust tell the story of a hugely negative interpretation of most if not all of what I do, say or simply am. It is a form of non-physical self-annihilation, where I reduce myself down to the least possible worth because of the apparent evidence accumulated against me from inside myself. If it's from the external, I have no choice but to believe it. Disregarding the one-sided nature of the judgement, the trap is to 'go with' the condemnation and build the story more.

Self-abasement is an extreme dislike for that which I attempt to be in the world. I am not important enough to love or even like. Loneliness abounds. It can feel like a type of punishment doled out by others or myself and wears me down. Despising myself is debilitating, but seemingly warranted as the only way to deal with my perceived ugliness, stupidity, wrongness or whatever is presented. I can even become self-derisive and mocking of myself, becoming my own worst critic.

ENTRAPMENTS: UNHEALTHY SELF-TALK – 1 – Self-hatred	GUIDANCE TO MOVING FORWARD TO A NEW MINDSET – 1 – Self-hatred
I am deeply ashamed of myself.	It is just a story, no one is perfect. How can I be better than this? What do I have to release? *Tile 63: Releasing – Keys: 1, 2, 3, 6, 7, 8.*
I feel putrid.	Where did this story come from? A judgement comes from a judge. The judge usually comes after an event. I am more than this. What can I do to change this? *Tile 63: Releasing – Keys: 1, 2, 3, 6, 7, 8.*
I am disgusting.	How do I step out of victim mode? That's only a thought and a thought can be changed. I don't have to believe it. What can I replace it with? *Tile 63: Releasing – Keys: 1, 2, 3, 6, 7, 8.*
Who I am is endlessly flawed.	Flawed is relative and collects biased evidence. Flawed is a judgement that condemns me. Where did this begin? Where did I get the idea? What do I need to do to no longer believe this? *Tile 63: Releasing – Keys: 1, 2, 3, 6, 7, 8.*

Self-loathing, 0

Self-loathing is full of misery. Self-hatred has deepened into extreme personal rejection of one or many aspects of self. Deep shame permeates this tile and the internal dialogue and belief system is both very believable and very repetitive. There can be a heaviness that permeates and pervades activities to such an extent that it feels it's best to stay away from others.

The rejection of self has deepened to a feeling of disgust. Disapproving of oneself this much can be described as feeling like an abomination and may result in self-harm. Criticizing myself with real vitriol occurs. Deep-seated hostility is experienced against self. Talking about myself with extreme derision, contempt and disdain occurs at this level of Entrapment. If someone offers a perspective from higher tiles, this tile is so focused on the reprehensible nature of self that the positive cannot penetrate the feeling of being disgraceful and deplorable.

ENTRAPMENTS: UNHEALTHY SELF-TALK – 0 – Self-loathing	GUIDANCE TO MOVING FORWARD TO A NEW MINDSET – 0 – Self-loathing
I have been a disgrace and everybody has had enough.	Is that real? What is the evidence for that? What can I do to show them that I am more than just this part that keeps me believing I have been a disgrace? *Tile 63: Releasing – Keys: 1, 2, 3, 6, 7, 8.*
I don't feel anyone could possibly need me around here.	Someone will need me in the future. In the meantime, I can help someone else feel noticed. *Tile 63: Releasing – Keys: 1, 2, 3, 6, 7, 8.*
Will anyone really care if I leave the team? I'm sure the answer is no.	There is someone I haven't met yet who is waiting for me. If no one really cares if I'm here or not then there is no one left to please. I can please myself now! *Tile 63: Releasing – Keys: 1, 2, 3, 6, 7, 8.*
My life is like a series of dominoes lined up. When one gets knocked over, they are all knocked over.	What evidence is there to this negative story? How do I create 'one gets knocked over and I find a way to bounce back? Six times knocked down, seven times stand up!' *Tile 63: Releasing – Keys: 1, 2, 3, 6, 7, 8.*

Let's review

- Long periods in the level of despondency can tip a person into more pronounced expressions of giving up on life. At this level, a person has bought into the belief that life is meaningless and so he becomes a victim to the effects of negativity with no way of recontextualizing events and finding positive solutions.
- This is a very isolating level to exist in and a person will need to address not only the lifelessness in the physical body but the charge stored in suppressed emotions and the toxic thoughts that keep this level in place.
- Less energy is available at this level for the activities that can rebalance the body, hence it becomes more difficult to make changes. Support is critical at this level.
- Some of the victim attitudes prevalent in our societies are ingrained in our bodies and the structures of our bureaucracies.
- From the mildest form of Lifeless at Inadequate, 9, to the most pronounced version of this level at Self-loathing, 0 the common thread is a desire to avoid participating in life as it is too painful and meaningless.
- Stepping out of the consuming negative beliefs that keep people trapped in the level of Lifeless begins with the Revelations outlined in this chapter. Begin with tile 60 at Realizing Truth and Releasing (63) the suffering through consistent therapeutic help.

Coming Up Next

What is the way out of the trap of negativity? What is empowered leadership and how do I nurture it? What are the qualities that signal the end of 'Ego' and the emergence of integrity? The following chapter reveals the antidote to the heaviness and hopelessness of the tiles below 29 and the Egotistical inflation of those below 59.

PART 4

THE BEGINNING OF TRUE LEADERSHIP

CHAPTER TEN

Stepping into Integrity

The Beginning of Integrity Starts with
Stepping into the Tiles of Revelation

This part of the journey helps people find a way through the maze of below-60 Ego and to realize or find a truth that can help them out of all the Entrapments. Seeking what I want by Controlling, being Egotistical or to avoid the pain of being a victim feels hollow and unsatisfying as it is soulless and self-centred. The repetitive cycle of victim and perpetrator is seen for what it is and discarded in order to focus on the real need at hand. The outcome is less important than the means through which that outcome is arrived at through the efforts of the team. The Code's power opens up at Realizing Truth (60), the doorway to integrity and inclusiveness.

Tiles 60–63 are the place where a type of metamorphosis occurs. Old behaviours are seen for what they are and relinquished so that new ones begin to emerge. There can be a period of intense readjusting at tile 64 and time out may be required, or seeing a therapist or simply calling a meeting to clarify how the way forward will be different. This dynamic will be explored in detail as we explore the approach taken at tiles 60–63. The tiles of integrity open at the level Stepping In and they are centred around 'us' and 'we' rather than 'I' and 'me'. The latter is left behind as a deeper truth about how to live starts to arrive.

The Truths

Before we take a closer look at the tiles in each of the development lines that reveal a more positive approach you will notice that after each tile description there is a table that identifies the truths that exist at each level and the tiles that make up the level. Repeating these truths and contemplating their wisdom begins to reshape the brain away from negative responses.

60–69: The Level of Stepping In

60 Realizing Truth	61 Ready	62 Preparing	63 Releasing	64 Reori-entating	65 Positive	66 Adven-turous	67 Convic-tion	68 Fearless	69 Fully In

Here, you are motivated by improvement in yourself, others and the team. You are looking for a win-win in all relationships and learning to respond through witnessing rather than reacting through Ego. You actually see your below-60 self and the below-60 self of others as being an endless drama. Finally, you can see just how much this is happening and how much people do not realize it, and if they do, many are not interested in doing anything about it.

You learn to slow things down and become increasingly disinterested in judging (characteristic of below-60 behaviours) and more able to be watching/witnessing/observing with increased wonder at what you are learning and how it relates to the Awareness Code and yourself, your team and your family. The level of awareness above 59 is packed with realizations, e.g. 'The people I dominate through Controlling in some way are more likely to become my enemy than someone I treat kindly'.

For the veil of 59 to come down and to have access to 60 and above, you need to find another state, a different way of functioning, perceiving, interpreting and understanding. You are shifting from Ego Mind to Witness Mind (*see also* Chapter 15, pp. 217–237), where instead of living from set beliefs, opinions and rules, you are going to feel more alive and in the moment.

Realizing Truth, 60

What was presented before and you couldn't see, understand, conceptualize or accept as having any benefit for you is somehow more palatable, available, reasonable or worthy of your time and consideration. You may have known it intellectually before but could not get past your Ego behaviours to actually live it. In realizing truth, you have some kind of 'shift' in perception, a breakdown of old reasons that just don't hold up any more. At 'Not Buying In', it's a 'no', but on hearing the truth for the first time or fiftieth time, there arises the 'maybe' or even the 'yes'. Silence helps as you are transitioning from Ego Mind to Wisdom Mind (*see also* Chapter 15, pp. 217–237) and initially this can take time and feel unusual, so the less interference the better.

Leaving the Ego can feel unsettling initially and the Ego can call you back to 'safety' or that which is known. But in understanding some kind of truth, a small crack or opening has occurred for you and a new understanding has entered. You need not know what to do, only that you are going to do something different and with more authenticity.

Somehow, the truth is getting in, regardless of how many times you may have heard it before. Something is being accepted or allowed in to penetrate past the Ego structure and into a more real part of yourself. You are adopting something that you couldn't before. Some kind of veil has been lifted, more context provided, an old habit has been realized, consequences have been faced or you actually feel how you are affecting others (empathic) and change in an instant.

You may oscillate between realizing the truth and reverting back into Ego. And you can oscillate many times. There is a feeling of discovery where instead of trying to get something, you have discovered more of what you are going to have to become in order to live with integrity. Eventually you will witness the intuitive, magnetic qualities of this new mind. The exact outcome will probably not be known but instead of scepticism and fear ruling the moment, you step forward into the unknown.

---

60 – Realizing Truth: Empowering Statement

Who can you ask for help to get some clarity on this? What does it take to get a truth you are not yet seeing?

You can feel there is a pattern you are acting from. You need another pattern to create many new ripples.

You feel you're not the negative thoughts and you ask to be shown another way. You're willing to learn a new approach that includes positive thoughts.

Ready, 61

There is a new truth to live by but so much can remain unknown. Stepping In takes courage. Below 60, we can rehearse and practise endlessly with an Ego Mind, trying to get it right and avoid getting it wrong. Here, at ready, we shift from right/wrong to doing the best we can but we may not know what our best is. Discovering how the new realized truth is to be actioned is part of the journey. You can be like a green apple that receives the new sunlight but needs a period of time to ripen or for maturation to occur.

More 'will' is available to proceed in a new direction. This direction may be guided or totally unknown. It is about going forward, not back. The tentative, undeveloped 'yes' from realizing the truth is now nurtured. Below 60 we may be negative, especially below 30, as resistance towards living the new truth is encountered. Game on! A new eagerness to be different has arrived. An inner drive or momentum is present that is not enforced by negative consequences of punishment and retribution, nor is it based on Ego's endless ideas of attention and promotion. It is a steady, underlying current that this is the 'best way forward'. What will be will be – 'Let me have a go!' There is a new zeal, a goodwill and an aptitude to find your new self. In this state of readiness, you are up to taking on life without knowing how to make anything happen yet. The moment is more alive. You are more alive. There is more spirit. Ready is a state of consolidating the realizing truth and stabilizing so as to enter tile 62, Preparing.

---

61 – Ready: Empowering Statement

Change is inevitable. You are a change maker rather than a change resistor.

It feels good being responsible for your own choices. You're able to see beyond the issue.

You have the resources inside yourself to respond as required. Whatever is presented, you will consider it before responding.

Preparing, 62

The motivation that courage provides is coming alive within you. Preparing yourself to welcome changes sets up the environment for courage to enter. Now that you are ready and the inner drive is activated, it is time to prepare. Ready is not enough, we need a way forward to channel that readiness into. There are two parts: (1) preparing the external and (2) preparing the internal:

1) Preparing the external. What action is required? What questions need answering?
   - If it is to travel to a new adventure location, you book the ticket. If it is to apply for a wonderful new job opportunity, you do what it takes to apply. If it is to have a courageous conversation with a colleague or your boss that you haven't ever been able to have before, because you find it difficult to set boundaries, you set up the meeting. Preparing the way and setting up the external requirements to action the new truth overcomes what was once too challenging. In below-60 tiles perhaps you were ignorant of the possibility of acting in a new way.

2) Preparing the internal. What action is required? What questions need answering?
   - Preparing the internal means you spend some time considering and understanding what it was that held you back and if and how it is going to stop you proceeding. You have 59 Entrapments to choose from, each one capable of restraining you by the nature of the stories at each tile. What are the Entrapment(s) most likely

to pull you back to below 60? Where does that feeling live within you? Own it, identify with it, invite it to the surface as it may be very subconscious. Where did it come from? How does it seem to be serving you? What story does it have? The key here is to spend time experiencing or feeling the limitation/Entrapment and bringing it to the surface, with the intention of realizing more truth about the situation and getting ready for tile 63, releasing the old story.

---

62 – Preparing: Empowering Statement

Let's gather some information and collect ideas. You need more, new context. Ask others how they see you.

The past is done. It was full of trial and error, let error be your teacher as a way forward.

Everything that has happened has prepared you for this moment. Everything you do is grist to the mill of your unfolding growth and learning. It is showing you what needs to be released.

Releasing, 63

The internal story is ready to be discharged, transcended or overcome in some way. There is no prescriptive recipe as to how to release it as it depends on context with so many contributing variables and inputs. It is not just a matter of when to release the old belief but how to release the build-up charge that belief/story has accumulated. This will maximize the potential to arrive at a new place or truth. It may be incredibly simple, such as seeing what has entrapped you, identifying the tile of Entrapment and reading the 'moving forward' suggestions offered to overcome the Entrapment. Such a framework can help to dissolve the resistance to releasing it. Or, the issue/Entrapment at one of the below-59 tiles might be a very complex, multi-layered, charge-ridden story and so requires multiple releasing attempts so as to purge, clear and be ready to Reorientate (64).

Generally, the deeper and older the story or memory, the greater the potential for core pain to surface as the story may have been believed thousands of times. The story will have to be recontextualized, which means seen in a different, more positive, above-60 way than was originally interpreted or received. By being with a trained therapist, or another person above 60, things can be realized, readied, prepared, transcended or broken through. Or you can give it your best effort by yourself.

There can be a lot of processing, pondering and remembering as the Entrapment is explored. You are now developing a Witness Mind so exercise it and let it have an opportunity to reveal things for you. This is not about forcing yourself to work it out, but sitting and witnessing the memories or feelings. They will open up for you to have the insight you need to release the story.

There can be an unleashing of charge, e.g. crying, a scream of frustration, a physical hitting of a pillow, a wild dance, a deep willing, a visualization of the 'old' leaving, a ceremony of burying a token of the Entrapment and many other possibilities. The intention is to drop, clear, liberate, let loose, separate, dissolve, detach, remove, discharge, peel back, strip away, erase, dispose, dump, break, close out, unlock, rid, lift off or liberate your awareness from the ignorance of below 60.

The process of releasing may all happen in one session, or it may take repeated sessions to gradually strip back old patterns of behaviour. Having a visual of the Entrapment and adding sound, such as screaming or simply telling the story, really helps. Once the release is complete, you are very present and ripe for reorientation.

In the early stages of using this new Witness Mind it will be advantageous to have someone else present, especially anyone trained to be present with an unbiased, non-judgemental Witness Mind to support you. In the preparing stage, you are forming an understanding of what it is that you are able to release to move deeper into letting go.

---

63 – Releasing: Empowering Statement

Allow the charge of old energies and patterns to move out of you accordingly. E.g. Sadness – cry, Fear – quiver and freeze, Anger – yell, etc. Allow this knowing that you are releasing, not growing the charge. The witness is present during the release.

Own that what is coming out of you is yours to take responsibility for – you're learning not to blame others.

Letting go of attachment to agendas frees you to be part of other potentials.

Reorientating, 64

Releasing (63) creates an internal space so you can feel less cluttered, confused and held back. You are now ready to move in the direction you set up in the Preparing phase (62). You are redirecting your willpower. Internally, it is now more about connecting to a more authentic self and to be that for others. You need a focus, a vision and a new story from which to operate. It is best to scan for the best way ahead. This is very individual and depends on a multitude of components that make up the context of your life. So, it is not about a right or wrong choice. That duality is Ego. This is about intuitively feeling for an above-60 tile and one Revelation that moves you and gives you a sense of wonder about what it would be like to live that way.

The power associated with above 60 means you are attracting that which is required to help you to be the best version of yourself so you can help others. You are realigning and your awareness is going through a period of witnessing what it is like to be more conscious of how to do that. Answers will come to you as to how to act, behave and live at the higher tile. The Ego is on notice that the change is not just imminent, it is now happening. The Entrapment may return but your increased awareness realizes this and you reorientate as soon as you can.

At reorientation, there is a change in how you organize yourself to accommodate the new Revelation and you now go ahead with the actions visualized back at Preparing (62). There is rebalancing and new guidance available. You begin to embody the qualities of the new Revelation that you are practising and as it takes hold, it begins to walk you through your life. This is much more than a feeling of Egotistical satisfaction, it is deeply moving as you learn to navigate this new psychological and physical experience.

Life has a new focus and there has been a shift. You can redirect your energy and effort, repositioning yourself towards greater integrity. It can be a break from tradition, overcoming a negative habit, redesigning your approach or a total overhaul of your attitude.

---

64 – Reorientating: Empowering Statement

Perhaps you can change one thing and see how that alters the outcome? How have other people done this differently?

You're beginning to see that it's not just about you. What outcome would allow everyone to feel empowered? How can you do this so others benefit?

It feels good to get into other people's worlds, value others, observe different ways of witnessing or seeing situations. What attributes make for a great mentor? Who can you ask to be yours?

Positive, 65

You start to focus on the upside while staying very aware of things that need to be addressed. There is a deeply moving experience that can accompany the inward reorientation. You now have a growing capacity to continue to expose and transcend Ego. Ego Mind is designed to resist, defend and dismiss (55–54). It puts up a fight inside of you and attempts to undermine your newfound freedom or reorientation. What is positivity? The magic ingredient that will overcome any of the below-59 Entrapments.

It can be an enthusiasm to stay witnessing during challenges and to keep Stepping In when before you wouldn't, or when others can't, won't or don't know how you have a go. It can feel good to model this behaviour, not for personal attention but because others are learning by your example. Ego needs to endlessly tell others how to live, but positive and above just lives it for others to see. Feeling there is an advantage to living this kind of life, the enthusiasm may even bubble over into eagerness. The uplifting buoyancy that comes with positive can be contagious. It feels beneficial to everyone. It's a great feeling to be acting from and being positive and you begin to know you can choose it more often.

Living consciously with positivity means being more constructive, practical, productive, helpful, optimistic, pragmatic, assured, welcoming, decisive, supportive, expressive, resolute and involved.

---

65 – Positive: Empowering Statement

Any below-60 thoughts, feelings or reactions are there to show you what you're to understand and overcome in that tile.

Below 60 is not an option any more. You're focused. Keep learning, improving and transcending the lower tiles.

You can do this. You're a capable person. You're Stepping In and having a go, learning and growing all the time.

Adventurous, 66

Can life really be adventurous or even a game? Can a person view everything happening as an adventure? Yes. Life, even challenges, can and will become an ongoing adventure at this tile. The below-30 Entrapments can see life as cruelty to be lived through and it is a necessity to seek safety and security at all times. The 30–59 Entrapments see life as full of things to get a hold of. So, what is the adventure? It can be a short-term risk, where instead of focusing on the potential negative outcome, you stay aware of those outcomes but they are not controlling you. So, what is controlling you? Nothing. You are being guided by intuition and positive reorientation. Initially, of course, it is not that well-practised, but eventually, it will become more precise and more accurate.

Take learning to walk, for example. Had we approached learning to walk through an adult Thinking Mind, we may not have bothered as an Entrapment could easily have held us back – 'I might get hurt', 'No adventure there', 'Don't try', 'Don't walk'. But as a child, the body needed to develop and a child has the spirit of adventure when learning to walk. To crash, fall, bump and trip is all part of the adventure and builds the skills to be able to walk. The child just gets back up and keeps going. Then the adventure opens up into running and jumping. A leader can take on a new project with Anxiety (26) or Adventure (66). The latter is the spirit of finding out who you are by constantly having a go. If it doesn't work out for you, then you have learned something and found out who you are **not**. If the lessons resonate with you, they can be incorporated into who you are. If you went with fear initially, you would never have discovered what you did.

An adventurous outlook is a gateway. You may feel like the adventure is a journey or a quest. Give the adventure a name and a vision and choose the Revelations that will be required and start living it each day with Positivity (65) as your foundation. Make it an enterprise, a voyage, a happening, a paradigm shift. Just keep Stepping In.

---

66 – Adventurous: Empowering Statement

Every new person or situation you encounter is now a new mystery unfolding.

Every new challenge is like a great game designed to test your resourcefulness. It feels so good to find those resources and to meet those challenges.

Life is a game of endless opportunities to move from stuckness to increasing flow.

Conviction, 67

Positivity is great! The feeling of Stepping Into an adventure is wonderful. As it unfolds and the Entrapments look like reappearing, conviction will be necessary to stay on track. This is Witness confidence, not Ego Confidence (57). The latter arises because you can get what you want. Witness confidence arises because you are sticking with the adventure and staying Positive (65). This is a gift that you are developing. While Ego Mind will create a belief, Witness Mind will feel a wonder, a presence of something beautiful growing within you (whatever the Revelation is). The assuredness or solidity of living above 60 is building. It is very difficult to be certain of anything and you are not trying to do that. You are living and learning by Stepping In. You are finding your own truth as you do that. You are letting go of right/wrong and good/bad. Everything has the possibility of being an adventure from which you can learn something and grow. Instead of judging, you are observing and waiting for more context and how the next challenge will grow you.

Condemning others is more and more difficult because you become convinced that is not who you are meant to be. Negativity is getting further away. A new strength of observation and connection to what is best for all replaces Ego judgement. A knowingness arises from always Stepping In for the good of all and there is conviction that this is the way to go. While Ego Mind creates belief and opinion and doggedly holds on, conviction here is the experience of being genuinely in touch with the highest potential and representing that. It doesn't have to happen if something else more appropriate is presented. As these potentials unfold, you continue to be the one who represents or is the ambassador for the good of all.

67 – Conviction: Empowering Statement

There is a way through this and you'll find it. You'll keep going until you feel solid inside.

It can be done! The way will reveal itself to you if you keep applying yourself and stay focused.

Consider it done.

Fearless, 68

Fear underlies the stress inherent in tiles 20–29 and seems to be wired into us from birth. The fight-flight-freeze reaction surely cannot be transcended? You can certainly learn to take on fear as a day-to-day ongoing learning experience, challenging and facing into it at every moment. You can be fearless in repressing it, or quashing it the moment Ego feels it. However, burying fear doesn't overcome it in the long term. Instead, take every fear as an opportunity to find out what lies behind it. Identify the Entrapment and return to tiles 60–64 in order to work with it and understand it. The body can still tense up, the impulse to run away or go into battle can still be there, but with time the reaction can be less severe and last for less time and recede into the background. Fearless doesn't have to mean absolutely no sign of fear. It can be that fear is attempting to register its Entrapment but the power of this tile reminds you to keep solid as you navigate your chosen path.

Other descriptions of this way of living are bold, intrepid and audacious. Stepping into life at this level is underpinned by a conviction born of experience. Undaunted by another person's Entrapment persuasions, fearless enters the challenge with the Witness Mind **very** engaged because at any moment, an old fear story may try to sabotage proceedings. Instead, when fearless remains present this awareness feels that the choices made were from a win-win perspective that considered all involved. It was intuitively felt as the highest potential. Witness confidence replaces fear.

---

68 – Fearless: Empowering Statement

It's up to you what attitude you have towards life. If life is now a game, instead of fear, what does it take to have wonder?

It's not about the outcome, it's about playing the game of life, being with life.

You're engaged in the present unfolding that fear cannot enter. You're focused on creating.

Fully In, 69

Fully In is a type of maturation and depth where it really does feel like you are on board with the adventure in a consistent, ongoing way and the saboteur has been put to rest. Completely in may be a real challenge as this means you align with the undertaking, but you may not be aware of all variables involved in the unfolding of the undertaking. It is more the attitude of Fearless (68) that prevails rather than a promise or vow to stay committed. This Revelation reveals a thoroughness to your dedication and a comprehensiveness to your consideration of all it entails. You are intrigued and captured by the bigger picture rather than worried about the 'dots or points or ideas' (*see also* pp. 239–241) that can be difficult to juggle. The bigger picture has a power that you're tapping into and you know your persistence is going to make a difference.

You are able to ensure your involvement and have the strength of will to stay with the highest potential that can unfold. In its entirety, as much of which is known to you, you can dedicate yourself to the endeavour. This type of Stepping In inspires others. Reservations have been examined and taken into account; the past is important in that you have learned what to do and what not to do in that particular context. The lessons learned may or may not be appropriate in the **new** context that is presenting. To be Fully In can hold more information without going down the rabbit burrow of over-thinking. Fully In can let go of the past quickly so as to be fully available for the project or team.

---

69 – Fully In: Empowering Statement

Every part of you is committed to staying above 60. You've faced the triggers that could pull you below 60 and they no longer have any power over you.

You're aligned with values above 60. This alignment consistently pulls you upwards as they are more powerful than the downward pull of the below-60 tiles.

You aspire to the higher tiles. This aspiration keeps you above 60.

Let's review

- A person able to realize that the truth at the heart of good leadership is service steps into empowerment.
- Witness Mind begins at tile 60, which is Realizing Truth in the Stepping In development line. This is the gateway to true power.
- Pause in order to integrate a new way of responding to a situation. Delaying how you act can be the difference between engaging an automatic defence mechanism and responding with clarity after seeking more context.
- Stepping In allows for the incremental movement towards being 'Fully In' whatever project is being worked on. Teams respond to this flow of positivity.
- There is motivation to step into improving oneself, teams or family dynamics as this creates a win-win for everyone involved.
- Stepping into integrity can be a process of identifying negative thoughts and releasing negative behaviour and replacing it with a quality above 60 that is manageable and appropriate for what is being released.
- Starting with an attitude of positivity increases the potentials that are available and what were once perceived as problems start to become opportunities to develop new skills.

Coming Up Next

Once living with integrity becomes part of a person's way of interacting in the world, more opportunities arise that deepen the capacity to affect more complex situations. In the next chapter you will learn how being open and transparent is not a vulnerability but an Incredible technique that helps to foster powerful and effective leadership. So, what are the qualities or attitudes of being open and transparent? How does a leader become solid in the face of ever-increasing complex and diverse situations? Read on to discover your potential as a leader who knows how to be a team player.

CHAPTER ELEVEN

Being Open and Transparent

The Heart of Integrity

It is important to know that the leaders who operate from the tiles 0–59 have limited ability to hold, support, build rapport, assist, sustain and advocate for their team members. Leaders operating from 60 and above 'have their backs', encourage, endorse, affirm, validate and promote their team members. As you access the tiles towards 100, the ability to **do** this for your team members becomes an ability to **be** this for your team members – the power of the tiles shines through you.

70–79 – The Level of Opening

70	71	72	73	74	75	76	77	78	79
Receptive	Witness-ing	Open-minded	Trustful	Connected	Collabor-ation	Emerging	Agile	Wow	Flowing

While Stepping In has a lot to do with developing the Witness Mind through developing yourself, Opening is now about preparing yourself for the greater potential that exists in collaboration and moving into 'we'. You feel for what lies ahead for others, the team or whoever is coming together under your leadership.

As you learn to step in, you will begin to learn how to be more available for the multitude of challenges and complications that a more complex life will bring. The more Stepping In you are capable of, the more you will need to know about what real openness actually means because authenticity is the key to moving into the energy of Transforming and we need to be open to being very real.

Receptive, 70

Being receptive to life and to people, especially those you were closed off to before, is going to multiply the number of opportunities that are created. A yielding attitude does not mean weakness. We are compliant when required and it enables us to navigate tricky situations that Ego would otherwise have pushed through regardless of the consequences or else Ego would have created a sense of failure. An easy-going nature is developed by being willing to stay present if the situation requires and to go with closing down the opportunity or opening it up, depending on what is intuitively known or sensed. Being agreeable and accessible in receptive mode encourages compromise in order to establish a win-win outcome, which is a wonderful gift.

Not being precious about Ego sensitivity and taking things personally means we can tolerate more and learn more in any given circumstance. Being broad-minded unlocks the Entrapment of narrowness. Being keen and willing to learn predisposes you to making more contact than closed-down could ever offer. Being cordial, friendly and conscious of others' needs and qualities helps you to be receptive as well. Being amenable and approachable are wonderful qualities that inspire receptiveness in others. Being hospitable, welcoming and responsive provides a favourable respite from the below-60 tiles.

---

70 – Receptive: Empowering Statement

You are genuinely interested in the other's points of view. Diversity is valuable.

You understand things differently. You share your point of view with others and listen to their understandings.

Within the team you have different ideas about how things might be achieved. Put all these ideas on the table and look at each one.

Witnessing, 71

Once Receptive (70) is in place, Witness capabilities can grow to a new level. Witnessing is not the same as looking in order to find ways to control or looking that invites the energy of doubt. It is at the level of Opening and so the effect is an ability to learn without judgement and this takes lots of practice as you were probably taught to judge from an early age and you may have been modelled judgement also. Witnessing does not add any emotional charge to what is being observed, it just lets it be and frees up the other person to 'be themselves'.

As the focus is no longer on what you can get but what you can learn, help or give by Witnessing, things can and will open to you in a way they will not when you judge. By viewing and taking in the unfolding without condemning it, more detail becomes available. Keeping old stories out of the equation means you see things with fresh, new eyes. Not Controlling, but just being with the situation shows you are willing to understand.

Another person can instinctively read this quality and feel more relaxed to open themselves in your presence. Beholding the scenario with a sense of the remarkable or impressiveness invites the other to be open too. Witnessing is gathering context to understand, whereas judging is gathering evidence for some personal agenda. Judging and Witnessing have a very different feel about them and you begin to notice more with Witnessing. To drop the old stories opens the possibility of seeing the deeper reality around you. The Witness attends to the essential needs of the team members and is capable of noting the many dots (*see also* pp. 239–241) or variables playing out in the team.

---

71 – Witnessing: Empowering Statement

You observe the unfolding without attachment. You're ready to respond rather than react.

Within the context, the most useful idea will be chosen. This may change at any moment as the context changes.

You watch with interest and curiosity about the unfolding potentials. In time, you can re-find wonder, but for now, Witness.

Open-minded, 72

Being open-minded is about allowing and accepting. Ego expects to control every single variable so that when something goes 'wrong' or was overlooked, the attitude of Controlling goes into overdrive. Blaming and condemning forces change and there are always negative consequences to forcing change. 'Left field' occurrences and overlooked aspects of a project are a way of life that need to be tabled as soon as they are noticed and brought to the attention of someone who can most likely deal with them appropriately. That person will need to be open-minded.

A liberal approach is more generous, magnanimous and tolerant. It invites others to stay, even in difficult times. The associated kindness and benevolent nature of open-minded permeates projects and relationships – 'Why put down anyone or anything?' is the attitude. Well-placed leniency and an unbiased nature promote others' opening. Impartial fairness and tolerance facilitate coming together. Equitable and just treatment of all concerned unlock the tension of prior mistreatment.

Broad-mindedness is the ground for inclusiveness. When our minds are open and inclusive, and we are approachable, there is an honesty and willingness to really get to know how another person functions and what they need to be their best. Encouragement and being open to new things promote creativity and breadth of vision. Creativity thrives as interest and enthusiasm is encouraged.

---

72 – Open-minded: Empowering Statement

You ask questions, seek insight and listen deeply when there is something you don't understand.

Even when you feel you understand something, you remain interested and curious about what everyone offers.

Your suggestions are always welcome and will contribute to the highest potential outcome.

Trustful, 73

Trustful follows Open-mindedness because the latter is building a capacity to operate from the Witness Mind, so that your ability to be intuitive is being promoted. The more intuitive you are, the more information, guidance and genuine insight into someone else's nature/intent/agenda you gather. So, trusting is more about trusting yourself rather than someone else. Have Open-minded (71) Witnessing to gather insight rather than Ego stories that gain evidence for assumptions. You can 'read' a circumstance/situation/person better so you can trust yourself more. Whether another circumstance/situation/person is capable of being genuine or agenda driven becomes more obvious the more you can use Witness Mind.

Trusting is Witness Mind confidence. It is not naive or gullible as this type of mind tunes in more than Ego Mind can. You can learn to rely on Witness Mind and the more another person is open, and therefore genuine and authentic, the more you can trust the person. Openness has a type of smart innocence and the Intuitive Mind can feel that. One can confide in such innocence as it is not hiding Ego agenda. There is a benign harmlessness to someone you can trust. Witness Mind remembers that whenever you are dealing with someone, you are primarily dealing with just one part of them so you may be able to feel you can trust that part as it is open and you are open, but there may be other parts of that person not operating in the moment of being with you and that part may be below 60. While Ego Mind guesses these dynamics and assumes, Witness Mind is learning to actually realize these dynamics by being very present.

---

73 – Trustful: Empowering Statement

You are to learn to trust yourself before you can learn to trust others.

Everything that happens is for your growth. You're never given more than you can handle.

Alignment with trust allows a responsiveness that is intuitive and innately protective.

Connected, 74

A trusting relationship is truly engaging and full of potential. Truly forging a link with someone else or with the situation sets up a flow of information and exchange that realizes greater potential than surface contact. Taking the time to get to know someone else is a priority because their value is in the person they are rather than Ego wanting something from them. You approach another person, whether a relative, colleague or friend, as someone who has something to offer you through knowing them. There are qualities that may be evident in that person, but some may be buried because of the stories coming from their Entrapments.

Being receptive, truly offering the support of the Witness Mind, being open and trusting all create the environment for others to flourish. Alliances can be forged that were not possible in Ego Mind, cohesiveness can activate, liaisons be established. Bonds that are formed create the groundwork for later collaboration. Synergy builds as exchange promotes generosity of spirit. Meetings can be deeply rewarding as the focus is how to bring the best out of each other through connecting. Relationships set the foundation or springboard for the work ahead that might need teamwork and cohesion that deep connections build. Solidarity, joint ventures and mutual alignment through deeper connection give rise to authentic rapport.

---

74 – Connected: Empowering Statement

There is a flow between the team that can be nurtured and developed.

Through the flow between the team, the shared goal is given power.

The number of potential outcomes rises exponentially to the number of persons sharing and connection around a common intent.

Collaboration, 75

From the deeper connection and trust, we can launch forward with the project or adventure with renewed vigour and a feeling of true partnership. We can all buy in on ways forward as we intuitively know more about each other's capacities, limitations and preferences through those deeper connections. Knowing how our partners/children/colleagues truly operate in life gives us more intuitive confidence of a way forward. The power of co-operation magnifies exponentially when we are all really truly connected.

Partnerships can do things that alone we cannot. Associating with those close to us promotes breakthroughs and working together is a delight rather than an Ego competition/confrontation.

Concordance, harmony, agreement and accord can be the atmosphere that the work is undertaken in. Consensus is easier, participation enhanced, absenteeism drops. Banding together for a common purpose, assisting each other, celebrating collective team efforts regardless of outcome. The emphasis is on the collective ability of the team and it is to be constantly witnessed and nurtured, not judged. Review and improvement replace blame. We have got each other's backs and celebrate others' learning and growth.

---

75 – Collaboration: Empowering Statement

In sharing our resources, we multiply our potentials.

We have such diversity, which, when brought together, creates something entirely new.

It is wonderful to be a part of deep sharing, which leads to growth and often provides higher outcomes for all.

Emerging, 76

From this collaboration of connectedness the team creates fresh new ideas and possibilities. 'What's next?' is full of possibilities and potential. We are backing ourselves to generate the new. There is a feeling of when we come together we are very capable of giving rise to inventions, discoveries, findings, solutions and breakthroughs. Trends can be established in this environment of 'anything goes', just put your ideas on the table. Openness is able to cope with any input, no matter how unusual or strange initially. There is support for a creative outlet being made available so that what was hidden before can now see the light of day. And it is not to be prematurely scrapped. Intuitive Mind needs time to digest it, understand it and penetrate the possibilities of it. Whereas Egotistical was resistant and dismissive, Emerging is inclusive and optimistic, regardless of the input. As we are doing our best to bring forth new input from the Witness Mind, we know it's about what is being given, not taken. Development, not rejecting things, is the primary focus.

---

76 – Emerging: Empowering Statement

As each team member brings forth their ideas in the spirit of building one team solution or approach, you are becoming an example to others.

No longer do you just state the problem and move on. You're growing together to emerge from your connection with a solution.

You start to feel a heart involvement alongside the head and that's the new motivation: the heart is emerging.

Agile, 77

New and emerging ideas can give rise to new and emerging complications, challenges and difficulties. Instead of this being heavy, dreadful and terrible and 'Let's find someone to blame', agile brings forth a type of acceptance of any or all of these things. It is the opposite of abdication, dismissive or a 'who cares' attitude. The deeper we go into the Revelations, the more responsibility, attention and energy we need to run the power of these Revelations. Agile does not lose energy to Stressed (20–29) or Despondent (10–19). It activates to swiftly and keenly deal with whatever presents that needs attention. Agile, fast responses are the order of the day, not panic.

The pragmatism is a quality to behold as the team or individual launches into an intuitive brainstorm at Collaboration (75), which gives rise through Emerging (76) to a new solution and agile springs into life and executes. It is intelligent in its approach, focusing all its capability to manage the new proposed solution. At the same time, it is flexible, light-spirited, vigorous and thorough. The skills of the collective shine through. To be agile feels uplifting, even buoyant. An agile attitude is alert, focused and always ready to learn.

---

77 – Agile: Empowering Statement

Your team is like an octopus. With numerous legs of ideas, each one contributes to the bigger picture and is not overlooked.

The ability to adapt to constant changes benefits our team. You explore outside the square and move from linear to abstract.

No contribution is overlooked or canned. Every offering has some potential or a key that can support the final outcome.

Wow, 78

The teamwork feelings that are associated with this type of openness promote a wonderful acceptance of any contribution. Enthusiasm abounds and perhaps a fervent, eager, burning keenness to be involved is what is at the heart of wow. To be involved, to contribute, to be alive to the unfolding of the intensity is the attitude of wow. Keenness is the key. This is a type of inner drive, different from wanting to get something. There is a heart feeling here that has arisen because of the collective Opening. The promise of always finding something new and surprising is very stimulating. Not stimulating in an Ego way for pleasure, but in a Witness Intuitive way as it is bringing something out of you that has always been deep inside, waiting to be found, nurtured and released when you had the people and circumstances around you that could validate this powerful feeling. It is a feeling of power, of passion. Wow is a burst or celebration of how we work together, of the potential that just emerged, and that we were Agile (77) enough to bring the potential to fruition.

There is a sense of celebration as 'work' gives way to 'entertainment'. Someone just 'knocked our socks off', we 'cracked up', momentarily we were 'electrified', we were 'enchanted' or we were 'delighted'.

---

78 – Wow: Empowering Statement

Wow! The team is achieving beyond what you imagined to be possible at this stage of the project. Keep the momentum moving.

It's awesome to be involved with this team. You are surprised at the level of performance achieved together.

You give 100 per cent to the task, unfolding.

Flowing, 79

This is the ongoing presence of the passion found in the Wow (78). It grows and gives rise to a smooth, harmonious life. Of course, there will be people or situations in your life that have one or more Entrapments present, but that does not affect your capacity to stay in the flow, it merely prohibits them from breaking into this flowing Revelation with you. However, at flowing, this is taken care of and easily negotiated. There is a power to explain, to invite, to include, to have conversations around consequences of continual below-60 behaviours. It does not feel like a burden, but part of the flow of life as you open to each situation.

Each encounter is teaching you something and each person, regardless of the entrapment, is showing you a face of humanity for you to learn and intuitively reach into. When the learning in that relationship has reached some climax or ending, it doesn't feel negative when you are in the flow. In flowing with life there is a sense that 'losing' is not an option, just learning. Whatever happens will be utilized for benefit and no one will be dragged down by judgement. It can feel like you intuitively know what to do next, or what is coming next, and make arrangements for that.

Life is a continuous stream of opportunities. There is an unbroken or uninterrupted connection to the team spirit.

79 – Flowing: Empowering Statement

When the team is in the flow, everything falls into place effortlessly. Things get done that normally wouldn't get done.

You've noticed a change in how the team are more open and alive when sharing their ideas. You really value and appreciate all contributions.

It's great to witness the team members achieve their personal work goals when they immerse themselves wholeheartedly.

Let's review

- At the level of Opening and transparent more life energy is available to participate in the change and projects that companies and organizations require. Energy is not wasted on unnecessary ruminating, Controlling the situation or feeling Hopeless (11). It is instead redirected to the challenges at hand and finding practical solutions for them through Collaboration (75) and seeking context.
- Connection with peers and an increased capacity to collaborate become effortless and rewarding.
- Life starts to flow and an ever-increasing ability to experience one's own agility in affecting positive change moves a person towards being a Transformational Leader.

Coming Up Next

When a leader is practised at consistently keeping open the door that invites change, growth is possible. Devoted to understanding himself and his teams at greater depths, he earns the devotion, super strengths and extraordinary capabilities of the people he leads. It's a team effort but it feels effortless!

CHAPTER TWELVE

Transformational Leadership

Moving Deeper into the Code

Inspirational leadership

As leaders solidify in their commitment to step in and be open to serving their teams with integrity, a particular environment is created that warms people towards the goals that are being striven for. The goals are life-supporting goals. A leader is aware of the collaborative approach that is required to bring to life these Incredible projects and goals. At the cusp of becoming a Transformational Leader the person is aware of the higher calling and the Incredible potential every team member has. Functioning at this level consistently opens up the more powerful tiles of Integrity (88) and Inspiring (89)

80–89: The Level of Transforming

80	81	82	83	84	85	86	87	88	89
Highest Callings	Realizing Power	Realizing Value	Fellowship Mindset	Embra-cing	Spontan-eous	Off-the-charts	Integ-rating	Integrity	Inspiring

These are the change makers, disruptors, inventors, change agents, movers and shakers and guardians with ever-opening hearts. Whatever presents in front of such a person is intuitively considered in order to find a way in, or the leader gathers around a team that can find a way in. Or, if it becomes evident through wise exploration that it is not the best way going forward, then such a leader can easily move out with no regrets and a wonder of 'what is coming next?' Such a person knows that when one thing closes down another is being prepared.

Increasingly, there is a 'living in the moment' attitude, which gives rise to a freedom not available below 80. Life is more a feeling experience rather than mentative or emotive.

There are three major aspects of the life cycle – (1) building up, (2) maintenance and (3) breaking down. A lot of people love building up and creating new things, developing, innovating and improving. There are those who prefer to maintain that which was created by themselves or others. But who really enthusiastically embraces the breaking down, death, finishing and ending? It's easy to grieve. In Transforming it's essential to take breaking down head-on as an essential component to make way for the new. Transforming embraces the shift that cleans out that which is decaying and welcomes in the new.

All major aspects of life have appeal and worth and value. You can start to feel what is required in the moment as you learn to live more and more in the moment. Lifeless (0–9) and Despondent (10–19) are more about the past. Stressed (20–29) is more about the future and the uncertainty of it, while 30–59 is more about the future and how to get something out of it; 80–99 is more about the present and the wonderful, greater good that can be found **now**.

Transforming is more about giving than receiving. At this level receiving takes a back seat and may even fall away as a requirement from the 'other'. Within tiles 50 to 59, a person will be led to believe that tiles 80 to 89 have been achieved and can convince themselves and others that this is the truth.

The awareness of yourself and others is growing and deepening, and you will automatically move into the Transforming level. What does that look like?

Highest Callings (80)

This level is the beginning of truly feeling and exploring what the bigger picture of your life, your family, the business or team that you are a part of, might be. What is the most important mission? How do you know the answer? Is there even a larger purpose for you, and if you envision that, what might it look like? What stands in the way or has stopped you in the past? Go back to Realizing Truth (60) and explore this. Deeper or higher potentials might be calling you into this space of exploration in order to understand yourself better and fulfil your greater potentials. Perhaps someone brings it to your attention and you can go to the source of where that potential lives. The potential is already there but not actualized by the Ego, which usually says either 'I don't know' or 'I don't have time for that right now' as it is too busy getting what it wants.

The greater good or highest vocations are usually found in silence once you ask the question. You meditate or take it into your sleep and rest deeply as you contemplate the higher callings. Slowing down and feeling for it is going to propel you along this level so you can experience life in a way you couldn't have imagined before. As you understand more and more tiles, you can be a more real and authentic version of yourself. What is your potential? Ego uses a goal or aim, which is Ego's way of motivating itself, but its agenda is to get something for itself. At highest callings, a person begins to access the Wisdom Mind and there is a knowingness that can access and begin to actualize the potentials. At this level, there is more than one higher calling to consider. Most people focus on the bigger life picture, which is a macro version and usually more difficult to access. Start with the micro version and consider, 'What is your short-term higher calling over the next few days/weeks?'

This kick-starts you into a very achievable short-term calling at a much deeper level. Who or what can you turn yourself into for others? Then there is the medium-term higher calling that is available in a few months. It's not a target or destination, but a journey of really finding yourself in giving to that which calls to you. Perhaps it is being more present for someone who is challenging for you to be around, or maybe it is learning to use your voice more creatively to inspire others.

---

80 – Highest Callings: Empowering Statement

Acting from your highest calling energizes you and connects you to the bigger picture that feels intrinsically whole and purposeful.

Your highest callings will challenge people around you who are unable to connect with their own highest callings. You are comfortable with this and can provide stepping stones for others aspiring to find their highest callings.

Living from a higher calling feels like connecting with a source of energy that is abundant and can support the endeavour.

Realizing Power, 81

This awareness is where you are required to find and focus on your qualities and gifts, which you may or may not be aware of as yet. Some are activated already, some are dormant waiting for awareness to shine its light on them. Power is what brings benefits to yourself and others and your team. It gives you an advantage through the challenges and provides support when required. Power comes through your inner assets, which shine forth and perhaps initially this is due to some effort but eventually being this power is a default or automatic way of being in the world. It's advantageous to ask others as well as to deep dive into what you might love most about yourself, especially when the situation requires a presence that you enjoy being for others. Continuing to use your power is like making a magical elixir, where the qualities blend to create your best efforts. Power is initially hidden in a leader's potential and as competence, capability, influence, authority and potency grows, the power shines through.

Bringing awareness to any qualities alive or dormant within you enhances their presence. This allows you to move from best efforts towards eventually becoming that super strength. Any of the 40 Revelations have many qualities embedded in them and have been alluded to or described in each overview of those Revelations. Choose a Revelation and envision what it would be like to live, breathe, walk and live that reality. Embody that power in a new, fresh way and at the end of each day, rest deeply, review the day and then fall asleep with the vision of how to improve or deepen in the chosen Revelation the next day. When it becomes who you are, move on to another tile.

Realizing Power, 81

You're able to witness any pull within you that may crave attention or wish to be seen as special, but you refuse to succumb to the test. Instead, you work with the underdeveloped part and seek to understand the lack from which it perceives itself.

Your power feels like a gift to others and it's a joy to share what often comes naturally and effortlessly.

You're getting in touch with your qualities. You review successes and the activities that feel great to be part of.

Realizing Value, 82

Now that you have Realized Power (81) as well as perhaps helping your partner/children/colleagues identify theirs, it's time to meditate on a few key questions. Ask yourself: 'With these qualities, what is my greatest, deepest, highest value to the team or family?' Consider too: 'How do I impact them/the situation/the project with full involvement using these qualities and how are they going to be affected by these qualities?' 'What are the greatest benefits that they can gain by you bringing these qualities to them?' 'How do you evaluate that? And if others had that attitude, also could you show them you treasure what they bring?' 'Can you cherish their presence and acknowledge they are bringing wonderful qualities to provide super benefits?' 'Are you/they maximizing the power of the qualities and utilizing them for the best outcome?' Contemplating these questions can help you realize your value.

How will another person be able to put your/their power to full use? Starting with realizing your own and others' value is a powerful step.

How can you examine the qualities of integrity at these levels and ask the best questions to obtain answers to these questions? These qualities we have and are bringing out of each other are priceless. They emanate from deep within you and provide a crucial role in maximizing potential. Do you have to ask the other person/team members or can you intuit what 'realizing value' you are to them? For example, 'Your quiet introspection is valuable to the team because you are the one prepared to go deeply into any challenge and they know you are looking for a new design or new innovation. Your quiet introspection is wonderful to have present at the meetings.'

Realizing Value, 82

You don't have to wait for others to appreciate your value. You identify this value yourself and seek to be that. When you do this, the intrinsic feeling of being your best just arises by it.

You're grateful to be gifted your power. It's a joy to share it with others.

Ask others what is the greatest value you can be to or for them.

Fellowship Mindset, 83

Being in this space is where you are open to enlisting anyone who is interested in assisting you to achieve the identified higher callings and to deeply value their contribution. The collective 'buys in' in a unified way where every person involved is not just following some recipe, dogma or script to avoid punishment from breaking the rules, but instead they have formed a common way of approaching and bringing the best out of each other. This assists in manifesting the higher callings.

When there is an understanding of what the Highest Callings (80) might be for you and the team, the next move is to gather around you all those with an interest in being the best version of themselves. This is the attitude that is required to invite transformation.

So, a Fellowship Mindset is to flush out any Entrapments, such as rebellion, doubt, being the renegade, insecurity, addiction, etc.

These would impede the ever-gradual alignment to moving forward. You are now entering the territory of the Wisdom Mind. You are still witnessing these Entrapments and letting them go weekly, daily, hourly or whenever they arise. As you do, more wisdom is arriving. Wisdom is the 'how' of transformation or connection without interference. It is knowing more what to do or who to be without Entrapments present. It is understanding through discretion and discernment. It is the artfulness of knowing what to leave alone and what to go with. It is gamesmanship, where no one is a loser. It is now natural to turn to others to offer opportunities to be a part of the great adventure of a higher purpose and to reciprocate efforts for others' higher purpose.

---

83 – Fellowship Mindset: Empowering Statement

A fellowship mindset encourages both diversity and creativity.

Fellowship mindset allows you to sit with all the potentials until one of them emerges as the most preferred option. No force is required, just equal sharing.

Within yourself, you will learn to organize all of your archetypes into one common higher purpose, and not only one part having conviction, but all of them.

Embracing, 84

Realizing power and then knowing and realizing the true value you can be for those whom you are leading or for your own personal endeavours means you are now able to embrace everything you have collected.

Really own the potential that these strengths and values can manifest. Hold them in your mind and heart more than ever before. Accept that this is just the beginning of truly espousing and embracing them. Be the advocate for these strengths and values. Champion the cause that you dedicate them to. Embody each quality and encircle each member as being crucial to the unfolding. Hold each team/ family member in such a high regard that without them, the greatest outcome for all could not be the same. Enjoy agreement, grasp the qualities and talk about them, promote them, celebrate them, surround the team with the embracing energy of acknowledgement of the importance of them all.

Have open arms and make it known that you notice when the qualities are shining forth and the great value that is being experienced because of them. Give credit where it is due. Wrap each other up in real acceptance. If for some reason you or someone else is not Realizing Power (81), embrace them with understanding. We all have multiple inputs to our performance and ability to shine. This is not a tile of using pressure to get results, it embraces the Fellowship Mindset (83) and allows for individuals to transition through their personal journey.

---

84 – Embracing

Embracing is an attitude of collaboration and fellowship. It is the foundation required to move towards being incredible. You're all-inclusive so as not to miss or dismiss anything that may be vital to moving forward.

At this level there is a willingness to work with triggers and uncomfortableness as a way to refine communication and reinstate fellowship. You embrace the keys.

The relationship becomes more important and is as important as the outcome.

Spontaneous, 85

Impulsive Ego Mind is **very** different from a spontaneous Wisdom Mind. The latter has the huge benefit of coming from a place where many of the Revelations of 60–85 are providing a very solid ground to be able to go with the flow of any new direction opening up. A lot of what you know about yourself is gathered by having a go at something new, by not holding back and then finding out that perhaps the venture was not you after all. You are closer to finding out who you really are, rather than having failed. Failure lives below 60.

Being spontaneous means you have moved past what people might think of you, which is one of the Ego's most potent retardants to being spontaneous. Allowing others to have opinions of negativity towards you is a key for a spontaneous life. Establishing empowered boundaries frees up your spirit to become impromptu.

Patterned, safe, robotic or prescribed ways of responding stifle creativity. When you arrive at spontaneous, it's like a breath of fresh air as **unthinking** downloads and 'ah ha!' moments become more frequent. You are not talking knee-jerk reactions but being in the space where the Wisdom Mind gets an opportunity to do its thing, unimpeded by the constraints of Ego Mind. Improvising, unmediated, ad-lib, off-the-cuff, suggestibility all live here at this level. 'Where did you think of that?' 'I didn't, it just appeared!' You're compelled to volunteer by an inner drive. Things can be very instantaneous and untaught. They arise of their own accord.

---

85 – Spontaneous

The spontaneity of ideas and follow-through into action leaves you speechless. This team is going places.

Not believing fear-based thoughts opens up a whole new playing field of potentials and directions to take off in.

The aliveness generated from spontaneous adventures has decreased absenteeism within the team. Yes!

Off-the-charts, 86

This is the zone where you take stock of accomplishments, efforts and application. You don't sit back on your laurels, believing it's enough or it wasn't good enough. No matter how well you have embraced the outcome, you still work on it or play with it until you feel its full potential has materialized. This applies not just to the project but to each individual and the team as well.

You are looking forward to and eventually becoming that which looks for and finds 'out of the square', 'out of the ordinary', 'off the scale' and 'above the average'. It is a way of life, not for Ego attention but because you can and you do. Aim sky-high. Innovate.

Go for the unusual or different. Be the agent of change. Let's 'go through the roof'? Be 'outside the box' to beyond imagination. Find the perceived limit and wonder what it's like on the other side. Search for what it is to be 'ahead of the game' and 'off the beaten track'. Get used to this territory. Off-the-charts is a type of celebration where there is an extension beyond the 'norm' and it either pays off or gives rise to a breakthrough that compels celebration. Any idea or suggestion that is unusual is kept in case it is needed at a later stage. Do not discard anything prematurely. Wisdom Mind can hold many dots (*see also* pp. 239–241) at once, even for years.

Off-the-charts can be a series of Wow (78) moments (*see also* pp. 170–171) culminating in a realization of how far the team has come and how they are now operating as a team together.

---

86 – Off-the-charts

You're witnessing yourself and the team reach results and outcomes no one was expecting.

You celebrate your remarkable achievements with humility. Your win is an organizational win, a professional win, a team win and a customer win.

You take the time to recognize, acknowledge and celebrate humbly any off-the-charts results, presentation, change or Revelation.

Integrating, 87

This is the coming together of the biggest picture or highest callings. At tile 80 Highest Callings was born, wondered about and kick-started. Through all the tiles 80–87, Wisdom Mind has been providing a wealth of capability and self-assuredness by direct experience. It is becoming second nature to 'wing it' and be humble about the synchronicity of events. Being in the Wisdom Mind connects you to an intelligence greater than yourself and greater than the group/team. This is an experience the Ego Mind doesn't have because it secretly and sometimes very overtly (Arrogant, 51) believes it is the 'something greater'. Events and unfolding start to be experienced as choreographed, have more meaning than some random, chaotic universal unfolding due to 'chance'. You can feel the co-createdness of what is going on rather than thinking about it as an idea or concept. Your role is to provide the power of 60 and above so that eventually Off-the-charts (85) happens. But your Wisdom Mind impresses the notion that it's not about being acclaimed or applauded, it came 'through you'. You were some kind of vehicle for Off-the-charts. You provided the stability and qualities and strengths, then it seems to 'all come together'.

Here, combining, including merging, amalgamating, complementing, harmonizing, co-ordinating, orchestrating and bringing it together describes the energy at this level. Synthesizing, arranging, reconciling, systemizing, synchronizing and attuning happen. For Steve and Wayno, authors of this book, the order of the 100 tiles was not initially known in the exact sequence but when they all came together it was an Off-the-charts moment. They looked at it all for a long time, taking it all in. Both witnessed each other spontaneously playing with how the levels and vertical themes were to come together. The integration process worked its magic.

---

87 – Integrating

This team has become an Incredible tapestry of Stepping In, Opening and Transforming tiles.

Every moment is a learning opportunity, a new tool to add to the tool kit for life.

The team's individual strengths combine to create a whole. The knowledge and wisdom of the team is becoming beyond measure.

Integrity, 88

It becomes obvious that you can live this life of constant transformation of yourself first, and then by being present that way, others around you are influenced by the power of presence. Being a person of integrity is more than just telling the truth. How honest you are to be, in terms of the other's capacity to receive higher truth, is determined in each and every moment (Spontaneous, 85) rather than a rule. Ego requires rules as it's too stressful to be spontaneous. Ego doesn't know how to be spontaneous. Instead, it is impulsive or compulsive, which includes an Entrapment. Spontaneous is freedom from Entrapments in the moment and can eventually become a way of life. Ego is not 'wired for complex, multipoint integration' (87) so needs a rule for everyone to follow. Integrity feels into every single exchange/involvement with a direct intuitive sense according to one's development and how clear the other person is.

A person with real integrity has practised consciously 'reading' the situation to best ascertain how much to stay as the witness and how much to be involved in that situation. There is no right or wrong, just the Wisdom Mind doing its thing of integrating as many factors or variables that it can regarding the situation it has in front of it. Fairness prevails as the intention is that everyone is included and although everyone may not feel a 'win', the greatest potential is where everyone has been taken into account. Here, there is purity of mind and heart. There is an incorruptibility because the focus is on little to no personal gain, being just, sound, virtuous and impartial. The focus is on veracity, reliability, allegiance, dedication and a constant grasp of the highest calling, along with realizing power and realizing value that are being delivered to the task/person in front of you.

---

88 – Integrity

Your word, thought and deed are your signature on this project, deal. The outcome will be win-win.

Your integrity is infused in your energy field and others will feel that. What you do and who you are when no one is looking is becoming more important to be aware of. Others may not know, but you do.

Your alignment to the highest in each moment is your goal and the team's goal.

Inspiring, 89

This awareness arises not by trying to be inspiring, but simply by being present and at the deepest level of Transforming. A life of positively and powerfully asking yourself and others to metamorphose out of Ego Mind into Witness Mind and then into Wisdom Mind is awesome and the positivity follows you around wherever you go. Watching someone remodel their life, divert from Entrapments and abstain from self-destructive patterns is inspiring. Then, when the person does that for others, it's compelling. It evokes admiration as it is irresistible in the absence of egotistical attention seeking and inflatedness. An inspiring person humbly offers a transformational space for others to grow at their own pace and into all the different types of Revelation and this is mind-blowing to be around. In other words, the Ego Mind takes a back seat and the Wisdom Mind activates. It's enthralling to be a part of, as well as humbling, captivating and mesmerizing, because to help transform your colleagues/team/company/ family is part of your highest calling and of Realizing Value (82). Wisdom Mind can be entrancing and absorbing to others. Ego Mind cannot comprehend the nature of the power. Being in the presence of someone inspiring helps you towards your own Wisdom Mind, then being a part of it 'rubs off' on you.

---

89 – Inspiring

The more you align with your higher purpose and who you're meant to be, the more your spirit shines through.

When you're being true to yourself, you allow others to be also.

It just takes one team member to be inspired to be the spark to set off a chain reaction.

Let's review

- Transformational Leadership serves life-supporting goals and is at the forefront of best practice. Being in Fellowship Mindset (83) and a global mindset become very important.
- At this level there is an ability to participate in the three main aspects of the life cycle: building up, maintaining and breaking down. Leaders at this level know the value and importance of the breaking-down process in order to create something new and more relevant.
- At this level there is an ability to live in the present moment and being what is required 'now', which leads to noticing and encouraging everyone's power to create an Off-the-charts (86) outcome for the company, team or family.
- Mastering this level means becoming the quality of Integrity (88) in all that is said, done and thought. This accountability inspires others to be the same.

Coming Up Next

When a leader becomes inspiring through the qualities he represents, something happens within the environments he participates in. What happens? What is the next level once Inspirating (89) becomes common practice? The following chapter shows you how the energy of the heart space is not something to hide, and that to lead from the space of lovingness is not incongruent with the corporate world. In fact, the health of teams, organizations and the wider world depend on leaders who are able to be devoted, sincere and compassionate. Find out how you can align with this style of leadership.

CHAPTER THIRTEEN

Incredible Leadership and Beyond

Entering the Mastery of Leadership

At this level, a leader is beginning to move towards mastering the craft of working collaboratively and with a deep sense of fulfilment in being able to be of assistance. Functioning from a sense of unity and common purpose becomes the norm.

90–99 The Level of Incredible

90 Grateful	91 Sincere	92 Heartfelt	93 Devoted	94 Thriving	95 Com-passion	96 Altru-istic	97 Heart-bursting	98 Extraordin-ary	99 Revealing Grace

When true transformation is unfolding and more spirit is being released to drive the changes, you cannot help but feel like it is a blessing to be part of the team, family or personal journey. There is a heart opening that can be difficult to explain as it is so much deeper and more rewarding than pleasure seeking. So, what is the language of Incredible?

Grateful, 90

At this level the heart opens and you can feel appreciation for what you are a part of and have been given. People, opportunities, even change itself – which was once going to create stress – is now enveloped with a 'Thank you for being in my life'. You know you will grow in wisdom from all that you have learnt by releasing one or more Entrapments. You are able to access the Wisdom Mind. It can be experienced as a type of celebration. In the 50s, Ego's efforts at saying thank you come with a hook and, consequently, attachment. Whatever behaviour or acquisition or thing that could be 'gotten' was driving the Ego. Below 60, there is an inherent pressure on the person being 'congratulated' because the thank you is laden with the expectation that the outcome needs to be repeated.

Whereas in gratefu there is an overflowing of warmth and connection and it is not reliant on something having to be repeated. The person is the focus, not the thing Ego seeks from them. There is a recognition that quality is more important than quantity. This acknowledgement is full of power as it affects the receiver and further validates the recipient. Having gratitude for yourself and others validates you and grows the power of this internal source. Indebtedness, validating, honouring and admiration are all ways to congratulate someone for being in your life and the gratitude is for who they are, not just what they do.

---

90 – Grateful

The support and opportunities that are made available to you and the team from this organization are truly a gift.

Arriving at work with colleagues who are also activated to work in the higher-number tiles has you feeling deep gratitude within.

You're not going to take any opportunity for granted. Things can change at any moment and this may not present again – seize the gift!

Sincere, 91

Being sincere is to approach life with a sense of honesty, warmth, vulnerability, attention, frankness, realness and truthfulness. 'Regardless of what may arise, I will give it everything to stay in this space for others' is a typical statement here. You stay true to the above-60 tile that you can now live from, no matter what happens in the external world. As you deepen into the Revelations, who you really are becomes more apparent because Entrapments are transcended, old stories are dropped and more valuable stories like your Highest Callings (80) are evident. When you are sincere in your approach in a consistent manner, others move from having trust in you to having faith in you. Faith is more powerful. Like trust, it must be earned by living at one or more of the Revelations and the space of sincere sits at the heart of someone having faith in you. While you can be ever-changing and spontaneous, sincerity means reliability can enter. You are true to who and what is required in the moment and instead of Scheming (34), you are compelled to stay sincere. Sincere stays connected during physical separation. Others are in your thoughts and it is like a part of their spirit is with you.

In the Entrapments, you hand over your power or spirit to an external situation or person. For example, the victim can say, 'Look what they did to me,' while at Egotistical, the statement might be, 'And I will never do that again.' The energy of sincere can see that a person may not have been able to hold someone else or even to hold himself together. Or there is a recognition that the other was abusive because of some veil of ignorance (59) and forgiveness is available. Sincere can cope with all these situations and transcend Entrapments as a person at this level has grown to the point where he has faith that the Wisdom Mind will find a way through.

---

91 – Sincere

You wouldn't be where you are today if it weren't for everyone's contribution – 'Thank you' to the whole team.

You're ready to do what it takes and look at any below-60 tile that hinders your team performance.

You're moved to change residual below 60 for the team and for your family, friends and everyone you meet.

Heartfelt, 92

At heartfelt, there is a flow from the heart to a person, situation or team. There may not be an actual reason for the flow, although you could find one to generate the flow, such as 'They are wonderful' or 'It is amazing'. But when the heart opens and the feeling of connectedness presents itself, no actual reason is required. Heartfelt is a constant presence of the wonder of it all and of genuine, unfeigned deep connection. It feels so real, poignant and expansive. It is all-inclusive and non-judgemental. The experience can also be quite acute and intense or gentle, soft and nurturing. There is an impassioned involvement, an involuntary presence that supports.

Relationships between two or more people in a family or team that are heartfelt have the special ingredient of beauty. Heartfelt radiates out from the Wisdom Mind and there is a feeling of its constant and innate presence that may not have been available and accessible until now. Deep sharing is possible as trust has turned into faith. Perfect frankness ensues and undisguised openness, that the Ego just cannot cope with, becomes the norm. Insecurities are flushed. Scepticism can be blown away by being with a heartfelt person. A heartfelt group is even more powerful. Relationships are joyful. All this can be experienced as beauty.

---

92 – Heartfelt

What you have achieved together brings a warm feeling to your heart and a tear to your eye. You may not fully understand how you feel connected to something much bigger than yourself right now.

This team has you wanting to give in new ways you haven't felt before.

This team/organization inspires you to want to give back more, be more.

Devoted, 93

As the heart is now really involved, it is easier for those who stay in Heartfelt (92) to slip into devoted. Here, without trying, the nature of the situation uplifts you into a place of dedication to the cause/person/

Highest Callings (80). It is like you have no choice, it is calling you and you commit because you can. As you are doing this from Wisdom Mind and not Ego Mind, it is not about being conned, manipulated, tricked or being gullible. You have constantly witnessed the situation and been able to forgive any transgressions. You may have had deep conversations to expose below-60 antics and Entrapment beliefs. The overriding presence of Heartfelt (92), however, is the key. Being fond is not enough. Affectionate is not enough. Keen is not enough.

Devoted signifies you are handing over some of your spirit to something bigger than yourself. It could be present in a group, person or team. It is not your Ego engaging in devotion, as Ego presents more like idolizing and attaching to a character, rock star, movie star or a group. Instead, devotion is non-attachment. It is both tender and strong. The person or group that offers the energy of devotion will not claim ownership of the devotion. A person who is devoted will know it is bigger than her. There is no fixed dogma to devote yourself to, just the presence of something wonderful that is not forceful, although it can be uncompromising because you need to stay well at this level. Everything matters here so staying well in order to be present for a multitude of inputs is an essential ingredient. Selfless steady reverence, every part of every day, leads you to a state of thriving.

---

93 – Devoted: Empowering Statements

You know this is where you're meant to be. Here, with this team, with this organization. Right now, no amount of persuasion will convince you to look elsewhere.

It's undoubtedly the right place and the right time. There is no explanation, it's a feeling.

The potential of this team blows you away. You're in 100 per cent to see you reach your goals collectively and how you reach them is more and more important.

Thriving, 94

Your resolve to be the best version of yourself has attracted a presence into your life that can be described as wonderful, beautiful, real and very intuitively intelligent. Entrapments that once ruled your life and veiled you down with a multitude of aspects of ignorance have been stripped back. There can be a flourishing. This tile is not in relation to finances, although you may be in financial abundance. It is about you, not the material world. You are flourishing by virtue of accessing so many Revelation tiles that add multiple faces to the Witness/Wisdom Mind that you can now live by.

Your health is prospering and your inner relationship with yourself is prospering too. You are paying attention to detail while holding the bigger picture of what it really takes to thrive in this world. Good, natural healthy food, drink, sleep, exercise, meditation and time out are all essential parts of your daily life and you are devoted to improving all aspects so as to be the best version of yourself and the natural state of this, just like nature, is wellness and aliveness. Relationships with others can thrive because you are thriving in a relationship with yourself. Listening to what your body is telling you rather than being pleasure driven means you can listen far more deeply to others when they relate what they need to operate at their greatest potential.

You have a prolific set of practices by now and constantly seek out those who do the same. It is as if you have had a seed of potential for so long and now you have been shown how to sprout. That is why you can devote yourself to this new version of yourself. You earn the 'thrive'. You can live the 'thrive' because you have transcended the Ego that held you back through the Entrapments. Your heart is open and plentiful. You have bursts of exuberance followed by periods of deep rest. You move from strength to strength. You smile a lot and are not fighting or coping with life, you are thriving within it.

> ### 94 – Thriving: Empowering Statements
>
> Thriving invites people. It's infectious in its sense of aliveness and fun.
>
> Ego Entrapments have been worked through to such a degree that more energy is available to focus on what helps you and others to thrive.
>
> Devotion (93) before thriving. Are you truly devoted? To what?

Compassion, 95

At this level there is an outpouring of kindness towards that which is focused on. A deep connection occurs in a natural, easy way. You now have access to abundance, a thriving of heart and goodwill. This means it's compelling to reach out and help. The heart is generous and full of goodwill and service to others. Gentleness and the capacity to be with others while they go through their suffering are central to compassion. There is no judgement, criticism or stories of condemnation for the other person or team. There is support and selflessness, tolerance and patience.

The awareness of compassion does all it can to understand the situation in front of it. Instead of running from an old story, having to fix everything because things are broken, compassion encourages a person to give more context to their predicament and as this happens, Entrapment statements and perceptions are revealed. Compassion also intuitively feels for the tiles of Entrapments involved so as to offer a more empowering above-60 perspective when the person is ready. 'Generosity of spirit' is the capacity to stay present with the situation in a big-hearted way. Compassion includes attentiveness and the 'hand of friendship' in times of real challenge. It's also empathy, which is being able to put oneself in another's shoes. Here, you can more easily understand and share the feelings of another but you are holding the Wisdom Mind instead of slipping into the negative pity or worried Entrapment. You really stay with the perspective that together you can work through things.

---

95 – Compassion: Empowering Statements

The focus to be of service that springs from the devotional heart creates a magnetic effect. What you require to fulfil your highest potential is naturally drawn to you and your team. Abundance offers resources and attitudes that can have an impact on the unfolding in the moment, whether it is in the team, company, family or relationship.

An intimate awareness of what is essential within the bigger picture and to focus on it begins its manifestation. The devotion required to attract it in is present.

Being able to be present with another while they release their below-60 charge, not taking it personally or feeling that it is bad in any way, is the best way you can 'hold' them.

Altruistic, 96

The nature of abundance is to flow to and fulfil the higher callings and as this happens, you and your team thrive. Eventually there will inevitably be an overflow. With Ego transcended in order to be kind-hearted, loving, devoted and thriving, a charitable giving rises up and the Wisdom Mind shows you how to redirect this abundance. The abundance can be financial or it can be experience, understanding or wisdom. All of these can lead to mentoring or distribution. It seems to be flowing to you and out through you to others. Humanitarian goodwill, magnanimous gestures and magnificent outpourings arise as a part of being Incredible. Living here is wonderful because you participate in helping the Highest Callings (80) manifest for the benefit of others. The benefits of altruism continue to shine well after the higher callings seem to be complete.

Fulfilment and contentment are definitely present, but perhaps another higher calling is arising through the abundance created by the infinite higher calling. There is freedom to be in the flow, both inwards and outwards. There is no 'getting' of anything, just a receiving for which there is deep gratitude. All true Wisdom Mind qualities are feeding and reinforcing each other. There can be a philanthropic flow of money but also generosity of song and sound, such as a free performance or the physical presence of one who has some mastery; provision of sleeping quarters to the homeless, a space to rest and recover. The list is endless. The ways of being altruistic are endless. Being Heartfelt (92) is growing and growing until one day it bursts.

---

96 – Altruistic: Empowering Statements

As more abundance is attracted in, there is an opportunity to share or redistribute resources, so altruism can be embraced. There is a feeling of being a co-creator in redistributing energy away from egoic pursuits to more embracing causes. This creates more abundance to share and redistribute.

Opportunities to be altruistic appear as there are no blocks to receiving and giving.

You constantly look for new ways to give, to be of service, to help make a positive ongoing change to other people's lives.

Heart-bursting, 97

At 60, we realized something. Now we recognize something. Since being a small child, you were subconsciously or consciously searching. You were looking for a true or 'most real' identity. Where do I fit? What am I designed for? Ego is a scattered, fragmented version that you gather in bits and pieces mainly from caretakers and siblings. You are this. You are that. But it was never truly you. It was a way of being in the world as an Ego. As soon as you learnt to Witness (above 60), you realized you had to release stories that entrapped you and find a new version of yourself. This will have been assisted by a person or group with Witness qualities. Perhaps movies, books or music help you identify with a deeper vision of yourself. You can be inspired by someone, a team or a group that has Wisdom Mind qualities (80–100). Instead of telling you what you are, you are modelled by how you can find yourself. As that unfolds, your Heartfelt (92) builds until it bursts open. You are finding who you are through inner contemplations and guidance and then a heart-burst comes along.

Wow (78) was a prelude, then at Off-the-charts (86), you were given more to celebrate. At this level of heart-bursting it is a deeper and longer-term experience that reveals your spiritual nature. This is the identity that sits behind all the identities. You feel a part of something very large, incredible and benevolent. You recognize the immensity of that which you don't know and feel very humbled by it. You are moved to a new level of gratitude we might call 'awe'. You are in awe of the mastery you can now see in those who have somehow walked out of Ego and through the maze of the Revelations to inspire you. You can touch your own capacity to master life. Not control it, but to be at one with it, alignment to the highest potentials that can now be seen to be everywhere. There is an unbridled joy in waking up and participating in the game of life.

---

97 – Heart-bursting: Empowering Statements

The energy of a big heart-burst can also reveal itself as a quiet, inner awe at the unfolding achievements.

You have Heartfelt (92) intentions. The feeling is remembered and can become a big part of your life. This creates a movement of living in the extraordinary.

It doesn't matter if it is one prolonged big Wow (78) or many small ones that lead to the bursting. Just be with it and grow it.

Extraordinary, 98

The Heart-bursting (97) is the doorway to extraordinary. Life feels exceptional. This is not the Ego, thinking and believing it is special. The Wisdom Mind has direct contact with the extraordinary. It makes no sense to the Ego, which has no way of interpreting the extraordinary. It perceives the unusual nature of extraordinary as weird or strange. It is secretly afraid of it, so condemns it. Extraordinary just gets on with exploring fantastic possibilities and fabulous ideas. The peculiar is welcomed and the unbelievable is achievable. Amazing experiences abound. When someone is watching extraordinary events in people they can be triggered into Ego Mind or lifted into above 60 and become curious and inquisitive (Open-minded, 72). You have entered the realm of genius as the Wisdom Mind is activated and this mind can reach in towards where the gold is, the unmanifest. While Ego Mind's identity is the physical gold, Wisdom Mind's gold is to assist humanity in some way by being extraordinary. Not trying to be (that is Ego), but actually being there by virtue of the path of self-actualization that 80–100 is.

Here, astounding things happen, astonishing is commonplace, awesomeness is the new normal. Superb events unfold. The unexpected wonder prevails and no direct credit is required. It is unconditional. It will be done. Why? Because it can be and we can all play our parts. Ego inflation is a long way away. Offbeat, spectacular, wondrous and unconventional are all what life is like here. Concern about what others think is unimportant. How people or some aspect of life are positively affected underpins everything here.

---

98 – Extraordinary: Empowering Statements

Loving at such depths becomes normalized so that the extraordinary behind all things begins to emerge or pop out in the same way a picture emerges from the 'Magic Eye' 3D games and images.

Alignment with the greater context in each situation gives rise to the highest potential to be seen and then the extraordinary can manifest.

Attempt to set a standard that is your best at all times.

Revealing Grace, 99

Here at this level, there is the constant feeling of being blessed, not only for those things and people that are in your life but life itself. To participate is full of wonder. To contribute is deeply fulfilling.

Generosity and compassion, goodwill and tenderness, strength and forgiveness all come naturally. Mercy prevails. This feels like the gateway to the sanctity of human life. A deep reverence for all of life's mysteries and that which makes sense to you. You are very aware you have access to one grain of sand of knowledge and all the other sand is for others to access and bring forth into the planet. Grace is felt as an overriding intelligence. It opens doors by virtue of knowing rather than pushing or forcing. You are tuning into its infinite wisdom and aligning with it and taking no credit for the appearance of Grace and what it reveals for you, or those you are in service to.

Life is enriched beyond words by Grace. Like all the other energies/qualities available through the 40 Revelations, it moves through you at its discretion and cannot be controlled. You can align with it, be mesmerized or entranced by it, be drawn to someone who is also playing with it – but you cannot own it or trade it. It is the doorway to Beyond Incredible (100). Realizing Truth at 60 was the doorway from Ego to the deeper mind and heart. Grace at 99 is like a vast ocean and you learn to surrender to it, knowing Ego must fight it, because Ego cannot comprehend Grace. Grace has no issue with Ego. It endlessly gifts people who are Ready (61) and facing into the Revelations. It oversees the journey towards and into being Beyond Incredible (100).

---

99 – Revealing Grace: Empowering Statements

A deep reverence for the immensity of what has been achieved and is still to be achieved. There is no attachment to Grace, only a deep feeling of humility and awe at being able to be a part of it.

Looking through the eyes of Grace reveals a mystery that all the tiles cannot understand.

You can't make or force Grace, you can ask or pray for it. Or you can diligently and devotedly practise all the Revelations that lead to Grace.

100: The Level of Beyond Incredible

United	Doing the Impossible	Breath-taking	Miracu-lous	Mastery	Superhu-man	Profound	Beyond Incredible

When your awareness is in this energy, it is difficult to articulate it. The expression cannot capture the experience. The Ego is a long way away and you can just marvel at what is unfolding around you.

There may be an ordinary event or situation, but in this awareness insights that were not previously available become possible. Because of the profound nature of this awareness, you may slip into rapture, ecstasy or bliss, which are all expressions of the awareness of the magnificence of the creation of life that is shining through into your awareness. It is not appropriate to order from lower to higher the qualities that are given for this awareness. All of the qualities here are brilliant, radiant, uplifting and amazing. Also, time loses its meaning here. It's like usual physical reality is still going on but the usual sequential linear unfolding is not as important. The delight at seemingly small things is very confusing to the Ego Mind. There can be laughter that is unexplainable and arises spontaneously for no reason at all. The drama of the Entrapments is clearly seen here for what it is. Changes can occur rapidly, even instantaneously. Being with someone who is in Beyond Incredible can accelerate your growth exponentially.

There is a deep sense of all things being united in some way, like a large ecosystem that is interconnected. This is experienced as a oneness where the separation of Ego melts away and everyone has a role to play. There can be moments when you feel like everything is contained in you somehow, which is of course not your physical body, but your energy field, and then there can be times when you feel like you are everything else (equivalent to you being somehow in a Universal or United Mind, as well as the Wisdom Mind).

Profound is the intensity of the very deep connection for that which is loved, studied or worked with. The abstract, esoteric complex is a wonder to investigate. The more abstruse, complicated and sophisticated the challenge, the more alive to it Profound becomes. A deep-seated knowing (claircognizant) can arise. The mystery of life unfolds with no pressure. What you are discovering was and still is unknowable to the Ego-thinking Mind. Luck and coincidence are replaced by karma, synchronicity, synergy and choreography.

United is experienced as things coming together towards one answer, one way forward, one highest potential, etc. Without Ego-thinking Mind involved, intense witnessing collects context and the Wisdom Mind builds the picture, while the United Mind holds it to 'download' into this physical reality. We usually need to have a daily practice to activate and support this capability. The separation of Ego and its consequent constant efforts to find something to bond, join or unite with (food, relationship, sport, etc.) is replaced by a sense of blending easily with whatever is undertaken that will benefit someone. The bigger picture is not let go of. All the team is interconnected. All play vital roles. All are essential to the one purpose.

Doing the impossible is breaking free of restrictions, limitations, stories and ideas that are around, keeping yourself small. The Ego is not involved at a higher calling so as you progress from 80–100 and beyond, there is a growing sense that what was deemed impossible before can actually be activated and there is a witness able to see how things unfold. It's like Adventurous at (66) and its witness is ramped up with a Wisdom Mind that is overseeing it all. It can feel like all of these above-60 Revelations are coming together. Some are Realizing Power (81), Spontaneous (85), Grateful (90), Devoted (93), Revealing Grace (99). All of them build a framework, a boat, that takes you across the ocean of Grace and into doing the impossible. Ego Mind cannot fathom this space. What appears to be stopping the team can be scrutinized under a powerful microscope and teased apart to reveal a way forward. Everyone in the team has part of the answer inside of them.

Breathtaking is the description of what happens when you are shown the highest truth. It is astonishing, mind-blowing (blows Ego Mind away!), mind-boggling (boggles Ego Mind), stunning, wondrous, ever-surprising, stupefying, mind-altering, spectacular, fantastic and unbelievable (have un-believe or let go of beliefs). What exactly has caused all this to happen? Your awareness is coming into direct contact with as much truth as can be coped with while still in a human physical body. Eventually you will be presented with gloriousness.

Miraculous is very subjective. Something marvellous. A shift in paradigm. Something that defies the physical laws or current perception of reality. The direct experience of synchronicity and choreography, where the idea of luck and probability fade and another, deeper law of how things unfold presents itself. Something astonishing or exceedingly rare. Spontaneous remission, which is the unexpected recovery that was not diagnosable or considered doable or even possible outside of common consensus. A scientifically unexplainable real-life happening or phenomena. These are available at Beyond Incredible but rarely advertised. Glamour is not part of this awareness. Awareness here just gets on with being of service and if fame comes, it is accepted humbly but not needed. It has been surrendered in Incredible (90s).

Mastery – Grace reveals that all along you have been attaining understanding, knowledge and direct experience of each of the Revelations. You may have been drawn to explore a specific Revelation as it was going to be extremely important for your higher calling. It is becoming apparent that you were in training all along in this Revelation as a major theme in your life. You were a master in training, finding out what it takes to be a master, which is to have access to some truth about the Revelation so as to pass it on. Mastery occurs when you have developed your Wisdom Mind so that when asked something you do not know in relation to your field of endeavour, you can access the answer in the moment. You do not 'own' the ability or answers as yours, you simply humbly acknowledge there is an inner peace that contains all the answers and potentials and that you are still in training to develop that ability. We do not stop 'mastering' our field of endeavour.

Superhuman – time to fly. Not having below-60 emotions is unfathomable to Ego Mind. It cannot understand this dimension of existence so does something below 60 with it. For example: Judge it (50s), be Sceptical of it (49) or Afraid (25) of it. The games or dynamics of all the below-60 tiles do not suck you into reacting anymore. Your energy can go towards creating the new and bringing the future to life with great intensity. You have been preparing to fly through the 60s and 70s and now you can soar. It's not just about what you can do, but how you can experience yourself when no one is around. Ego puffs up, but superhuman feels the huge potential with great humility.

Spirit seems to be underlying everything. It has been in the background the whole time and life appears designed for humans to find a way to bring more of it into earthly life. It is still there in Self-loathing (0) but like a trickle, as most of the thoughts, feelings, etheric and physical bodies are tied up in Entrapment ideas, beliefs, emotions and poor eating and no exercise. Spirit grows in presence as you move through the Code and makes its presence felt everywhere at Beyond Incredible. Every person, organization, location and team is felt as having a different level of spirit. Beyond Incredible people make a study of the spirit of their country, locality, family, team and individuals close to them. You are really starting to understand this at Inspiring (89) as you are in spirit more than before. At Beyond Incredible, you are aligned with spirit – that which is your deepest truth and reality.

Beyond Incredible Truths

Full alignment with the mastery that unfolds each moment in its full karmic beauty.

Entering the drama being played out with the full awareness that is a drama. Roles are taken on and there is awareness that they are only roles.

Everything that occurs is a win-win as all is unfolding towards knowing and feeling the depths of that which lies behind all creation. There is more awareness of the unknowable, deepest intelligence. The depths of the intelligence are more accessible or closer through the qualities of benevolence, lovingness, Grace and countless other positive qualities that demonstrate unity.

Mastery is ongoing, it never stops.

Miracles defy definition and are open to interpretation.

Keep going until life itself is a miracle.

In the deepest stillness of meditation, the breath is barely perceivable.

What took your breath away below 29 was perhaps something 'shocking'. Now it is spellbinding.

Doing the impossible is a wonderful life journey. You can be human doing the possible, or superhuman doing something impossible.

United is where duality of right-wrong and good-bad all starts to fall into the background, and you are present with the amazingness of all the drama and can start to see it for what it is.

Profound is where you have 'found' your deepest nature and it resides where all of your deepest nature is to be found.

Let's review

- Incredible Leadership understands the importance of balancing everyone's needs and contributions through the wisdom and compassion of the heart space.
- There is a deep sense of the blessing it is to be able to collaborate in teams to affect social change and create a more balanced world.

- The language of Incredible Leadership is tinged with deep gratitude and humility. This is a felt experience as genuine sincerity, compassion and gratitude make people feel uplifted and part of a bigger picture.
- Nothing is taken for granted at this level and there is an ever-increasing ability to notice where improvements can be made in self and in teams.
- Companies thrive at this level of service and it becomes possible to action extraordinary results for many.
- When this level of unified service becomes the status quo there is an ever-increasing amount of potentials that can be activated to address global challenges and redirect energy towards projects that promote life-sustaining principles. This is a powerful place and leaders at this level of mastery understand the collaborative and unified nature of truly devoted leadership.
- Beyond Incredible Leaders are global players in that the energy from which they function assists humanity.

Coming Up Next

Now that you have explored the content of the Awareness Code from above the integrity line, would you like to see these qualities in action? In the following case studies, you will meet people who have empowered themselves into the energy of living a life of integrity. They have done this not by shunning or avoiding the tiles of limited awareness but by embracing their lessons and building a scaffold that registers the lesson but does not allow the negativity to permeate.

CHAPTER FOURTEEN

Case Studies

Based on Real-life Case Studies

Anastasia – Open

A small and successful group of 20 people come together regularly and are co-ordinated by a group leader. Anastasia was to organize the work at various volunteer places in their local community. She was fair, kind and had the team's best interests at heart. Almost all of the time the atmosphere of the group and its work was harmonious (75) with little outbreaks of emotional drama or conflict in the team (below 60). And if there was, it was dealt with in a way where all parties felt it was a fair process with a reasonable resolution (Positive, 65). People were prepared to step in and be open. Sometimes group members could amicably sort through conflicts with relative ease and flow (Collaboration, 75).

A new person named Robyn arrived. She quickly set about learning the processes of how the group worked for the community and also how everyone worked together in the organization to move things forward (Receptive, 70). Robyn was shy and introverted and found it hard to speak up and give her ideas or opinions to help the running of the group. Nevertheless, she still fitted in to the group dynamic well. It became apparent, however, that when being confronted by situations with aggressive customers or people (43), Robyn began to cry uncontrollably (16).

Anastasia took Robyn aside and with Compassion (95) and patience began to ask questions like, 'Where is the murky feeling inside your body?', 'How old do you feel in this feeling?', 'Can you remember the earliest time in your life you felt like this?', 'If we could go to the deepest part of this feeling, what would it say?'

Robyn found herself feeling strangely comforted by these non-threatening questions – and found it relatively easy to answer them. She found that each time she answered Anastasia's questions, there seemed to be more of an understanding from earlier in her life. The exposure of her story (60) seemed to create an understanding (61) and the more she talked it out (62, 63), the more there was an easing of tension inside her body.

Anastasia asked Robyn to feel for the trigger when someone was aggressive towards her. Robyn found it quite easy to get to that memory. She found that she was speaking from a part that was about six years old and it was her grandmother in front of her in the memory. When she was six years old, for six months she stayed with her grandmother, who would be consistently aggressive and forceful with her. Robyn would cry uncontrollably while being forced to do things for her.

Once Anastasia had assisted Robyn to diffuse a large amount of the crying 'fear' charge around the early childhood feelings with Grandma, she felt no charge when asked to think about her grandmother. She could see Grandma was unhappy and Controlling (40s). Anastasia gave Robyn some quick tips to help her with future aggressive people that may trigger her into the past again. For example, saying to herself it is now the current day and she is not six years old any more, she is an adult and can ask for more context or request help, or as the exchange happens, slow herself down and breathe away and charge and do her best to Witness (71) and learn.

After speaking to Anastasia, Robyn had much more success in dealing with the public in the various volunteer places and actually looked forward to going to work there. Although she still felt fear when potentially aggressive situations came up at work, she also felt like she had more understanding about how to cope with each situation rather than an overdramatic reaction based on past unresolved pain inside her. This understanding made her feel really fulfilled inside her heart (Grateful, 90 and Heartfelt, 92). Robyn received much feedback on how she had changed, which really helped motivate her to practise using this new behaviour.

This experience with Robyn helped make Anastasia more Open-minded (72) to dealing with new people and this leadership experience also allowed her to magnify her connections (74) and work in the local community with a much wider group of diverse people, who all wanted to help.

Attalia — Incredible

Attalia is from Jamaica. She is a lead actress, mental health advocate and a part of a new production. Her success has enabled her to have the finances to establish a foundation in her name. It helps those in her homeland to access better mental health services and provides wonderful assistance to many Jamaicans (Altruistic, 96). During one of the first meet-and-greet production table meetings she shares a bit about herself. She notices around the table the people who enjoyed what she said and some who are sceptical (49). The judgement triggers a hot flush to her cheeks and a feeling of being Anxious (26) and Hesitant (29).

Later that night, Attalia sits down to reflect on the emotions that came up during the day because this trigger is one she has felt before. She finds a part of her that still cares what some authorities think about her truth and life interests. She knows that her work is of a high professional standard and her foundation is built on Integrity (88) and Sincerity (91), but there is still residue and charge around what people think of her.

Attalia begins to feel into what the best way forward is to fully be Fearless (68) around who she is now. She begins to feel for an imaginary situation (being an actor, this is her job) similar to the previous meeting. She remembers being in school at about eight years of age when she is asked to share about her holidays. Her response evokes humiliating laughter and she regrets sharing her world. She feels tight and mentally fatigued from excessively thinking about why she let herself be so open and vulnerable. When the adult Attalia asked that young part of her to speak out her feelings, the younger part expressed: 1. 'Be very, very careful who you share with'; 2. 'Watch them carefully because they will be judging you'; 3. 'They will laugh and you know that hurts'. Attalia realized (60) that this part had been inside of her all these years, causing tension and tightness when she was asked anything about her personal life.

'So,' she told her young self, 'let them laugh, you can't stop them. They don't understand so let's focus on sharing with people who have Integrity [89] and like your adult, and who actually enjoy helping others.'

Attalia began to realize when you are in love (Heartfelt, 92) or a positive space, it doesn't matter if someone chooses a negative thought about her. All she has to do is stay focused on her heart. She made an internal decision (Reorientating, 64 and Conviction, 67) that it's more important to be real if the moment calls for it and if someone chooses to judge you based on their personal opinion, despite being a great professional actor, then that's their choice.

Attalia began to feel more centred, open and joyful again instead of uneasy. It was important to release this emotional charge because as an actor, she works best in a Spontaneous (85) heart space. Her acting became more powerful and successful and this in turn gave fresh momentum with her new production, which then created additional funds for the foundation (96).

Becoming an Incredible future US presidential candidate or business leader

Frederick (not his real name) did not fully Realize (60) he had a Highest Calling (80) to be the president of the United States of America. It was not until he was presented with the Awareness Code, and his attention was drawn to tile 80, that he fully began to take in the understanding. It was also during this Awareness Code session that his son rang him and referred to his dad as the next potential candidate for the presidency, which stunned all present (Wow moment, 78). In follow-up sessions, we started to help him develop a much deeper understanding of his below-60 behaviour and what he would have to work through to consider pursuing this role.

Frederick aligns strongly with the 'American Dream' and the ideal that anyone, no matter what their background is, can achieve Incredible success if they are willing to make sacrifices and work hard (Positive, 65, Conviction, 67 and Emerging, 76). He grew up in a working-class family and neighbourhood, rather than the wealthy and privileged background with which so many political leaders identify. He witnessed first hand the difficult lives his parents and grandparents had, scraping by every day to put food on the table for their family. He understands the struggles of so many Americans today, who have little hope and for whom the 'American Dream' is just that, a dream.

Frederick expressed the view that America seems adrift, largely the result of a lack of true leadership in the political arena. His reflections on past presidents informed him that over the past century, the United States has displayed some truly historic moments of leadership, from President John F. Kennedy sending a group of anti-Castro fighters to the Bay of Pigs in Cuba to end the Cuban Missile Crisis of October 1972 to President Richard Nixon becoming the first American leader to visit China in 1972 and meet with Mao Zedong, to President Ronald Reagan telling Soviet Union President Mikhail Gorbachev to 'tear down this wall' during a speech in front of the Brandenburg Gate in 1987, two years before the fall of the Berlin Wall.

Frederick was aware of all this and also of the below-60 pitfalls previous leaders had fallen into, as well as the above-60 tiles. He also reflected on leaders whom he had admired, such as Abraham Lincoln, who had inspired him as he brought to life his Highest Callings (80) with Compassion (95). His education and observation seemed to inform him that now the United States was turning inwards, becoming a protectionist country at a time when the world most needed true Stepping In (60s), Opening (70s) and Transformating (80s) leadership.

Frederick shared his vision with the authors of this book, along with his passion for creating a new style of leader and what that leader could be. Discussions were focused on identifying a great leader as someone who is on the cusp of becoming an Incredible Leader (90s), someone who has Integrity (88), who can inspire others, who can build a Fellowship (83) of people around him with similar beliefs (86), someone who is Grateful (90) for everything they have been given in their life and grateful for what America has given them. Someone who has the ability to unite a country that is hurting and divided. Before the COVID-19 challenge, meetings with Frederick focused on helping him to examine himself and the world around him in light of the Awareness Code and to consider what the motivations for success have been in America and what his own motivations were. Are these motivations actually steeped in insightful awareness or based on self-interest (below 60)?

The path to becoming the U.S. president is not an easy one and Frederick has some significant dilemmas and personal challenges that he needs to face if he is to elevate himself to the highest office. The initial meetings with Frederick aimed to help him explore his personality (below 60), his goals, ambition and values. The result so far is that he is able to clearly identify some of his personal dilemmas and the lower tiles that could prevent him from being the leader he aspires to be. He demonstrates touches of Ego Confidence (57), Arrogant (51) and Know-it-all (52) and can be Dismissive (54). At the same time, he has already demonstrated an ability to be Fully In (69), armed with a Positive (65) attitude, an Adventurous (66) spirit and plenty of Conviction (67).

He has a Conviction (67) for building community-based models, bringing people together, connecting them in meaningful ways to live potentially Incredible lives. There is a melting pot of American people who want their freedoms, but who have become consumed by nativism and xenophobia (Resentful, 45 and Malicious, 40). Frederick dreams of 'dialling down' the tribalism and to provide the Transformational Leader (80) that he perceives the country is hungry for: 'We need to recognize that the country's first name is United and over 30 years, people have divided the place for their own interests,' he says. He is already a successful and wealthy businessman, so could himself be a poster boy for the U.S. capitalism he seemingly seeks to dismantle.

It seems then that his first challenge is to overcome the limited Entrapment tiles as he moves towards his highest callings. Perhaps the training ground is to first take on a more impactful political role as a stepping stone or it might be more around becoming an Incredible Leader and beyond in his existing business role. The authors will continue to work with him towards the goal of becoming an Incredible Leader, either as president or as a businessman.

Let's review

- These case studies show that consistently identifying and acting from the qualities above the integrity line reduces the victim mindset and reduces the likelihood of being seduced by the pay-offs of the perpetrator mindset.
- More energy becomes available to access the activities that rebalance the body and so it becomes easier to make changes and be motivated by the joy that arises from living and leading from a space of integrity.
- People who are able to consistently live in the tiles of empowerment do so by embracing the lessons of the Entrapments. They build an inner resilience based on integrating the lessons without the negativity taking hold.
- The Witness Mind and Wisdom Mind are increasingly made available as the higher tiles are stabilized.

Coming Up Next

To proceed any further, you will require an understanding of the human mind and how it functions within the Awareness Code. Let's take a deep dive into these dynamics, learning how to transition from the Ego-thinking Mind towards the Incredible power of the Wisdom Mind. Along the way we will see why the Witness Mind is so valuable. Just being exposed to this knowledge alone is transformational.

PART 5

FURTHER INTO THE CODE

CHAPTER FIFTEEN

Diving into How the Mind Works

Undertaking the Dynamics of the Awareness Code

The Awareness Code has the potential to take you into being a Transformational Leader, then to Incredible Leadership and beyond. The following section outlines the different minds awareness can operate through so you can begin to identify the mind you are employing in any given moment. In the same way you would not employ an unqualified employee to complete a complex task, awareness cannot shine forth the power of spirit by employing an unqualified or underdeveloped mind. The Awareness Code shows you which qualities are the domains of each of the minds so you can cultivate the qualities that employ Higher Mind.

The Levels of the Mind through the Lens of the Awareness Code

Awareness requires a mind to operate through. A very Undisciplined Mind, Judgemental Mind or Fearful Mind is so blocked that awareness is limited and the power of spirit is unable to work through it. At Higher Self level, the leader accesses a mind that is much more powerful, liberating, discerning and capable of higher potentials. A United Mind is something that is Beyond Incredible. Let's take a closer look at the levels of the mind.

What happens at Egotistical level?

Ego-thinking Mind

Operates below 60 and is 'I'-centred. At this level it is all about the leader and what they want. The leader plays the game of pretending it's about someone else but really it's about the leader. This may be in the leader's awareness or operating outside of awareness. If it is the latter and the leader is challenged, there can be a lot of resistance. Below 60 is characterized by 'not being aware of what you are not aware of'. All below 60 is seen as a type of ignorance. Ignorance cannot see what it is not aware of. For convenience, let's divide Ego Mind into two...

The below-60 Thinking Mind uses the past and limited current context to calculate, approximate or estimate what is happening and what is about to happen. It works on conjecture and speculation, belief and opinions that tend to 'look in', 'box up' or 'pin down' things based on judgement. Ego-thinking Mind tends to work by separating, pigeonholing, labelling and comparing. It looks for evidence to support its ideas, theories, expectations, opinions and bias and will tend to find the evidence, even when it's not there.

Unempowered Ego-thinking Mind – Lifeless, Despondent, Stressed, 0–29

Here, there is a belief from which a person operates that is victim orientated ('I am worthless'), which works against the individual or group or idea. This mind is unsure, uncertain, and cannot grasp the bigger, complete picture. It creates a feeling of inferiority so it is constantly disempowered and reacting with a victim mentality. Beliefs are packed around doubt and constant references to the past when things have not worked out in a way that was perceived as positive. So, evidence for negativity abounds and reinforces the way the mind interprets the world and self.

Judging Ego-thinking Mind – Wanting, Controlling, Egotistical, 30–59

Here, there is a belief that promotes an individual or group or idea and stays separate from what others 'think'. A team member may feel superior when another team member is being put down. Judgement is applied and superiority/inferiority hierarchical comparisons abound. It is a win-lose mentality. A pride is established so as to get something, often at the expense of someone else, their idea or their contribution. Beliefs are based on what and how you can get things. You reinforce the belief by Controlling. This type of thinking 'forces' things to happen and sets up a win-lose mentality. Based on the past, it predicts or guesses rather than connects. It projects, expects and assumes rather than asks for more context so as to feel into another person's experience.

What happens at Higher Self level?

When awareness moves above 60, it doesn't mean the Thinking Mind switches off. It is still there operating but now there is a different, more powerful mind that begins to function, called the Witness Mind.

Witness Mind – Stepping In and Opening, 60–79

Witness Mind creates gentle enquiry, spaciousness to respond and a no right/wrong perspective. There is an asking with intent to incorporate and validate the other team members. The mind changes from Ego-thinking, which is a concrete, locked, limited judgemental mind, to a Witness Mind, which is an open, hypothetical (positive), complex mind capable of holding onto a bigger context. It sees the patterns and feels into things that the Thinking Mind cannot grasp. It reasons not through Ego-thinking but by joining dots together after asking for more context. Answers start to 'come to you' by the power of witnessing.

Let's divide the Witness Mind into two…

Liberating Witness Mind – Stepping In, 60–69

Liberating Mind is the way out of Ego Entrapment. It can realize a deeper truth to a situation and start to see the antics and Entrapments of the Ego and the Ego in a way Ego Mind cannot. Intrigued in any challenge, it is internally nurtured to grow and develop rather than repeat Ego patterns. It is the beginning of awareness of the Higher Self, known also as the True Self, Soul, Ultimate Self, or Deeper Self.

Courage lives here and when we experience the need to change, we 'step in' or 'step away' in order to make a powerful statement or expression that we are now more aware that something is to change. It's the beginning of knowing a higher potential or win-win exists and moving towards that. It's much easier now to simply ask for more context. Not to provide more selective evidence for the below-60 story, but to shine a light on what is really happening.

Reorientation (64) is then available and instead of projecting negative past events on to the future possible events, life becomes more Positive (65), Adventurous (66) and freeing until the leader has more willpower or Conviction (67) to be fully in.

Discerning Witness Mind – Opening, 70–79

Discerning Mind is open without feeling vulnerable, which is Receptive (70). Then deeper Witnessing (71) can really occur and Trust (73) can operate. More truth becomes available so that connections are established that share information. Thinking orientates to giving and receiving, not the Ego-thinking Mind's attitude of 'What can I get?' New fresh ideas arrive through deep Witnessing because this mind is an attractor field so that the leader can personally evolve with new fresh perspectives. The leader is now internally motivated to receive these ideas for the benefit of others.

The Discerning Mind can join dots together to get new perspectives. These 'new ways of seeing things' are generated the more you can witness through contemplation, meditation, observation and sitting with the extra context asked for. An unbiased, impartial, unprejudiced, neutral, calm approach is cultivated.

Increased powers of consideration, contemplation, listening and non-bias are available. Greater degrees of complexity can be understood as the Stepping In process activities a sense of 'knowing' or 'feeling' of what is required. As we move through the tiles above 60, our ability to see outside the box and possibilities other than what was in the past or directly in front of us begins to flourish.

While the Ego-thinking Mind was trying to grasp or get, the Witness Mind acts like a magnet, pulling new fresh ideas to itself. The concentration is deeper and more meaningful and is moving away from separateness to togetherness and a win-win for all involved.

While Ego thinking still occurs, it is overpowered or overshadowed by a new type of Witness thinking, which can cope with the obscure, abstract, hidden or underlying aspects of any situation. Patience replaces reactive, emotional (tiles 0–59) Ego thinking. The answers to any situation are experienced as within us and we are to learn to witness the external unfoldings by deeper listening and watching, as well as learning to witness the internal unfolding by contemplation and meditation. What was incomprehensible, problematic or too complicated for the Ego-thinking Mind is seen as an opportunity to utilize the power of Witnessing. This ability is experienced as a deep sense of achievement and replaces the need to win that operates below 60. Witness Mind replaces reactiveness with responding.

The leader who witnesses becomes the one most responsible in the room, considering all dots/views/jigsaw puzzle pieces for their uniqueness and importance. With practice, the pieces will come together automatically. That's the power of the Witness Mind.

Wisdom Mind – Incredible, 80–99

This mind grasps the bigger picture, the higher calling and the deeper meaning to all it encounters. It sees into things by being much more Embracing (84) and attentive. The heart is involved, bringing Compassion (95) and deeper understanding. Wisdom Mind is even more intuitive than Witness Mind – while the Witness Mind brings the jigsaw puzzle pieces into place, the Wisdom Mind can bring fresh new perspective or insight because it is connected to the future. The unmanifest holds that which is about to be created or invented. The great disruptors access this mind to bring though new inventions and innovations. Important answers just arrive of their own accord with little or no effort. Increased alignment with a project or team initiates the activation of this mind. Ego-thinking Mind and Witness Mind are still operating, but now awareness can activate through this Wisdom Mind for deeper penetration into the truth of the challenge or situation that is presented.

As you engage above minds, there is a silent strength and authority that activates. Ego thinking can secretly or loudly rebuke, denigrate or reject the authority of the Witness and Wisdom Minds because it doesn't understand it. It is the increased Wisdom Mind presence in the person that opens the above-80 tiles and this provides more power, insight and understanding than the Ego-thinking Mind is capable of.

Ah-ha moments, revelations, epiphanies, insights, discoveries, inspirations, innovations and illuminations describe the Wisdom Mind space. Life-altering, life-changing moments occur here. The great new ideas movements and paradigm shifts arrive through this mind. Living life from above 80 invites answers and provides a team and its leader with new opportunities, vision and promotions of greater things to come.

What happens at Unity Mind?
Unity Mind or 'Oneness Mind' – Beyond Incredible, 100
It's very difficult to use words to describe this mind. Here, the leader feels 'at one' with the team and celebrates the amazingness of all collaboration so that stress drops away and a great 'wonder' replaces it. The solutions and creative ideas that are generated by true team humility are second nature. Feeling blessed is normal on a daily basis. The combination of Fully In (69), Flowing (79) and Inspiring (89) opens doors previously unimaginable. The power of this mind is a strong magnet because of how the focus is to assist at a global level in the field of the passion chosen.

Your relationship with time changes and there can be a sense of no time, just in the flow without effort. It's like there is direct experience of the unfolding of things.

You might ask, 'Why would a leader have any interest in accessing this mind? What is the point?' This is an example of Ego-thinking Mind asking and it cannot and never will understand Unity Mind. However, a brief experience of this mind can initiate profound and dramatic change in your overall awareness and it can have a dramatic shift towards more Witness and Wisdom tiles on a day-to-day basis. There can be a deep realization that there is much, much more than you had ever perceived or even conceived of before the 'oneness' of Unity Mind was experienced. You may invoke a dramatic change in your lifestyle or take a totally new career direction.

Once experienced, there cannot be a forcing of that experience to return again. That would be Wanting (30s), so instead there is a continuation of the 90s Incredible Leadership development until Unity Mind is once more Graced (99) upon you. Here exists endless peace, balanced harmony and access to non-personal questions that can benefit humanity on a global scale.

Let's look at an example of how each mind works

You, as a leader, begin to feel that a career change would interest you. What does each mind do with this? Here is an example…

Ego-thinking Mind – Disempowered, 0–29

The leader would think of all the things that would block this move – 'I am not ready yet', 'I don't want to let the team down', 'I will wait and see what happens', 'I don't have a new direction', 'I haven't got enough time right now', 'I'm too stressed', etc.

Ego-thinking Mind – Judging, 30–59

The leader would first want something: 'I want a job with more money', 'I want a team where I am respected', 'I don't want to feel undervalued'. The leader would suggest, on behalf of his own agenda, how the new team could benefit. They would try to control: 'I deserve more money',

'I am not interested unless I get…' The leader would also be egotistical: 'They need me more than I need them', 'I don't need anyone who can't recognize my brilliance', 'Prove to me you need me', 'Of course, I am the best person for this job'.

Witness Mind – Liberating Mind, 60–69

The leader notices feelings arising in themselves or others, notices exhaustion creeping in, notices other team members not having gratitude for the team, etc. Patterns of behaviour are noticed that do not align with the level of awareness required from the team and leader. There is a courage to step in and remain open to learning and growing – 'Help me understand what is happening for you', 'What do you really need from me for you to be your best in this team?'

Witness Mind – Discerning Mind, 70–79

The leader is beginning to trust that the resources for change are within themselves. How to connect and collaborate will come forth from within (Emerging, 76). Let's stay together with this challenge, let's keep talking from a win-win perspective, let's keep flexible, stay with possibilities, bring in more dots (*see also* pp. 239–241), paint the entire picture, contemplate all the landscape.

Wisdom Mind – 80–99

This mind recognizes when the surroundings are inconducive to the higher calling. Perhaps the fellowship is not evolving. The leader or team members' power may not be able to flourish and wonderful creative ideas are not embraced. Instead of being triggered into a reactive Ego Mind, where the leader would start wanting, Wisdom Mind intuitively knows how to plan and prepare for a new, spontaneous adventure. There is aliveness as to what that might be.

'Let's learn from the past and move on quickly to what is in front of us now.' 'In our discussions, let's focus on contributing with a view to creating and innovating, not fixing.'

What are the origins of Personality, Thinking Mind?

The degree to which a person is locked into particular ways of Ego thinking and behaving is determined by many factors. Ego ensures the survival of the human species at a physical level through the fight-flight-freeze response. Once physical survival is ensured, the impulse to relate with each other beyond survival begins. Through the hard-earned lessons of the foibles of humanity, which are recorded in history, people develop more of a capacity to distinguish between the disempowerment and judging of personality, which is forceful and life-sustaining attitudes that ensure survival through above-60 tiles.

The Stories We Create

As we move through life, gaining early programming and conditioning, we start making up stories to help us understand ourselves and 'life'. These Ego stories can be personal about our internal landscape or non-personal about others, family or work, for example.

We carry these stories into leadership and are a lot of them we are actually unaware of. All our below-60 awareness comes from our own or someone else's stories. We swap them, borrow and replace them constantly. For every story – for example, no one really likes me (Unlovable, 3), we are endlessly collecting evidence. You might hear 15 people thank you and one person shows their dislike of you or your effort, or they might simply forget to say thank you and the negative comment is the one you remember. It activates or triggers the stored emotions and thought that Unlovable collects since the start of the story.

It's clear then that a leader must change stories that don't serve us, but is that possible? Yes, it all depends on the leader and if they are able to move past Not Buying In (59) and arriving at Realizating Truth (60). If they are very deeply embedded in Ego and have been all their life and are convinced they are always right – for example, Narcissistic,

50 – it can be complex to help them know that other stories are not only possible but are waiting for them to find a way to step into them.

The below-60 tiles are all present in every person at all times but the Ego is usually only capable of being aware of any one or two at the same time. After the Ego has been 'triggered' or has 'reacted' its feeling and thinking may be in stress or at tile 25, Worried. Dismissive (54) is still present of course, but that part of the Ego-judging Mind is not active. In order to get out of the Ego disempowered tile of Worried, awareness is shifted to Dismissive and the worrying is dismissed. However, the charge and 'unfinished' content of that tile is still there. A more aware leader will bring awareness through the 60s Stepping In, activate Fearless (68) and Release (63) the content of the worry in a liberating way. Awareness can then come through Positive (65) and Adventurous (66).

Repetition of Thoughts

Once a thought has been activated in a layer, e.g. Wrong, 6, that thought might be 'it's all my fault'– this will then activate an emotion of wrongness or badness that in turn affects the body's ability to produce adrenaline and this may serve to tighten the body into contractions and cause tension headaches.

If you get to tile 63 and you are able to let the thought go and not 'believe it', then the pattern dissolves for now but may trigger again at a later time. Every time you believe or buy into the below-60 story, you grow it, feed it and entrench further into it. It makes sense then that every time you DO NOT believe or buy into it, it will start to shrink or decay, depending on many variables that we look at through this book.

The original, very early stories that we carry are what we call 'core beliefs and emotions'. For example, this may be an underlying tendency or core belief that might be 'I am Never Enough' (8), because you were unfavourably compared to the oldest sibling and should have known better and you may have been guilted in an attempt to make you a better person. This can be said to be the child part of you. If, however, you 'go with' or identify with the belief that the child part of you has, it becomes a default pattern. This means you have just identified with the story and you may have done this hundreds, maybe thousands, of times. You may not be aware you are doing the default story, you build the charge of the pattern each and every time you think and feel this way.

Repetitive thinking and feeling promotes awareness of the layer you are in. Above 60 of course, this is a wonderful thing because 'what you focus on you become'. If your core is Adventurous (66) because this was promoted and accepted as a child, your default will be to take a positive risk in order to learn about yourself. Within the Awareness Code, the layers ending with a '9' when below 60 have a low repetitive nature to them and are perhaps more easily let go of, but those layers below 60 ending in a '0' have a very high repetition and will usually be more difficult to break.

How strong is your sense of self and what mind is that sense of self employing?

All the stories you have inside of yourself about life, relationships, self-worth, leadership, parenting, health, finance, etc. create your sense of self. This is your Ego self. Your identification in the world that arises from the stories you have about your life and who you think you are, and how you treat yourself and others comes from these stories. Have you been like a sponge and just accepted your caretakers', teachers' or peers' stories of you, or have you been able to create original stories based on your own personal experience of yourself? This will be critical when challenged in a leadership role. You may want (39) to be respected or admired or listened to as a leader, but what if at your core, you doubt yourself and are anxious (26)? This doubt will present when you are challenged by your team members. It will undermine your leadership performance. You can see from the Code that any above-60 tiles will provide you with greater 'solidity' or 'sense of actual or real self, not Ego self' in times of challenge because this sense of self is a direct experience of who you really are and not the stories others have asked you to believe.

All team leaders will be faced with their team presenting with one or more of the below-50 Ego tiles. A leader's understanding of 'where they go' on the Code is required, if not essential. The more awareness you have, the deeper towards 100 you can be, and the more solid you are within yourself and the more powerful you are to inspire others towards letting go of old stories and creating new ones that will assist the team to flourish.

Is your sense of self stronger, deeper and more solid than any of the hierarchy of structures around you in your role as a leader? The Narcissistic (51) leader will automatically send their creative team members in a direction where the leader will have an opportunity to be credited with the outcome. Wow (78) moments will be claimed by the Narcissistic and this style of Ego identification can eventually dismantle an organization.

Entrapments cover or blanket our spirit. Another new perspective is that spirit is very fluid and can be loaned out to whatever your Ego or wisdom self 'invests in'. For example, a new member joins your team and if you are Worried (25) and Competitive (35) with that person, not much spirit will flow between the two of you and you will not inspire (in-spirit) them. However, if you are free of these Entrapments and operating at Realizing Power (81) and Realizing Value (82), for example, you will notice or help them understand their strengths and feed back their Realizing Value. There will be much more of an exchange of spirit. This bonds and creates rapport and so much more powerful chemistry than Ego and self-centredness in the team.

A little bit of someone else's spirit can really lift a team member. 'I am thinking of you and what's best for you' is a strong promotion or validation to help someone move to 60. When you know someone is investing their spirit in you because they intuitively feel you have the capacity to move deeper into the Code, this actually assists you in doing so. A more solid sense of self can initially be built because you have the spirit or a mentor/coach/CEO 'with you' in spirit.

The Different Types of Confidence

In 0–29 Lifeless, Despondent and Stressed, there is a lack of esteem or confidence. Instead, there is a constant self-putdown and self-abuse and self-doubt. To escape this drama, the Ego sets up a way to help itself feel good and seeks pleasure or a sense of self that is 'happy' with getting what it wants. As it learns to get what it wants, it develops a separate identity and sense of achievement and the more it can get something, the more 'confident' it becomes in its capacity to predict getting what it wants for the next time. Feeling good about getting something gives it an Ego self-esteem, based on the ability to generate wants that it thinks it has to have to feel good and then it gets that and becomes even more Ego Confident (57).

All this changes as we get to Realizing Truth (60), where it is now about reading the situation for how you can contribute and achieve that which provides a win-win. Not getting what you want can actually be experienced as a win because not being attached to the want feels like a win and is an above-60 feeling. The newly negotiated outcome replaces the 'have to have' and feels uplifting. Witness confidence and esteem replaces below 60 and here, it feels authentic and full of Integrity (88). We need Ego self-esteem and confidence to help us out of lack (below 30) and then Witness self-esteem and confidence lifts us out of 30–59 and towards Wisdom Mind (above 80).

Essential Ingredients to Cultivating the Above-60 Mind

1) The dot and circle
   A dot is anything that is present (or absent) in any situation/project or relationship that can have an influence. Any situation can have

many dots. Some are trivial, some can be important but delay is appropriate and some are to be attended to.

So, what do we do with the dots or variables that we think are important? Below 30 is always in a confused state; 30–59 tried to control every single one of them. At 60–100, we do our best to identify the various dots and witness them AS WE PROCEED with the project/task. Above-60 awareness is more focused on NOW and is capable of monitoring and adjusting to eventually be very Agile (77).

A circle is the bigger picture that holds all the dots or at least as many as you can be aware of at the same time. Below-60 awareness is limited in how many dots their circle or bigger picture can hold. As we move from 60–100 awareness there are more pieces of any jigsaw puzzle available and your awareness can hold them without stressing (20–29). It's challenging, but Witness and eventually Wisdom Mind are designed to have the capacity to cover more variables and the challenge is both invigorating and uplifting.

At a meeting, below 60 will narrow down to defend a person's dot, which might be an idea, opinion or a guess. Or they might attack another person's dot. While this is going on, a leader who is in above-60 Witnessing (71) can see the importance of the dots and which has more merit. A leader with above-80 Wisdom Mind can feel the significance of each dot intuitively and feel for the bigger picture (circle) of which dot to include and which one to exclude.

A person who is dot-focused can narrow down under a microscope but may miss the bigger picture or lose contact with it. A circle person can hold many dots but may miss specific content.

Awareness 0–29 is about finding a dot and narrowing down on how it can't happen, whereas 30–59 is about finding a dot you think is the most important, narrowing down on it and trying to control things so you get whatever the dot requires. You try to make or force the dot to happen. Between 60–100 is about finding a dot and narrowing down on it so that you increase the likelihood of it happening and there is an awareness of the greater context. The dot will in some way help yourself or others so that you are promoting its probability to occur. It feels like you or the team represent a positive power that has identified the most likely best outcome and are working towards achieving that. Eventually, you will be Devoted (93) to the dot unfolding.

All below-60 levels tend to lose sight of the bigger picture as they narrow down on the dots (those multitude of things present in any situation/project/relationship).

2)   The lens of yin and yang

Leaders in any field of endeavour have many jobs or dots to address or complete. They 'do' so much, they become very competent and familiar with doing a lot. They can become human 'doings' – up early, late to bed, all day doing. Not much time, if any, for just 'being'. So, we lose touch with our human being-ness. When we attempt to just be, it can be reading, television, sailing, etc., which is still doing.

This doing part of humanness is the yang or masculine principle or aspect of all things and is seen as active, moving and doing. It is sharp in that it can penetrate or cut through things. This is great when we need precision and answers and need to focus on one thing. The yang of Ego can be like a laser beam. It is driving and associated with the heat of doing. Yang is emitting energy and gets things done. Yin is the female principle aspect of all things and is seen as being calm and relaxing. It is soft in that it supports, nurtures and holds many dots like the big picture. This is great when we need to be creative, connective and receptive. It is inactive and associated with coolness. Yin is absorbing energy and comes alive when the bigger picture is required. It's great at providing the circle for the group.

So many leaders can become yang-orientated and move out of balance into yin deficiency. Hyperactivity is an extreme yang and while you can get a lot done, the deficiency of yin rest can catch up with you through the appearance of yin deficiency symptoms. These physical symptoms will appear where you are most susceptible. For example, if you use your masculine yang Thinking Mind excessively, you may feel brain symptoms like a headache or migraine, kidney problems, exhaustion, sleeplessness, nervous conditions or irritability.

It's rare for a leader to be extremely feminine or yin but if we burn out or move into Despondent (10–19), especially Lethargic (13), we can become very yin and just not want to participate or initiate anything. This type of yin is driven by 'What's the point?', which is not a beautiful deep resting, meditative, dreaming yin state that would nurture you. Instead, it is a judgemental state working against a balanced, healthy you.

Each person, male or female in gender, has both feminine yin and masculine yang. We are all on a journey to find out which balance of both works for us. Every aspect of our lives must involve yin and yang. Take conversation, for example. As a leader, there is a tendency to listen to things in order to 'fix' it. Yang listening is all about listening to provide a solution to a problem. This is great if the person talking actually has a problem. Sometimes they don't and would just appreciate being valued by being listened to. Masculine yang can think this is a waste of time and a waste of its ability to come up with solutions. The talker can feel not listened to or understood, especially if the 'solution' masculine yang comes up with has been too dot-focused. In Ego, masculine yang listening can happen as a default unless they are alerted to and become aware of a different type of listening being preferred.

That would be to listen as feminine yin would listen. Not to fix a problem but just to be with the story. A sounding board. As the person with a problem talks, they themselves are hearing the problem expressed and may themselves get to Realizing Truth (60) to start to have some fresh intuitive insight as they get to witness their story unfolding.

The feminine yin listener doesn't solve anything, just supports the transition to 60. If the leader with the problem is stuck in blaming themselves, or blaming others over and over but not able to Realize Truth (60), it can be a real challenge to stay at yin as the problem is not being solved. Sometimes we really require the other person to be a masculine yang listener and we are discussing the problem with a view to the listener providing a possible solution. It is important to know which listener the leader with the problem is looking for.

We are innately wired to have cycles or phases of activity followed by rest, masculine yang followed by feminine yin, then back to yang again. If we wake early and push our yang for 16 hours and collapse into bed for eight hours of yin sleep, eventually symptoms can arise to let you know of the imbalance. Can you find time to rest/nurture yourself in a feminine yin way in cycles through the day?

You might have been programmed to think that feminine yin is 'doing nothing' and is associated with wasting time and not contributing, and think that 'I could be doing a lot of other more valuable things'. Going to above 60 will help you realize that the Revelations usually all arrive in yin/meditating/contemplating, deep rest time. Can you create more of this in yourself so that Heartfelt (92) is your underlying great feeling while you go about your doingness, rather than exhausted or stressed as the underlying reality?

3) What does karma have to do with leadership?

Karma is a Sanskrit word meaning 'consequence'. It is an underlying psychological law, much like gravity is an underlying physical law. If you plan an object 2m (6 1/2ft) above the ground, it sets up a higher potential for it to return to its original position. Karma is similar in that what you 'put out there' in terms of a thought or action or behaviour sets up a huge potential for it to return to its origins, which is you.

Another example in the physical world is the elasticity law, which says that when you stretch a rubber band, it has the potential to go back to its original shape. Karma is the underlying law that will assure in some way that how you act and cause what you say and think about others is going to come back to you. Like gravity, karma is not the course but its mechanism. It works behind the scenes just as gravity does. Because you cannot see, feel or touch it, then you may be sceptical that it exists. There is no good or bad gravity. If you leave an antique object on a ledge and you knock it over, it is not bad gravity, it is accidental on your behalf. But you could blame gravity (Annoyed, 47). Similarly with karma, there is no good or bad karma, but there are choices that you make that set up certain things happening to you and if you don't understand karma, you will probably just blame or judge yourself or others.

If, as a leader, you engage excessively in a particular back-stabbing activity against a colleague, team member or friend that sets up some type of malicious activity back towards yourself. If you are unaware of karma, it is easy to blame the other person (Resentful, 45) and not link it to your original behaviour. The idea of karma is difficult to comprehend for Ego (below 59) because it just wants to be able to get away with whatever Controlling tactic it can to feel good. All about getting whatever it wants (30–39), Ego avoids not feeling good (0–29). Ego doesn't want to know about the consequences/karma of its actions – it's easy for Ego to reject the truth of karma.

So, we undergo some type of suffering similar to what we have inflicted on others until such time as we Realize (60) that it is time to stop judging, Deceiving (44), being arrogant (51) or any tile behaviour that causes suffering to others. If we have accrued below-60 negative potential, karma does not mean you MUST suffer the same consequences you helped others feel. You can Realize (60) that all the above-60 Revelations are pro-life and then help others by increasing your service so the negative potential can be neutralized by positive potential.

The more 'good' and wonderful things you do as a leader in the world, the more potential for that to be returned to you from your team members. However, a person's karmic patterns are complex because we have participated in more than just personal behaviour. There is a team, family, company, friendship karma that plays out as well. As you become more intuitive in the Witness Mind, the Wisdom Mind becomes available so you can start to feel and read karmic patterns. Ego does not understand or interpret karmic patterns.

To move through the tiles towards 100, leaders must be accountable and learn to take responsibility for everything that they put out into the world. Karma ensures that. Great leaders learn from consequences. Realizing (60) that karma is very real and operating at all times, just like gravity, means you can have awareness to witness more aspects of karma. There is a point when a child realizes gravity will operate, although that child might not understand the mechanisms of gravity.

Leaders using Deception (44) means that potential will stay in their psychology and energy field and it will pull out Deception from others in the team at some stage. In Witness Mind (above 60), you can start to realize this as it is happening, accept it and release Deception as a way of living.

'I hate you, you moron!' said with vengeance can be Bully (42) and that sits in a leader's psychology and energy field until someone returns the insult and you directly understand what it's like to have that done to you. This has the potential to cause you to resolve (Conviction, 67) to not to do that any more to your team. If you become a victim (0–29), you suffer. If you remember and realize the consequences of your previous actions you can move into above 60 and Reorientate (64) to not doing that again.

4) Your sphere of influence

This term generally applies to a field or area in which an individual or organization has a power to affect events and developments. Every leader creates a sphere of influence by means of the tile that they operate in at any given moment. Tiles below 30 offer a sphere of negative disempowered influence of the team/organization. Languaging the Entrapments influences others in a similar way and gives them conscious or unconscious permission to be that way too. Tiles 30 to 59 provide a forceful sphere of influence and persuade the team members to align with the leader for below-60 reasons, such as fear of failure or not wanting to upset the leader, etc. The greater the engagement in the tiles language and energy, the greater the force felt in the room when the leader walks in. Alignment can be achieved but there are consequences, e.g. resentment.

Above 60 is the first association with true power that comes from the leader realizing the truth. The sphere of influence is positive and uplifting and empowering to the leader and team members. As you progress from Stepping In through to Incredible, the sphere of influence magnifies considerably and operates through entrainment. Team members are drawn to the power of these tiles because they promote growth and development of all concerned and look for the highest outcome for all. A leader who walks into the room living, breathing, talking and relating from the higher tiles automatically fills the room with that power. There is no need to impress or control others. This type of sphere of influence acts like a magnet, pulling to it that which is required to fulfil win-win outcomes. This type of attracting response comes with the territory of the higher tiles. Once you enter the higher tile and learn how to stay there, you earn the power associated with it and carry this everywhere with you.

A Final Contemplation

As you have become more aware of the different types of mind available to you, there may be a spark within you to really understand why you are compulsively called to employ the Lower Mind in various situations. Identify the situations where Lower Mind, whether unempowered or judgemental, dominates and forces its way in. Can the Witness Mind be asked to enter the situation? What are the stories you live by that are never questioned? Can you identify programmes these stories impose on you? Do you have a robust sense of self that comes from self-esteem?

See if you can identify the dot and circle approach throughout the course of one day. What do you discover? Deliberately track the yin and yang aspects of yourself throughout the course of one day. Study karma by watching the day's events.

Can you identify the karmic messages in your life?

Let's review

- You have access to awareness through your mind but the question is, from which mind do you operate? We recommend you limit the time spent in judging Thinking Mind and transition to Witness and Wisdom Mind, which is where the power is.
- Like Ego, Soul is not a dirty word. Both show the energy dynamics of limited connection and deep union in connecting with others through the heart. Leaders who function at this level transform all they encounter.
- Once practised at staying connected with others through the Soul body there is an opportunity to develop Unity Mind. This is a very powerful energy field.

Coming Up Next

How do the lower tiles play out in the corporate world? What is a 'Wounded Warrior' and why does the 'snake' try to control situations? In the next chapter you will learn about some of the personality types that can be encountered in the workplace and how some function below the integrity line while others above it, with very different results.

CHAPTER SIXTEEN

A Practical Application of The Code in Leadership

The Awareness Code as a Leadership Tool

The Awareness Code breaks down 100 dispositions or tiles available to people and the consequences of behaving from tiles that fall below 60: the Entrapments. If you are leading your team in sport, medicine, politics, the corporate world or any other arena of human endeavour, any movement towards unpacking and understanding rather than vilifying negative dispositions is movement towards addressing some of the biggest challenges we face globally. Everyone has a role to play in this. The Code alerts us to leadership qualities we all have access to and are called to develop by focusing on dispositions above 60: the Revelations.

The following section addresses some of the ingrained patterns of behaviour that can plague leaders. For example, policy making that is harmful and does not carry with it the spirit of Fellowship (83) and the benefits of Witness, Wisdom and Unity Mind. For the Awareness Code to make an impact in leadership, current leaders are asked to address their leadership at a personal level and to take responsibility for the spirit imbued into their teams. Are teams dulled down with personal agendas or thriving in a spirit of Collaboration (75), where people are encouraged to nurture their Realizing Power (81) become Agile (77) in problem solving and delivering Altruistic (96) outcomes?

In this chapter we look at the amalgamation of various tiles that create two types of personality and leadership style: the Snake and

Wounded Warrior. Both create a specific dynamic that influences people and teams in negative ways, but the Code shows how people locked in this dynamic can be assisted out of it. We also look at two other, more powerful expressions of leadership to make a contrast. The juxtaposition alerts us to the very real consequences of choosing leadership with or without integrity.

Activating the tool

A starting point for the practical application of the Code is for each individual to rank each tile on the Awareness Code. The ranking is to be on a scale of 0 to 10 Evaluate yourself across the tiles, marking how each one resonates with you on a scale of 0–10: 10 would reflect 'this absolutely resonates with me' and 0 'this does not resonate with me at all'.

Please see below an example of an emerging leader. Often when we ask people to complete this, there is a natural tendency towards giving yourself a higher awareness ranking than is true and also, leaders can underestimate their own levels of lower awareness. The higher scores highlight strengths in higher awareness or visible areas to develop in lower awareness.

The table on p. 240 represents the ranking of an emerging leader. The leader has significant above-60 dispositions across the levels of Stepping In (60s), Opening (70s), Transforming (80s) and Incredible (90s), which demonstrate the existing leadership. Also, the leader has identified some limited awareness, which is spread across the tiles below 60.

The leader has a lower ranking in Opening – Receptive (70), Witnessing (71) and Open-minded (72) – which can be a key window for working out how he can develop his leadership. He also has a Stressed and Despondent block, which includes Wounded (14), Hurt (15), Saddened (16), Disconnected (17), Frighteneing (24), Worried (25), Anxious (26) and Over-pleasing (27).

AWARENESS CODE

			United	Doing the Impossible	Breathtaking	Miraculous	Mastery	Superhuman	Profound	100 Beyond Incredible	TOTALS
											0
Incredible (90)	(5) 90 Grateful	(5) 91 Sincere	(5) 92 Heartfelt	(6) 93 Devoted	(3) 94 Thriving	(3) 95 Compassion	(4) 96 Altruistic	(5) 97 Heart-bursting	(5) 98 Extraordinary	(4) 99 Revealing Grace	48
Transforming (80)	(5) 80 Highest Callings	(4) 81 Realizing Power	(3) 82 Realizing Value	(4) 83 Fellowship Mindset	(3) 84 Embracing	(4) 85 Spontaneous	(5) 86 Off-the-charts	(3) 87 Integrating	(5) 88 Integrity	(5) 89 Inspiring	41
Opening (70)	(3) 70 Receptive	(2) 71 Witnessing	(3) 72 Open-minded	(5) 73 Trustful	(6) 74 Connected	(6) 75 Collaboration	(6) 76 Emerging	(6) 77 Agile	(6) 78 Wow	(6) 79 Flowing	48
Stepping in (60)	(6) 60 Realizing Truth	(6) 61 Ready	(6) 62 Preparing	(6) 63 Releasing	(6) 64 Reorientating	(6) 65 Positive	(7) 66 Adventurous	(7) 67 Conviction	(6) 68 Fearless	(7) 69 Fully In	64
Egotistical (50)	(1) 50 Narcissistic	(4) 51 Arrogant	(6) 52 Know-it-all	(4) 53 Self-centered	(4) 54 Dismissive	(4) 55 Defensive	(2) 56 Pretentious	(2) 57 Ego Confidence	(2) 58 Complacent	(1) 59 Not Buying In	30
Controlling (40)	(1) 40 Malicious	(2) 41 Enraged	(2) 42 Bully	(3) 43 Confronting	(1) 44 Deceiving	(1) 45 Resentful	(2) 46 Passive-aggressive	(2) 47 Annoyed	(3) 48 Frustrated	(2) 49 Sceptical	19
Wanting (30)	(0) 30 Infatuated	(3) 31 Perfectionist	(6) 32 Addictive	(3) 33 Over-ambitious	(1) 34 Scheming	(2) 35 Competitive	(2) 36 Attached	(1) 37 Narrowing Down	(1) 38 Identifying	(1) 39 Ego-requesting	20
Stressed (20)	(2) 20 Numb	(2) 21 Terror	(2) 22 Dread	(2) 23 Trapped	(5) 24 Frightened	(6) 25 Worried	(6) 26 Anxious	(5) 27 Over-pleasing	(2) 28 Insecure	(2) 29 Hesitant	34
Despondent (10)	(2) 10 Inconsolable	(4) 11 Hopeless	(3) 12 Unfulfilled	(3) 13 Lethargic	(6) 14 Wounded	(6) 15 Hurt	(4) 16 Saddened	(6) 17 Disconnected	(3) 18 Discontented	(3) 19 Disinterested	40
Lifeless (0)	(0) 0 Self-loathing	(0) 1 Self-hatred	(0) 2 Pathetic	(1) 3 Unlovable	(1) 4 Burden	(0) 5 Embarrassed	(0) 6 Wrong	(1) 7 Regretful	(1) 8 Never Enough	(1) 9 Inadequate	8

> ## Your personal ranking
>
> Rank your own scale of awareness from 0–10 and feel where the blocks occur. Be spontaneous and feel rather than think about the ranking. Perhaps ask a colleague to rank you too and compare the findings. Work with the 25 keys in Chapter 19 (*see also* pp. 267–299) and over a period of six months, track your progress.

Egotistical and Controlling Leaders

Through reading the cases studies presented so far and completing your own personal ranking you may have noticed that people are complex and function from an amalgamation of various tiles at both the victim and perpetrator levels, as well as the deeper tiles.

Here, we will look at four prominent personalities in the Ego world entrapped in the Limited Awareness tiles. In the previous chapter we looked at the different types of mind, which are: Ego Mind, Witness Mind and Wisdom Mind. To recap, the Ego Mind operates through the faculty of thinking and its domain is the Limited Awareness tiles that are Entrapments and create duality. The two opposites created in this mind are:

1) Disempowered Ego-thinking Mind – Lifeless, Despondent, Stressed, tiles 0–29

The Wounded Warrior, tiles 0–29

This team member seems to be champion of the cause in an Egotistical way (50s), but they may be hypersensitive to comments of encouragement or criticism. Being encouraged can trigger a feeling of Resentment (45) and the question 'What's wrong with how I'm doing it? Why do you have to pick on me?' This arises from the warrior wanting to be seen as the go-to person, the one who will 'save the day' (38). Deep down, this is a leader who is judging themselves or who has been judged before and still has charge around that judgement. They may try to Over-please (27) to not feel the Wound (14) and deeper Pathetic (2), or even Self-hatred (1). When on task and contributing, the warrior can be really engaged, connected and involved, but any hint of not being appreciated or valued can send them into a spin of emotions. Work can be a way of containing the Wound (14), but if the wound opens at work, the pain can be overwhelming.

To be able to grow, the warrior needs to be able to identify his lowest level of awareness and be prepared to begin development work, which involves being very honest and open. For example, a Wounded Warrior may often feel Hurt (15), taking any criticism personally and to heart, struggling to operate when he feels others disapprove of him. The person may feel as though he has been left out or rejected. Within the Awareness Code, we have developed techniques to help someone in this situation to move beyond this tile as part of their growth. Someone feeling Hurt can ask himself some questions that will help him to move out of Hurt, first by asking whether there is actually any truth in what others are saying or doing that causes him to feel pain. Perhaps the Wounded Warrior is using any criticism to hurt himself because he hasn't found the core of the Hurt and discharged it. If he is feeling left out or rejected, the warrior can explore joining a volunteer group, which will help him learn to give without expectation. There are many and unique approaches that can be taken to address the specific beliefs that drive the Wounded Warrior.

Example: as a leader of a team, when his workload builds up, or deadlines approach, John's stress levels increase significantly and he becomes Worried (25) about not being able to deliver his project on time for his team manager. John is already an anxious person, but this additional stress only increases his feeling of Anxiety (26). These circumstances often trigger a reaction that John believes demonstrates he is on top of things, but can be viewed as Over-pleasing (27). John responds immediately to emails, indicating to his team managers that he is working on something specific, when in fact he is just adding to his list of things to do, which feeds back into the worried and anxious cycle as he feels disempowered to take the appropriate steps forward to reduce the workload. He cannot hide his anxiety and as he is the leader, others are given permission to be anxious.

However, by identifying his inability to take steps towards managing his workload way before the deadline, John has the ability to move to higher awareness. By being able to recognize the triggers for his anxiety and identifying the point at which he became the victim of the lower tiles he has the power to recontextualize the story and act on his behalf to manage the workload. John can move vertically towards greater Collaboration (75), to demonstrate some Emerging behaviours (76) and become more Agile (77).

How to help the Wounded Warrior

The warrior's underlying pain will drive them to be Competitive (35) and Dismissive (54) so as to not feel that pain. Taking someone's warrior away from them can expose the pain. To overcome this, the warrior would need to be shown above-60 ways of being in the team. They may seem to have Conviction (67), but it's actually Ego Confidence (57). Wounded warriors are best taken to a therapist as the wound can be very deep and there may be a lot of defence and protection around it.

Questions to help the Wounded Warrior or anyone struggling in below-60 tiles are:

1) How do you feel about the team members and your status in the team?
2) Do you feel you are heard? That others value you?
3) Do you feel you hear them? Value them?
4) Do you feel they are dismissive? Is dismissiveness a problem in the team? Do you feel you are dismissive? If yes, would you like

the team or yourself to do something about this and operate as a more powerful leader? Are you interested in/open to learning how to be more inclusive of your team members and be a more powerful leader?

5) Do you feel the team is transparent? Are we evasive? Are *you* evasive? If yes, would you like the team or yourself to do something about this and operate as a more powerful leader? Are you interested in/open to learning how to be a more powerful leader?

2) Judging Ego-thinking Mind – Wanting, Controlling, Egotistical, tiles 30–59

The Snake, tiles 30–59

In many organizations it can be difficult to identify the Snake because there are often flashes of higher awareness. They appear ready and positive, there are occasional moments of Wow (78) and they talk about their Highest Callings (80).

These leaders can display all manner of behaviours that serve their Ego and they may not even be aware they are doing it. In particular, Deceiving (44) can take on many forms, such as betrayal, disloyalty, double-dealing, two-faced deals and subversive behaviour. This undermines the team performance, output and connectivity. It can be likened to a 'snake in the grass'. This Controlling attitude is often hidden by another part of the person in Egotistical. If we capture this 'snake-in-the-grass' leader on the Awareness Code we can see that the body of the Snake will be at Deceiving (44) and the head will be somewhere in Egotistical. However, this leader is always covering up their behaviours below the 40s. Therefore, a typical 'snake in the grass' might look like the imbedded snake found in the below-60 tiles in the Awareness Code, shown in the diagram opposite.

AWARENESS CODE

			United	Doing the Impossible	Breathtaking	Miraculous	Mastery	Superhuman	Profound	Beyond Incredible (100)
Incredible	90 Grateful	91 Sincere	92 Heartfelt	93 Devoted	94 Thriving	95 Compassion	96 Altruistic	97 Heart-bursting	98 Extraordinary	99 Revealing Grace
Transforming	80 Highest Callings	81 Realizing Power	82 Realizing Value	83 Fellowship Mindset	84 Embracing	85 Spontaneous	86 Off-the-charts	87 Integrating	88 Integrity	89 Inspiring
Opening	70 Receptive	71 Witnessing	72 Open-minded	73 Trustful	74 Connected	75 Collaboration	76 Emerging	77 Agile	78 Wow	79 Flowing
Stepping in	60 Realizing Truth	61 Ready	62 Preparing	63 Releasing	64 Reorientating	65 Positive	66 Adventurous	67 Conviction	68 Fearless	69 Fully In
Egotistical	50 Narcissistic	51 Arrogant	52 Know-it-all	53 Self-centered	54 Dismissive	55 Defensive	56 Pretentious	57 Ego Confidence	58 Complacent	59 Not Buying In
Controlling	40 Malicious	41 Enraged	42 Bully	43 Confronting	44 Deceiving	45 Resentful	46 Passive-aggressive	47 Annoyed	48 Frustrated	49 Sceptical
Wanting	30 Infatuated	31 Perfectionist	32 Addictive	33 Over-ambitious	34 Scheming	35 Competitive	36 Attached	37 Narrowing Down	38 Identifying	39 Ego-requesting
Stressed	20 Numb	21 Terror	22 Dread	23 Trapped	24 Frightened	25 Worried	26 Anxious	27 Over-pleasing	28 Insecure	29 Hesitant
Despondent	10 Inconsolable	11 Hopeless	12 Unfulfilled	13 Lethargic	14 Wounded	15 Hurt	16 Saddened	17 Disconnected	18 Discontented	19 Disinterested
Lifeless	0 Self-loathing	1 Self-hatred	2 Pathetic	3 Unlovable	4 Burden	5 Embarrassed	6 Wrong	7 Regretful	8 Never Enough	9 Inadequate

A team with a Snake in it can find it hard to grow because there will be constant conflicts. It's all too common to see leadership succession being handled poorly and this is the result of a number of people at the top jostling for the CEO role, which creates a lot of snake-in-the-grass-like behaviour.

Example: a team member undermines the team with his Arrogance (51). Somehow, he has been allowed to get away with it, probably because he has value in some way or is close friends with someone at the top of the hierarchy. Behind the scenes he is a Bully (42) because he is Over-ambitious (33) and constantly has a personal agenda (34) that is more important for him than team cohesion (75).

He is unable to Embrace (84) the team members and their potential because he actually has a deep Dread (22) of not being in control. Even more subconscious are his feelings of being Unfulfilled (12), which he just doesn't want to feel as it's too close to an even more painful feeling of being Unlovable (3). So, the Snake goes behind people's backs, sabotaging team progress and morale by being immersed in their own priorities, issues, Entrapments and ignorance.

Activity: insert your own example

Allow a current leader to enter your awareness. Does the leader have Snake qualities? Is the behaviour of the leader driven by his Ego? Does he display a high level of Arrogance (51), which may often go unchallenged due to his seemingly strong position of power and the unwillingness of many to take him on. At any stage does the leader become Enraged (41) when his rivals criticize him or his policies, particularly if he perceives it to be a personal attack? Are there any Bullying (42) tendencies? Can you identify Ego Confidence (57) and what are the statements spoken by the leader that alert you to this disposition? Leaders who are in the Snake personality are often Not Buying In (59) to any suggestions

> that involve changing known and unworkable structures. Is there evidence in the leader of pursuing more of a personal agenda (34) rather than working as a team? Being able to identify the Snake in your work environments or even on the global stage is half of the journey. The next move is how to approach them.

The Legend, 80s, 90s

In contrast to the Snake and Wounded Warrior there are leaders who leave a legacy that captures our hearts and minds and we wonder, 'How did they do that?' They become folklore around and through the team connections. The qualities of the legendary leader are ones that we admire, idolize or of which we are in awe. They are indeed awesome (Extraordinary, 98). Usually through deep dedication (Devotion, 93), they break through barriers and bring a new era, a new paradigm to the team. They function outside the duality of Thinking Mind.

The Legend is centred, grounded and represents many of the above-60 tiles, especially when the challenges arise. They Thrive (94) on challenge and bring everyone in the team along with them if they can come along. Sometimes a team member cannot see the brilliance in the proposed way forward and retreats into Stressed. Time and time again the Legends lead the team into unchartered territory (Spontaneous, 85), with Wisdom Mind leading the way. They know it's not always about being 'right', but instead, always getting the team to see and feel and know that they are all on a path to finding the absolute highest potential outcome for all involved.

The Hero/Heroine Leader, 60s, 70s

This personality type appears when the leader moves into Stepping In (60s) and displays the courage to be disruptive, different, unique and standing more in their power than when they were acting and leading from Ego. This leader begins to live in the 60s tiles until they overcome all their negative stories. These may be about being scared of authority figures, not being liked, or any of the Entrapments below 60. The Hero/Heroine can eventually exhibit Fearless (68) and Fully In (69), going where others fear to tread and holding the values of the team as a priority (Fellowship Mindset, 83 and Realizing Value, 82). In the face of the challenge, this leader may even get into Thriving (94), where they revel in the opportunity to dive deep into a situation where others may 'play it safe'.

This leader shows us an aliveness that is inside each team member but they may not either know that, or are aware of how to bring that out through the layers of conditioning. The Hero/Heroine models transparency (Trustful, 73) and is so Agile (77) that Wow (78) moments are just waiting to happen.

Corporate Transformation and the Awareness Code

The Code is applicable not only to individuals and their teams, but to companies as well. Entrapment levels of self-awareness are as equally prevalent in older, traditional companies as they are in newer purpose-driven enterprises. However, such altruism does not automatically lead to accompanying heightened awareness. If these companies could harness the Awareness Code, it would turbo-charge their humanitarian and purpose-driven efforts because the map offers a way to understand where the loopholes may be occurring in the company and how to address them.

Senior management can operate at the Egotistical level and below – Arrogant (51), Know-it-all (52), Dismissive (54), Deceiving (44), Scheming (34) – with devastating consequences in the long run. A leadership team driving above-60 behaviours would have avoided a significant number of the issues these companies face. Increasingly, companies will not have a choice about driving increased levels of self-awareness throughout the organization. They will find themselves disrupted or displaced by companies who have grasped the nettle.

Organizations that operate below 50 in awareness and lack integrity can only have a limited period of success before this plays out in a negative way. How the company operates externally or internally in the culture and the business then goes into decline or fragments. The company would then need to recruit new leaders to step in to take the company to a higher level.

A 2019 McKinsey report on 'The State of Fashion'[1] discovered that two-thirds of customers globally would switch or refuse to buy products depending on a firm's position on controversial issues. Social and corporate responsibility is being demanded in equal measure by the public. Its related by-products of transparency (Opening, 70s) and empathy are cherished. It follows naturally that leaders must be equipped to address this push towards Integrity (88). They must be able to intuitively tune into the customer's growing awareness and understand and empathize with these deeper human needs (Witness Mind).

A leader who does not listen (Witnessing, 71) to the reminders that the planet will not sustain unethical practices is a leader who is unable to enter Witness or Wisdom Mind. In these cases, it is up to people who can access these states of mind to find empowered ways to remove the person from leadership.

Modern leaders are being asked to step up and the Code can be used like a prism through which day-to-day and long-term strategic objectives are viewed.

How to apply this chapter

Fun-time Awareness Adventure

This activity is about developing a less serious approach and inviting a spirit of playfulness that can open parts within that will not respond to logic or an approach based on reason. The following are suggestions and you may have other approaches that affect you deeply. This is more about FEELING rather than THINKING.

---

[1]McKinsey, 'The State of Fashion' 2019. https://www.mckinsey.com/industries/retail/our-insights/state-of-fashion

1) Notice what inspires you. Perhaps start with music. Make a playlist of your favourite songs and listen to them over the course of the week. Scan the tiles and identify any tiles that apply to the songs you are listening to. Are there any messages for you in this approach?

2) Choose three songs that inspire you to MOVE. Dance non-stop to those songs until you are completely exhausted. Lie on the floor and as you allow your body to integrate the movement, scan the tiles and identify where the process took you. What have you discovered?

3) Take a walk – in nature. Watch how the body responds to a stroll in the green, lush forest, the beach, the desert, the snow, the wind, the rain. In each of the responses, can you identify a tile that is present? Is it limited or deeper awareness? What have you learned?

Let's review

- Both the Snake and the Wounded Warrior act out the perpetrator tiles of Controlling, Egotistical and Wanting, but they hide the victim holding the pain of being Stressed, Despondent and Lifeless.

- To assist anyone in these personalities it is wise to do so in moments when you are able to offer support from a place that does not judge the protective mechanisms.

- There are many other personalities beyond the ones we introduced into the chapters, some of which people come from above 60, such as teachers, pioneers, and others from below 60, such as the controller and the judge. We also can have personalities around the business roles we play; for instance, the doctor and pilot have strong personalities.

- It is important to understand that we shouldn't try to identify ourselves or others as a fixed personality, instead we are a blend of many parts and that changes over time.

- The corporate world is ripe to bring the Awareness Code to life in service to the planet and its people. What is your role in this?

Coming Up Next

Would you like to explore the mechanics of **how** to move closer to tile 100? Are you prepared to cultivate self-enquiry and let go of long-held and stale stories about your life? Realizing what is old and needs replacing is the first part of recontextualizing old stories. In the coming chapter, you will learn how to stop taking things personally, how to communicate more effectively and how to help others do the same. It's a win-win above 60 and that is where you are heading.

CHAPTER SEVENTEEN

Advanced Techniques

Be the Tile You Aspire to

Choose a Revelation tile from above 60, where you feel you are underdeveloped. Ask yourself, 'What is going on for me that holds me back from fully expressing the power of this tile? What would it look like to step more into this tile?'

Imagine Stepping Into this above-60 tile. There can be an **increased** feeling of lightness, relief, optimism, truth or freedom. Being aware that this can be a new story for you is powerful.

If I ask, 'Would you like to be a wonderful leader when you grow up?', what would you have said during the various stages of your life? All tiles are present at all times so imagine that this question only activates stories of you becoming an Incredible Leader, parent or partner and you are reaching your full potential, not hindered by below 60 or underdeveloped above 60. You need to be breathing, walking, eating, sleeping, living those qualities and virtues that are present above 60 and then Incredible can open to you.

Sometimes a crisis or sudden exhaustion or sickness promotes the activating of Realizing Truth inside of you and you realize you **must** change. This can often make Receptive (70) open up and Highest Callings (80) follow on with answers.

Level 30–59 usually does not want to go into any story below 29 as it is perceived as a weakness. It is covered over with 'I am doing okay' and 'I will work it out'. However, our stories tend to stay in there until some part of us awakens (60) to the possibility of actually really doing something about our life/situation/wellbeing.

Level 30–59 has multiple ways of not Realizing the Truth (60) of the higher tiles. Addictions to pleasure, avoidance, denial, pretending and blaming others are all in there. Changing a below-60 story starts at 60.

Something has arrived in my awareness. Instead of returning to an old pattern of below 60, I am now aware of a possible different way of being with what is happening. There is an individual and group/team commitment to GROWTH, but it is not Self/Ego growth, it is Self or Witness growth. There is a growing ability to perceive through the clouds of below 60 and start to see there is an ongoing 24/7 wonderful way of being in the world (the sun-behind-the-clouds analogy). More meaning is derived as the awakening deepens and over time remains as a constant.

Courageous Conversations

Below 30 is disempowered and courage is not available. Levels 30–59 can feel like courage but it is best termed 'false courage', or bravado. At its mildest, there is a tendency towards impressing others and at its extreme is to boast, brag, swagger and be cocky through a conversation. This drops away at 60 and there is a realization that a new power is available. Stepping In generates will and a determination to represent something more important than Ego. All through the tiles of 60 to 69 you will notice more will, determination or courage to represent a personal truth rather than an Egotistical or fearful position.

The emotional charge of below 60 cannot participate in a courageous conversation. Above 60 might provide this statement: 'There is something I have been meaning to bring to your attention after our conversation' is not attacking, condemning, controlling or accusing. 'I have noticed something that requires our combined attention' moves towards Fellowship Mindset (83) and Witness Mind and is not Ego-requesting (39). It implies observation rather than judgement and gives the team every indication that you are responding from above 60, not reacting from below 60.

For courageous conversations to be successful for a leader, all participants are to be above 60 otherwise it will have Controlling elements within it, or perhaps an Egotistical false courageous conversation. A healthy degree of Receptive (70), Witnessing (71) and Open-minded (72) also assists a courageous conversation.

As a leader, which would you rather hear: 'Here is what I feel...' or 'Here is what I think...'. It can depend on what you value and others may not value the same approach. This is not a dot that a below 60 would usually consider, but above 60, every dot is important (*see also* pp. 239–241). As you move through your courageous conversations, have you given consideration to the preferred (noticed not desired or scheming want) outcome that would benefit ALL concerned? Do you have one or more suggestions as part of your approach? We are moving from complaining (Ego-requesting, 39) to alerting other team members to a new direction so it has a feel of Embracing (84) instead of judging.

Justifying Below 60

As a leader, the liberating and discerning mind is required to be activated so we can catch when you or the team is justifying any below-60 behaviour. What the leader says and does gives permission for others to say and do the same things.

Each of the below-60 Entrapments, when viewed or perceived by below-60 awareness, will be seen to be appropriate behaviour, thinking and feeling because that's all that awareness is capable of understanding/experiencing. Being Hurt (15) or Competitive (35), for example, can be argued as required and a 'good' thing so that the behaviour is perpetuated. It may even be congratulated and seen as the cultural/family/company norm to behave in this way. Remember, ignorant (59) stands in the way of transcending below 60. It is only when you have your awareness above 60 that you can understand that each below 60 is a form of Entrapment and each Entrapment has to be lived for as long as it takes to be able to find the Revelation that will take you out of the Entrapment.

It becomes a journey of identifying the defence mechanisms, pushbacks, denials, projections and confusion of below 60 in both yourself and others. It's easier initially to identify it in others. If you find yourself reacting to someone else's below 60 in a judgemental or victim way, this can be pointing to this Entrapment as still being inside of you so that the other person is actually mirroring for you. When you eventually do not react to this Entrapment it is showing you that you have found the Revelation to be released from this Entrapment.

'It's okay to be frustrated, everyone does' is an example of saying below 60 is justifiable. And it is, until you know the Revelation that is going to get you out of frustration, and that can be different for everyone.

'I am Reorientating (64) my frustration into seeing each situation that I went to frustration with as a new opportunity to stay empowered. It feels great to be empowered rather than frustrated'.

Compare that to 'You would be frustrated too if...' followed by blame.

Another example: in a meeting, at Disinterested (19), I might believe there is nothing in it for me so I tune out and create separation and negative emotional charge. I might go into 'boredom' or lack of connection to justify it by an Entrapment belief about myself as less than in some way. At Ready (61), I couldn't do this as the Revelation of Ready opens up a space inside of my psyche with a new realization, perhaps 'If I just listen, there is always something to learn about myself or the other person' and thus the Witness Mind is activated.

This intensifies at Receptive (70), where active listening has replaced Disinterested and the witness is much more willing to receive and to be open to that which would have been missed before. At Highest Callings (80), that which has been received can now be utilized and often the missing piece of the jigsaw puzzle can be found.

At Grateful (90), there is a big thankful expression from deep inside that being Receptive has provided the consideration that led to the insight. As the above-60 Revelations become available, Intuitive Mind improves so that you do not have to be receptive to EVERYTHING but instead develop an intuitive feel for that which is being presented and you become selective, always looking for the best in the situation rather than being tangled in the blocks.

Instead of Disinterest, there will be a Realization (60) that the situation has released its potential and that it is time to move on to the next situation with an understanding of how moving on may impact the other.

A leader's Witness Mind has an ability to prioritize according to the potential of the situation rather than judging it. The potential comes to the intuitive Witness Mind rather than the Judging Mind. The latter looks to stay in the situation, or not, according to personal gain.

Communication Through the Below-60 Tiles

All below-30 tiles are disempowering and accompanied by a feeling of lack of understanding, not knowing what is right, who to believe, not trusting self and so on. The more-aware leader is looking for how to identify the Entrapments so as to then have a courageous conversation about what has come to light. Every life has its own unique expression. Here, we look at indicators the leader can become more aware of with practice. This lack is pain associated with it. The pain of loneliness, depression, uncertainty, rejection – the list goes on.

All below 30 cannot communicate effectively so the pain grows and accumulates.

The type of communication patterns existing at the first three levels of Entrapment are:

1) Depressive – Mostly internal negative beliefs. Listening to an inner belief system that is denigrating to self. Belief others will not understand, or if we speak, we will embarrass ourselves further, so instead we withdraw.

2) Condemning – What's the point in communicating? No one really understands. If I do communicate, it is through complaining, moaning, whinging, whining – poor me!

3) Stressful – Things are confusing so it is best to retract, pull back and say little.

So we gravitate towards 30–59 to escape this pain. We generate wants to find happiness and to be proud of our success in getting what we want so communication here looks like:

1) Wanting – An expression of the Ego letting the world know what it thinks it has to have to be happy.

2) Aggressively demanding, ordering, yelling, insisting, expecting, screaming.

3) Puffed-up self-expression of how good you are or how you do not need anyone or anything to tell you any more about how to get something because you think you know already.

4) 'I did this', 'I am good at that', 'Let me show you', 'No, not that way, this way'… All these expressions say one type of message: 'I am very good at one type of thing, why aren't you? What's wrong with you? What's your problem?' Meanwhile, I will completely ignore what I am NOT good at or pretend it's not important. The only thing that is important is what I am good at, which is why I am so important', says Ego.

Communication Through the Tiles Above 60

Stepping In, 60–69

'Let's talk so I can have more context.'

'Tell me more to flesh out things we may not yet know.'

'Can I help you understand who I am (not what I want) and can you help me by explaining how you best work, then we can be more for each other.'

'The past is history. Let's learn from it and move on to greater things.'

'What is still hindering or within you that is stopping you from being connected to this project/person so that eventually you will be fully in?'

'What am I not doing to help you be more pragmatic?'

Opening, 70–79 communication

'Let's watch the situation, without the charge of judgement, and get a good FEEL of where to go.'

'As you talk, I can practise having a huge dartboard and FEELING where your ideas land and there is no expectation that you MUST land a bullseye, but if you do we WILL celebrate it!'

'The more we collaborate, the more we can learn to truly connect and from that, things will emerge that could not if it were just me.'

Transformating, 80–89 communication

'I am learning to find a space within me that surrenders all positions temporarily so as to welcome in any and all possibilities, no matter how strange or unusual initially, in the spirit of freeing myself up internally. Then this radiates to the room and colleagues/my team will feel this as an experience available to them so that they can Step In (60–69) and move.'

'The spirit of fellowship is important to keep alive at each and every encounter/meeting.'

'Newness, innovation and pioneering are incredibly important measuring sticks for the new perception of success.'

Incredible, 90–99 communication

'Your value and worth are in the quality that you imbue the atmosphere with'; 'Your presence contributes'; 'Integrity permeates all we do'; 'This is the place to work, these are my people, let's co-create greatness here.'

How to apply this chapter

Choose someone whose behaviour you DON'T UNDERSTAND.

This week is all about noticing behaviours or situations you judge. Sometimes, a person's behaviour may trigger you because it is a mirror of something you do not own or accept about yourself. In other situations, the other person's behaviour is NOT something you do personally and it does not mirror any unconscious patterns in yourself. However, the trigger is there because rather than accept the behaviour in others and engage in dialogue about it, you JUDGE it as bad and so it will continue to follow you around until you can witness without judging. Perhaps the following activities may help:

1) Identify a person who triggers a response of confusion, frustration or any other response that is not above 60.

2) Look closely at what the person does, says or doesn't do. Can you match this to a particular tile?

3) What is it about this tile that creates the negative response?

4) Is the behaviour something you engage in without awareness?

5) Is the behaviour something you judge? What is it about that behaviour that creates the response you have?

6) Identify the higher tile that is required for you to empower yourself into a higher state of mind.

7) Can you reconcile within yourself that the person is learning about the game of life by playing with a particular level of consciousness?

8) Do you have a role to play in lifting or assisting the other person?

9) Has the process helped you reclaim a projection that did not involve the other person at all?

Let's review

- A young consciousness is easily programmed to ensure survival, however outdated programmes become harmful.
- You have been given techniques to recontextualize the old stories or programmes.
- Self-enquiry, realizing, witnessing and releasing the old are important keys in recontextualizing stories.
- Taking things personally points to a hidden Ego programme that can be changed.
- Effective language to assist with above-60 communication is a powerful, in-the-moment tool that can be harnessed with practice.

Coming Up Next

It all sounds good on paper, but how does the Code work in real time with real challenges? Part 6 reveals how the various responses to the COVID-19 pandemic reveal much about the levels from which many leaders addressed the situation. The Code provides a way to track how leaders are faring.

PART 6

LIVING THE CODE

CHAPTER EIGHTEEN

A Case Study of Living the Code During COVID-19

COVID-19 Leadership

In 2020 in particular, the start of the COVID-19 pandemic provided us with an opportunity to watch leaders at every level and where they operated from within the Awareness Code. The mechanics, dynamics, type of power (or lack of) and overall presence were on view for all to see: leaders of countries, states, territories, sporting teams, retail companies, IT start-ups and armed forces. In fact, everywhere teams or groups of people were looking to someone for leadership guidance were on view.

We would have noticed a reluctance to do anything from some quarters (Lethargic, 13). For others, the situation might have appeared to be too big (Hopeless, 11) and a doomsday overlay might have occurred (Inconsolable, 10 and Inadequate, 9). Even Regret (7) may have been experienced at not being more prepared (6), or Embarrassed (5) at not having the expertise or answers. Inactivity like being a bystander or abdicating responsibility abounds at these levels.

Stressed

Insecurity (28) and Fear (24) can keep leaders from making strong decisions. Instead, they may have felt Trapped (23) into maintaining an economic focus instead of seeing the bigger picture, which included human welfare.

Wanting

The Over-ambitious (33) and Scheming (34) leaders may have provided fake news or reassurance when that was not the advice offered by experts. Avoiding a recession, bankruptcy or financial difficulty, even not being re-elected, could be part of the agenda.

Controlling

These leaders were seen to be dictators in their attitude of how and what and where and when things were to happen. Little choice was given to the team as the hierarchical system was firmly established. All of this is justifiable to the leader in Controlling mode. These leaders are Sceptical (49) that the team or population they are leading have the choice. This may be the case, but the attitude here is harsh and directive (Confronting, 43) without compassion or care. Those being ordered what to do wither and comply, feeling disempowered.

Egotistical

Some leaders made it all about themselves and used the situation to promote their persona or agenda (Self-centred, 53 to Narcissistic, 50). Disdain for others' expert opinion, accusations, exaggerations, ignoring the facts, downplaying the gravity of the situation, highlighting personal achievements all show us where these leaders are on the Awareness Code. Flouting the guidelines, focusing on lost revenue to justify behaviours, transgressing agreed-upon group behaviours and feeling imposed upon rather than inspiring the team or how to be Positive (65) when a challenge arrives were all evident.

Stepping In

Leaders who could 'read' the situation responded early and led the way. The intuition that is available in Witness Mind could 'read' patterns of how the world pandemic was unfolding and didn't hesitate to initiate lockdown (Realizing Truth, 60 to Reorientating, 64). When some leaders were reversing the lockdown, those leaders were strong in

Conviction (67) and Fearless (68) in their patience to wait and see if there was going to be a 'second wave'.

Opening

Taiwan's President Tsai Ing-wen is one of the female leaders who was immediately open to expert assistance through Collaboration (75). With Chen Chien-jen, vice president, and an epidemiologist, they quickly created a well-planned response. They were Open-minded (72) and bore in mind what happened with the SARS (severe acute respiratory syndrome) epidemic, back in 2003.

Transformating and Incredible

New Zealand's Prime Minister Jacinda Ardern has Inspired (89) the people of her country and many from outside of New Zealand to join her in lockdown and set up a feeling of Fellowship Mindset (83) as she implored them to stay home and famously asked everyone to 'Be kind to each other' (Compassion, 95) as she reached out on a Facebook post in her tracksuit amid family duties and putting her kids to bed. She imbues every communication with a sense of Sincerity (91) demonstrated through the Collaboration (75) and Fellowship Mindset (83). The decision for her and her Cabinet ministers to take a 20 per cent pay cut for six months in April 2020 in solidarity with those affected by COVID-19 was lauded. Incredibly, her country responded with very low levels of infection as a consequence of such an approach. The aim to eradicate COVID-19 from within its borders was an outcome to be attained in a compassionate way. Her Heartfelt (92) approach to the people, which put their lives and wellness above the economy, has Inspired (89) people and leaders worldwide.

A special mention

Li Wenliang was a Chinese ophthalmologist who worked at Wuhan Central Hospital. Li demonstrated Conviction (67) when he sent a message to his colleagues on 30 December 2019 to warn them about a possible outbreak of an illness that resembled SARS, later identified as COVID-19. When local authorities heard of his report, he was called to the police station, where he was reprimanded for spreading rumours, threatened with punishment, made to sign a form admitting he was wrong to have messaged this to his colleagues and that he would not repeat his error. He contracted the disease himself and continued to report on social media from his hospital bed until the virus took his life. His Sincerity (91) to follow his heart and disclose what his intuition suggested, and his devotion to help others, lives on.

Let's review

- The Awareness Code (AC) offers people the opportunity to explore their Highest Callings (80) and to do so in the spirit of realizing their full potential and service to others.
- The spirit of the AC is uncompromising in asking people to let go of negative dispositions and to embrace positive change and this is done without any force being applied.
- Many companies and organizations are becoming aware of the practical approach that the AC offers and reaping the benefits.
- Complex situations, emotions and belief systems can be opened up because the AC provides a map for how to approach the Entrapments.

Coming Up Next

Would you be interested in 25 practical keys that help you unlock the witness and wisdom mind? Many of the people you read about in the case studies have in some way engaged in many of the keys explored in the next chapter. They created a plan based on the 25 keys and actioned it in a consistent manner to create wonderful solutions to the challenges they faced. You too can create your own way forward using the 25 keys.

CHAPTER 19

The 25 Keys to Living the Code

25 Keys to Strengthen your Shift Towards Powerful Leadership

Apart from the Guidance for Moving Forward to a new mindset provided at each of the four Entrapments shown at each tile, here we provide some powerful keys that will help you move from these Entrapments. Some involve physical activities while others are more psychological. After each Entrapment, positive statements and alternative attitudes were suggested and you were provided with keys to help you move towards the higher tile. Here are the keys…

1. Seek professional therapists, medically trained experts, coaches and educators

As you have been working through the Awareness Code, and as you continue to work through it, there may be issues, or more questions that arise and it is advisable to seek assistance. You may already be receiving help from trained professionals. If you are, the Awareness Code is designed for you to use or to work alongside these professionals as you move through the Code and begin to integrate it.

If your professional help is not aware of the Awareness Code, you could take the Code to them and if they are interested, they may undertake training at The Awareness Code Global Training Centre which has a website at acglobaltc.com.

Accessing the Core of a Story with a Therapist

A young child is shown a mirror image of themselves with a dot on their forehead but does not relate to the dot as anything to do with them. But at a certain point of development the child will point to the dot on their own forehead when placed in front of the mirror, acknowledging that it's them in the mirror. This is example of Realizing Truth (60) through the maturation process. Realizing Truth (60) is similar to becoming more aware or more 'real'. Peeling back the stories of below 60 with a therapist means you are realizing what you have been is a limited version of yourself. It's a similar feeling to 'This is what I am meant to be' or 'Now I can create all my own stories if I can just expose (become AWARE) of the Entrapments'.

A lot of psychology does not get to the core of the story, which is like a dentist scraping out the obvious decay and filling it over but not going down to the root canal, so the underlying problem stays, releasing toxins and building its presence. There is nothing wrong with the many approaches that attempt to implant positive suggestions, but it can be like trying to build a skyscraper on a refuse site without preparing properly. Deeply penetrating below-60 tiles with someone trained to assist you can accelerate understanding of the underlaying Entrapments that are to be flushed and replaced by the higher tile Revelations.

Action you can take

- Seek medical advice from your GP;
- Book an appointment with a counsellor;
- Book an appointment with a therapist or life coach;
- Book an appointment at acglobaltc.com with an Awareness Code Global Psychotherapist.

What is the DSM-5?

The DSM-5 is an authoritative guide created by the American Psychiatric Association and is the most common diagnostic system for psychiatric disorders. At the time of writing, there are 265 diagnoses in the DSM-5, so it is very comprehensive. You could undertake a DSM-5 test with a trained professional to receive the feedback that this provides from the perspective that this will assist you to grow as a person and not to find out what is wrong with you.

The Awareness Code will still be incredibly valuable without the DSM-5 results, however, since using both in tandem will provide great insight into understanding your personal psychology. Both are extremely valuable techniques that will assist you to understand who you are, how you operate, how you would like to operate and who you would like to become. The more deeply you understand yourself as a person, the more deeply you will understand your team. Utilizing both may assist you to gain a profound understanding of how to progress from being the leader you are today to becoming an Incredible Leader of tomorrow.

Here are some of the most commonly diagnosed disorders and an indication of the AC tiles that a person MAY be in if they are diagnosed. Every person's context is different, so this is indicative only (*see also* Medical Disclaimer, p. v).

Common adult mental disorders from DSM-5
- Alcohol and substance use disorder (Addictive, 32);
- Anxiety disorders (Trapped, 23, Despair, Dread, 22);
- Generalized anxiety disorder (Anxious, 26, Worried, 25, Frightened, 24, Trapped, 23);
- Panic disorder (Dread, 22);
- Phobias (Anxious, 26, Worried, 25, Frightened, 24, Trapped, 23, Dread, 22, Terror, 21);
- Social anxiety disorder (Insecure, 28, Over-pleasing, 27);
- Bipolar disorder (involves swinging from below 30 to above 30, maybe even to 100);
- Depression (Lifeless, 0–9, Despondent, 10–19);
- Postpartum/postnatal depression (Despondent, 10–19, Lifeless, 0–9);
- Seasonal affective disorder (Despondent, 10–19, Lifeless, 0–9);
- Eating disorders (Controlling, 40–44);
- Narcissism (Egotistical, 50–59);
- OCD (obsessive compulsive disorder) (Addictive, 32, Perfectionist, 31, Infatuation, 30);

- PTSD (Post-traumatic stress disorder), 26–20;
- Schizophrenia (extremes of any level and incognate, 0–50).

Source: Diagnostic and Statistical Manual of Mental Disorders: Diagnostic and Statistical Manual of Mental Disorders, American Psychiatric Association, Fifth Edition, 2019, Washington, VA: American Psychiatric Association, 2013

2. Undertake the Awareness Code Global Training Centre (ACGTC) courses or, if you have a company, connect with Xinfu to learn more about Transformational Leadership

The ACGTC provides online courses for professional and personal development, careers or anyone interested in having a deeper understanding of The Awareness Code. There are two types of courses:

- The Mentor/Coach Certificates – these are two certificates, one for general Mentor/Coaching and the other for advanced Mentor/ Coaching. Both are in the form of online video recordings. There are 30 hours of video detailing how to help someone, including yourself, move from below 60 to above 60 as well as five hours exploring the 25 keys in great detail.
- The postgraduate ACGTC Certificate in Psychotherapy, for anyone with existing psychological training who would like to assist their clients have deep change during a therapy session by using The Awareness Code.
- If your business is a Fortune 500 company or one of the fastest-growing companies with global potential and you would like to understand more how your company can be transformed, connect with Xinfu (www.xinfu.com).

See more at acglobaltc.com or connect with Xinfu at admin@xinfu.com

Action you can take
- Book in for one of the available courses;
- Speak to a trained Awareness Code Global Therapist, whom you will find at acglobaltc.com.

3. Speak to another team member who has read the AC, completed an ACGTC course, or worked with Xinfu

In addition, a Transformational Leadership masterclass has been developed by Steve Tappin, who has worked with thousands of leaders over the past 25 years. He has developed the latest best practices and encapsulated many critical elements into becoming a Transformational Leader. There may be an opportunity to participate in the Transformational Leadership Masterclass at www.xinfu.com.

With the Transformational Leadership Masterclass we have also included past episodes from the BBC's series *CEO Guru* hosted by Steve, including interviews with more than 90 executives of companies who have led their industry and the business world, from Sir Richard Branson (Virgin), Liu Chuanzhi (Lenovo) to Meg Whitman (HP).

Action you can take

- Organize a meeting with a colleague and share how the course has impacted the person's life;
- Seek additional feedback from another colleague in a different department;
- Speak to another colleague and share the impact of the Transformational Leadership Masterclass.

4. Find a mentor

Finding a mentor can be life-changing in a positive or negative way. If the mentor is operating from below 60, they will be entrapped, therefore modelling and teaching you how to be entrapped. Long term, this will work against achieving your highest potential. If, however, you Realize Truth (60) and use this realization to empower yourself to above 60, then this can really work for you and your team. If the mentor brings their above 60 upfront to you, this is only going to benefit you. The mentor can point out your weaknesses and it will be constructive and purposeful rather than from below 60, where it would be critical and judgemental. Their feedback, advice and experience can help you excel. They can be a sounding board because they are non-judgemental and above 60. They can take your challenges and critique them in a neutral, supportive way. You might even have a 'council of mentors' for multiple above-60 tile access.

Action you can take

- Reflect on who may be a personal mentor as you learn about the Code;
- Contact the proposed mentor and ask if s/he is available.

5. Your daily review

A review is where you go to a place where you can be alone, at any time of the day, and close your eyes. We can use 80 per cent of our energy through our eyes to observe and understand the external world and we will need all of this to look internally. You may review something that has just happened and you are ready to understand it more or you are working on an issue/theme/behaviour and are looking to penetrate further into knowing about that. Recall the event like an internal video and do your best to watch yourself (Witnessing, 71) and how you behaved. Can you identify the tile? Were you stubborn (Defensive, 55), or did you assume you were incorrect (Wrong, 6)?

Below 30, you will condemn yourself as your internal judge is full of stories like 'I messed up again', 'This is embarrassing', 'I will never get this', 'What if I never change?', etc. This type of review is disempowering. If that's all you can manage then it needs to be taken to someone above 60 to get yourself to above 60.

If your review is from 30–59, you will not really be able to see yourself from a detached witness space (remember Self-delusion in Chapter 1, *see also* pp. 15–32?), so you will end up confused or just wanting to be different but not knowing how. Then you can get frustrated because it is not clear why the issue keeps happening. This will turn into blaming others or the situation around you. It may escalate to egotistical defending and justifying.

Do your best to review from above 60. True Witness awareness is available and you can be free of judgement. Here, there is observation without interference of below-60 background emotions or thoughts arising. Below-60 presence of emotions or thoughts is of course okay and to be accepted as a reality for now. However, if there is still too much charge, the suck or explosion or knot or whatever the emotional/ mental charge is will drown out the Witness Mind and it will not be an empowered review.

With the Witness Mind activated, we can look at the review and ask:

- 'What was going on for me during that time?'
- 'Where was I on the Awareness Code and what takes me there instead of deeper in towards 100?'
- 'What would I need to let go of to be able to perform at a higher level?'
- 'What would it look and sound like to be operating from that deeper Awareness Code?'

It's like you are inviting in a video from an internal source rather than 'thinking' the answer. 'Feel' for what a preferred way of being and doing would 'feel' like. Put yourself IN the video, not just watching it. Going off to sleep doing this is very powerful. The process can keep going during the dream state and you can wake up just 'knowing' how to be in that situation the next day.

You may not even realize you have the answer until that situation arises and then you 'flow' through it in a different way. Instead of living in the past, the review invites the future into your awareness. This promotes premonition and connectedness to what is about to happen, which at its full expression is a type of clairvoyance that we all have. It just needs a daily discipline to activate it and keep it alive.

Action you can take
- Organize in your schedule 15 minutes to be on your own each day;
- Write your daily review in a journal *or*
- Spend time with your eyes closed and reflect on the day;
- Note any states of mind that require modification.

6. Engaging more Mind
Re-read Chapter 18 (A Case Study of Living The Code During COVID-19, *see also* pp. 262–266) and contemplate what it might mean

to engage more mind. Being sucked into Ego drama narrows down into Ego-thinking Mind below 60. This is a small part of the entire mind and when this happens it is similar to pulling down the blinds of a room, whereupon there is more darkness. Eventually, Lifeless is present when the blinds are nearly all the way down and you are only aware of your perceived problems, issues or lack. Moving to 60 and above, you step into Soul and use Witness Mind and it provides more awareness of tiles above 60 that were not available before. Try it. Activate Non-judgemental Mind by contemplating something existential. For example, climate change, gun control, privacy problems and many more possibilities. You may have judgemental beliefs for or against, which is Thinking Mind, but when you let that recede into the background you can notice how this will take you out of personal Ego drama and into a bigger picture, a more holistic way of thinking about life.

Read each of the descriptions of tiles 60 to 79 and new, fresh ideas of living in that space will begin to arise from deeper within. Tiles 80 and above will allow me to access even more empowering ways of being a pioneering leader by accessing Wisdom Mind.

Action you can take
- Schedule 15 minutes in your day for meditation;
- Practise being in Witness Mind by watching your thoughts;
- If the mind is busy, bring the focus back to the breath;
- If the mind will not settle, go for a walk;
- Go to acglobaltc.com and choose one of the guided meditations for any of the above-60 tiles;
- Use the meditations available on the AC app that are designed to assist you to access above-60 mind.

7. Select an above-60 tile and 'take it on'
Which above-60 tile would you like to become more aware of and bring into your life? The benefits of this tile will then be passed on to the team and all those in your life. Let's say you choose Connected (74). You now read the description and sit down to contemplate what

it would be like to be open to greater and deeper connectedness in your life, especially in the team where you play a leadership role. What would that look like and what would you do differently to what you do now? How can you REALLY be more connected everywhere you go?

Is that better listening, valuing, trusting, reaching out, being vulnerable? What does it mean for you to live and breathe and represent how to be wonderfully connected into this team? Ask others, 'Am I connected enough?', 'How can I be better at it?' Keep going until you feel you ARE connected.

At Egotistical (50–59), the Ego THINKS it knows best. It must do this to have an impact on the world, to get attention, to feel good about itself. Its opinions dominate proceedings (57) and it is required to Dismiss (54) others as they pose a kind of threat to the dominance of the Ego. The Ego represents and maintains itself by all the Entrapments of 50–59.

When we choose a tile from above 60, we will invite our Witness and Wisdom Mind. Each Revelation has a quality or essence about it that grows and becomes the true nature of the person. This replaces personality or Ego identification. So, a person then represents authentic (88) or Heartfelt (92) and simply becomes that quality. This quality that is always available to each one of us but is hidden like the sun behind clouds reveals itself and there is a period of adjusting and learning **from being that**.

When a person begins to live the above-60 tiles, he starts to feel within himself a team and any part of his inner team unable to stay above 60 is addressed in order to maintain inner collaboration and integrity. This inner life is then applied to the outer experience. People can experience themselves as a team with partners, friends, family, colleagues and company. We become team orientated while holding very firmly to the growing internal requirements to organize and transcend all underdeveloped inner parts expressing below-60 dispositions. In the inner you, it is like the witness is the CEO, pulling all the other parts into alignment and connecting them.

Wanting, controlling and Egotistical means of doing this become defunct. At Collaboration (74), for example, there is an experience of each part contributing a quality so that greater potentials can be attained that were not possible when below-60 reactions were running the show.

There is a feeling of 'we' inside, constantly moving towards deeper alignment and eventual harmony at Wisdom Mind, 80–100. Below 60 is a landscape of rebel, renegade, pushback, rejection, sulking, independent, 'what do you know?' and other negative responses, all operating in their own Entrapment domains and all competing for time, energy and other resources.

Some of these lower parts within a person can be too absorbed in their own antics and do not even know that other parts exist within that person's psyche. And when the it activates, this lower part can say and do things that cannot be remembered at a later time when a different part of the person is present. So, Stepping In at 60 is the beginning of real internal organization so as to harness more power and presence in the world. For each of the tiles 40 to 60 there is a 30-minute meditation available at acglobaltc.com to help you go in deep to understand more about each tile.

Action you can take

- Choose a tile to contemplate;
- Journal your discoveries;
- Identify two actions you can implement immediately;
- In one week, review the process;
- Find your chosen higher tile meditation at acglobaltc.com;
- You can also check out a timetable of lectures on tiles at acglobaltc.com.

8.   Re-read, re-listen, re-watch

Hundreds of studies in cognitive psychology have demonstrated that spacing out repeated encounters with the material over time produces far superior long-term learning than one burst of learning. One such study by Sean Kang[2] provided evidence that spaced-out receiving of

---

[2]Kang, Sean, 'Spaced Repetition Promotes Efficient and Effective Learning: Policy Implications for Instruction', *Policy Insights from the Behavioural and Brain Sciences*, 13/01/2016

learning material provided double learning compared to back-to-back repetition. It also enhanced memory of the material, problem solving and transfer of the learned material to new context.

Repetition can impress into the mind that which is important. The Egotistical person (50–59) can believe they already know something, but it is a thinking process, which is different. Repetition is one gateway to move from Not Buying In (59) to Realizing Truth (60). When we hear or see it many times, this has the effect of breaking down the subconscious that has heard and seen things perhaps thousands of times as a child. We are creating a new story when we move away from Sceptical (49) and Not Buying In (59) to Realizing Truth (60) and Receptive (70). The new story requires repetition to create new neural pathways so it becomes the default story rather than the old, limiting, entrapped story. While Ego Mind might think it's boring or unproductive, the deeper truth is that repetition is essential.

Action you can take

- Set aside time in your week to read around topics that are of use to you;
- Read *The Awareness Code*;
- Re-read sections of the book that particularly interest you;
- Re-watch videos in the Awareness Code App;
- Research Awareness Code material and other topics;
- Re-read multiple times teachings that resonate.

9. Finding key Entrapment words

When we REALLY stop and listen to the Entrapment story from below 60, we will begin to Realize (60) that we are using terms of expression or words that we take for granted as meaning something. When looked at closely, we get a clue to how to break it down. For example, 'I am always the one left out'. 'Always?' Are you definite about that? Below 60 distorts the truth, often without awareness because it happens so frequently or quickly and there is no review, or the emotional charge is too strong to

Realize (60) the distortion. 'Left out'. Question: what does that mean? Answer: not included. Question: what does that mean? Answer: I feel rejected. Question: what does that mean? Answer: I feel not valued and that hurts. Question: which tile above 60 would help you value yourself?

'Always' is an example of a generalization. Others include 'never', 'totally', 'absolutely' and 'forever'. For example: 'This team is forever waiting for my direction'. There are deletions where convenient, there is a deliberate or unaware leaving out of key terms or sentences so the focus falls on the one thing to be emphasized. This is prevalent in Narrowing Down (37). For example, a leader may say: 'When you forget the key elements of the agenda, you compromise the meeting's efficiency', but the team member turns it into 'I am not good at running meetings'.

Action you can take
- Reflect on your common negative language;
- Connect the negative words to the appropriate tile;
- What belief do you hold around the language used?
- Journal key findings;
- Replace the negative words with above-60 language.

10. Learn and practise the Awareness Code for Leaders Mastery Techniques

Co-author Wayno has been training with the Mastery Techniques for more than 20 years as a daily discipline. These techniques have been practised by master practitioners for thousands of years and many of them cannot be found in a book. Even if they were, learning from a book does not have the same 'power' to help you to absorb the technique into your system. The Master also assists you in utilizing the best part of your mind to receive the Mastery Techniques and become dedicated to using them.

A Master in this sense is like a student who has gone to university for seven years to study and become a doctor. Wayno took longer than seven years to become a Master. He would sometimes spend a whole seven days straight doing 11 hours a day. Of course, when you know you are born to be a Master this is how you can be so dedicated.

Becoming a leader with these techniques only asks of you that you create time each day to practise the current technique. From all the Mastery Techniques Wayno has received, he has chosen a select few to pass on to those leaders willing to take this next step to develop themselves towards Incredible. Here is a list of some of the benefits from using the Mastery Techniques:

- Increases the supply and flow of energy throughout the body;
- Improves both quality and quantity of energy;
- Induces calmness and capacity so you are able to access the Witness and Wisdom Mind;
- Enables you to be stronger in any tile you choose from above 60;
- Assists you in identifying below-60 Entrapments. Promotes connection with the intelligence that is greater than your Ego, Witness or Wisdom Mind.

The Mastery Techniques are taught directly from Master to Leader either face to face or live on the internet. Learning from a book or watching a pre-recorded video will not have that vital element of Master/Leader direct awareness exchange. How to access the Mastery Technique is through The Awareness Code App or visit acglobaltc.com.

Action you can take
- Visit acglobaltc.com for information on Mastery Technique online teachings times;
- Access guided meditations on each of the 60–100 tiles.

11. Scaling the Entrapment or Revelation

How entrapped we are can be understood by creating a scale of 0–10 for tiles below 60. Zero means I do not engage in any behaviour, emotion or thinking around that tile at all. A 10 means I am fully displaying the characteristics of that tile, e.g. Lethargic (13). Let's say I allocate 3 but I ask my team and they all say above 5. That's something I need to look at. What are some questions to ask myself?

- What is happening for my team to see me that way?
- Why am I a 3 in my opinion and not a 0?
- Have I been a 0 before and how did I manage that?
- What have others done to achieve a 0?
- Can I reduce the number by myself by raising my awareness?
- What is my belief/story around this number and what would it be at zero?

In a team meeting, people may be reluctant to be forthcoming about how they 'feel' about something, so 0–10 scaling quickly gives you a flavour of where they are:

1) At the start of the meeting;
2) After discussion of the important topic;
3) When finalizing a way forward and determining where people 'are at' – 10 is Fully In (69).

At any stage of a meeting or project the leader can ask, 'Where is everybody on the scale of 0–10?' If, for example, a member is 7 out of 10 for Collaboration (75) or the team average is 7, the question to ask is, 'Who has any ideas on how we can go to an 8?' Scaling provides subjective measurement of progress and is used for leaders personally and for their teams and for entire companies and eventually even countries could measure where they are on the Awareness Code.

Action you can take
- Take yourself through the process described above;
- Journal discoveries made and improvements you can action;
- Review your process monthly;

- Seek assistance if your progress is limited;
- Study an above-60 tile through the App.

12. All tiles are within you

Every tile exists within, it's just that they may not have been modelled or you may not have been interested enough to find out the more powerful, deeper tiles. Awareness of a tile's content and qualities isn't necessarily immediately available just because you read about them. Deeper contemplation of any tile means you are putting in the effort to access Witness Mind to find that tile within you. The Ego emotion and thinking tiles (0–59) are relatively easy to access. Revealing Grace (99) is not. We have to build an inner interest and wonder that supports the Witness and Wisdom Minds before Revealing Grace will temporarily open.

Action you can take

- Spend 15 minutes engaging in journalling daily;
- Identify the below-60 tiles you are trapped in;
- What events trigger these reactions?
- What charge is in you that requires releasing?
- Review the relevant above-60 tiles;
- Study an above-60 tile through the App.

13. Remember a time above 60

This is similar to Realizing Power (81). What tile above 60 am I already good at or even great at? For example, I am Adventurous (66). I sit and ask myself, maybe even write down some answers:

- How did I become good at that?
- When have been the peak times I was adventurous?
- Do I promote this in others?
- Do I celebrate this as a gift to bring to the team?
- Can I activate it with more awareness from now on?

- What will it take to be even more adventurous?
- What gets in the way or blocks my adventurous spirit?
- Did or do people reject or dismiss or judge this adventurous spirit? If yes, how do I empower myself to be more adventurous?'
- Reconnect with the feelings of that tile. REALLY feel it. Let it permeate your whole self. Use your mind to spread it.

Action you can take
- Select a relevant tile to work with;
- Take yourself through the process described above;
- Practise being in the feeling of this tile;
- Change your face or body to reflect the feeling;
- Repeat this process when you are experiencing a stressor;
- Commit to doing this a few times a day every day until it becomes a new habit.

14.   Create a shared-value uplift
Above 60, there is enough energy, intent and passion to feel for others. What can we do or be for others? Although full-on Altruism is at 96, we don't have to wait to get there to be generous or kind. Can we have more corporate social responsibility? Can the individuals and the team Collaborate (75) for social problem solving to Emerge (76) to generate Wow (78) moments that galvanize people? It's more than sponsorship. Networking is promoted and the invitation to participate (64) gets things going. For example, National Australia Bank (NAB) in Australia Assist put a human face to the difficulty of recovering debt collection. It supported customers from 60–90 days, giving them the opportunity to turn their lives around.

Action you can take
- Identify a behaviour in you that is not kind or generous;
- Identify the want and the feeling of lack;
- What can you offer others instead?

- Write a long list of how you are going to help others;
- Show your list to a colleague, ask for more ideas and ask them to join you;
- Create a team within your organization that has a focus on helping others;
- Journal your experiences around this.

15. Move the body

Studies provide compelling evidence that regular physical movement like swimming, walking, hiking, cycling, climbing, gardening, stretching, bouncing, trampolining, paragliding, juggling, etc. all turn on the production of endorphins or 'feel-good' chemicals in your body. This can assist you to elevate into above-60 tiles as you have more endorphins to help your biology into elevated states. As well as biochemical changes, movement releases stale, stagnant chi from our body and we take in fresh, natural, balanced energy and store it in readiness for the next leadership project. More oxygen in your system affects the level of serotonin and brings it into balance. This promotes the ability to access tiles above 60.

The physical (including ether), emotional and mental bodies can dysfunction in conditions where this is excessive air conditioning, Wi-Fi or Electro Magnetic Radiation (EMR). Being around other people below 60 or even your own below 60 can be stressful. Things left field that you missed or cannot control can trigger you. Moving and action in exercise has an effect of shifting, breaking down, stirring up, breathing out all of the above-mentioned unwanted energy. It is the drive to move blockages and negative energies out of you or the team and bring in life-enhancing energy.

When you exercise it is important to be aware of how low your energy is. If you push yourself hard, you may feel free or a lot better at the end, having negative energies, but rest is also important. Do whatever exercise makes you feel energized, whether that is taking a walk in nature, doing yoga, running, spinning, or swimming, but build in time to rest to conserve and gather your energy, by meditating or even napping if that's an option. Exercising in nature can be a great way to bring in healthy energy and push out accumulated negative energy.

Action you can take
- Identify how energetic you feel right now;
- What do you require right now?
- If it is stillness, meditate for 15 minutes;
- If it is movement, identify what your body needs;
- Move daily and vary the activity. Can you get to Adventurous (66), i.e. play music and dance to it?

16. Connect with someone/something uplifting

Entrainment is the effect of having one person attaining an above-60 tile quality and by being present in the room, others will benefit by their presence. The presence of the above-60 tile quality has the power to activate that tile in other members who are present. One person's great news in Embracing (84) even in an online meeting can be everybody's great news and we are all uplifted. Instead of news, though, which can rise and fall depending on the external circumstances, someone's constant Embracing (84) of the team, of challenges and life itself provides an ongoing environment that nurtures the team towards expression of that life. A leader at Thriving (94) can uplift everybody into that tile and the team can operate at a new, powerful level.

Action you can take
- Identify people who uplift you;
- Negotiate time with them that suits you both;
- Identify what it is about the people that uplifts you and whether can you develop that quality yourself. If so, how?
- Journal daily to bring that quality into your life;
- You can check out the timetable of lectures on higher tiles at acglobaltc. com.

17. How do I realize all the answers are within me?

When I am below 30, I CANNOT realize all the answers are within me. I am operating with a mind that cannot grasp that. Awareness of that truth is not possible between 30 and 59. As mentioned in the introduction to this book (*see also* pp. 1–11), self-deception in the 50s is very present and in Wanting and Controlling, we are too narrowed down on what we want. I 'think' I have the answers, especially at the level Egotistical. Just ask me and if I don't know, I will make something up so you think I know the answer. I will ask endless questions to try and find out the answer and when I find the answer, I will then know, but it's not my answer, it's someone else's. I borrow it and own it as mine, but it's not derived from my intuition. From 60 and above, I access my Witness Mind which IS intuitive and feel for the answer and it seems to have more truth to it the further towards 100 I access.

Action you can take
- Write down the question you would like to have the answers for;
- Now choose an activity that promotes Witness Wisdom Mind, i.e. a long walk, a drive to or from work in silence, a hot bath, meditation, a nap;
- Take the question into the activity. Do not think about it, just have it there and invite a vision or imagine what the answer might look like.

18. Spend time in or near water

We collect energy everywhere we go. Water has the property of dissolving not only physical but also mental energy, so that it has a cleansing effect. This is partly why so many people choose oceans and rivers and lakes to holiday near or in. We utilize this property of water externally as spas, baths, showers or swimming. It is important to stay adequately hydrated so that we can perform at our best in all areas of life, so make sure you drink enough pure, clean water. It is a great idea to shower or swim or have a bath after coming home from a day where you feel you have 'collected' energies that weigh you down.

Action you can take
- Plan a bath;
- Set time aside for a swim in the ocean, a river, pool or lake;
- Book a sauna or a spa;
- Drink plenty of water;
- Schedule time to be near a waterfall or breaking waves. These are very high-energy places to spend time near. If you do not live near these, plan a holiday or visit to be near them.

19.   Spend time in nature

Science has provided much evidence that nature assists us to recalibrate and rejuvenate. Being in nature provides:

- Natural light that helps regulate your body's melatonin levels. Melatonin is a hormone that looks after your internal clock;
- A lowering of the stress hormone cortisol;
- The opportunity for deeper, slower breathing, which stimulates the parasympathetic pathways that calm us down;
- Rest for the brain. The human brain can use a lot of your daily energy. When you are task-orientated, it uses even more. It is very advantageous to alternate periods of brain usage with periods of time in nature so it has downtime and is not stimulated to think. Nature promotes meditation, calm, pondering, contemplation (without thinking), Witnessing and, Wisdom Mind (not the brain). A relaxed mind leads to a relaxed body. Focusing on nature's stillness, wilderness, perfection, harmony and purity can instil these qualities in you. Colour, sounds, interconnectivity and organization are all other qualities of nature that you can sit in with more awareness;

- Inbuilt self-correcting mechanism. When it is disturbed, an innate intelligence is activated that works towards that disturbed area in its former pristine, original state. Sitting in nature and being aware of this activates a similar dynamic in you.

Nature has an inherent inbuilt capacity to heal itself. This means when disturbed, it has a capacity to rebuild, regrow, regenerate. It's like there is a spirit to nature, much as we have a spirit, where each place has a different feel and you may be attracted to: (1) water, such as oceans, rivers, lakes; (2) earth/land, such as a mountain, forest, desert; (3) fire, such as volcanoes or tropical sunshine; or (4) air, such as mountains and tropical rainforests. Each of these four ethers are found in natural places, or you can go to the local park or your backyard vegetable or fruit patch.

This simple act can take you out of the emotional, mental drama of below 60 and help you to reset yourself so more of your spirit is available by being in the spirit of nature, e.g. going to above 60. We can be glowing with all the healthy minerals and vitamins and natural spring water and air from nature, or we can be clogged up with fat deposits, additives and heavy metals, sugary drinks and air-conditioned recycled city air and appear not to be glowing at all.

The etheric part of our physical body is energy gained from nature essentially, so a vibrant awareness will come from activities in and around natural settings. One of the Mastery techniques (key 10) specifically addresses this key to improve your ability to absorb nature.

Action you can take
- Spend lunchtime in the park;
- Walk barefoot on grass or sand;
- Meditate in the park or garden;
- Go for a walk in the rain;
- Watch the night sky for 15 minutes;
- Schedule two hours on the weekend to be in nature.

20. Have a break

The Thinking Mind uses LOTS of daily energy. Short bursts can be supported by having breaks in between. But what if Stressed (20–29) is operating in a constant, ongoing way, e.g. worried about the team results. This 'burns' your energy and once the Thinking Mind gets into a rut or old story programme, it may get stuck there. Break the cycle in any way you can by creating a diversion or passion that uplifts you and is good for others. You will feel rejuvenated by any above-60 tile project or personal wellness activity. During the break you may find Thinking Mind is wound up and won't stop. The Mastery Techniques (key 10) addresses this. At acglobaltc.com you will find a 30-minute meditation available for each of the 40 to 100 tiles for you to listen to during your time-out.

Action you can take

- Shift your focus and move your body;
- Sit up straight and take five long, deep breaths;
- Go for a walk;
- Spend 10 minutes stretching your body;
- Have an afternoon nap;
- Sing a song.

21. What's love got to do with it?

When in Ego Mind, the version of love is want and desire, but we can use the word 'love' because we think that's what it is. It is very conditional on getting what we want. In Egotistical, I love you because I can get you to be or do what I want – 'I love you because you help me feel good'. What can happen is that when we don't get what we want, the 'I love you' disappears, showing us it was actually desire. In Heartfelt (92), resides the power of love because you have let go of Wanting. When things don't turn out in accordance with the highest potential for all (not just yourself), heartfelt love STAYS and works through a solution by accessing Witness Mind.

At Realizating Truth (60), there is an understanding love is about releasing these wants from another person. Then it's more about listening (70 and 71) and being there for the other team members, not for what they can do, which is very important, but for who they are. In love, we see deeper into a person and eventually see and feel their spirit, which 'inspires' us. So, as many times through the day as you can, ask yourself, 'Am I operating from Heartfelt right now?'

Action you can take

- Book a massage;
- Create something for yourself; for example a small garden patch, a new recipe, a daily morning stretch routine that listens to the body rather than someone else;
- Have a nurturing bath;
- Schedule a date with yourself;
- Write about gratitude and how to grow it in your life;
- Engage in a heart-centred meditation;
- Where and how do you nurture others?
- Visit acglobaltc.com and choose any of the 90–100 tile meditations to listen to;
- Considering how to give to others is a heart-opening exercise. It may start off as conditional, i.e. What might I receive back? But with practice it can evolve into unconditional and you are able to feel wonderful just by giving.

22. Listen to music

Many studies and your own personal experience show that music affects the way we feel and our state of mind. Let's incorporate that into the Awareness Code by saying that music can assist in moving you up or down through the AC. A study at the University of Groningen in the Netherlands provided evidence that the sounds you listen to can change the way you perceive emotions and the world around you. (Jacob Jolij, Maaike Meurs: 'Music alters visual perception', PLOS ONE, 2011). People who listened to happier tunes (in Awareness Code terms, an above-60 tile tune) not only felt happier (above 60), but they also see happier faces around them. When they listened to sad music, they spotted sad faces much faster and saw sad faces even when there were none. This helps explain the nature of how we find evidence for the stories we have created at each tile.

In the Awareness Code App you will find suggestions for music that potentially activates each of the 100 tiles. What is the benefit of activating a below-60 tile? Answer: to explore it to understand it, not to judge it, but experiment with its content and multiple forms of expression. Of course, one song can have multiple tiles and a very different response or reaction for one person compared to another. This is why the music provided is suggestion only, not prescriptive.

Action you can take
- Explore YouTube for high vibration music;
- Meditate to instrumental music;
- Dance to your favourite music;
- Sing out loud to your favourite music;
- Motivate yourself through music;
- Schedule time to play your instrument *or*
- Learn to play a musical instrument;
- Go to the opera or a live show or concert.

23.   Getting RUDE And RAW with The Awareness Code

There are many leaders who struggle to alternate between effective executing and deeply resting.

RUDE – The executing part of a leader's life
How many times have you read a great book, knowing it has inspiring content but you didn't Integrate (87) the practices or theory into your life? You may have great ideas but poor to no execution. The Financial Brand wrote in a blog on 23 September 2014 about a Microsoft study

that highlighted that the optimal number of exposures for audio messages to be effective is between six and 20[3].

You have an internal audio voice going on all the time, running an old programme. To create a new programme, you need to tell yourself to do something new at least every day for a week, preferably for three or more weeks. The Ego cannot imagine an amazing new you by getting above 60. Become the highest version of you (80) by actioning RUDE and not putting it off with the statement, 'I'll start tomorrow'.

The first question many of you will be asking is 'how do I practically take all that I have learnt on the Awareness Code and bring it into my day-to-day life?' The following acronym will help:

R – Relentless
U – Unimaginable, unstoppable, unwavering, unthinkable or
    unbelievable
D – Daily
E – Execution

Ego has a habit of sabotaging any new above-60 programme you will put in place. It values all below-60 programmes so will get you to make excuses for not being able to adhere to the new programme. The acronym begins with:

- Relentless, which is essential for Stepping In (60s) with increasing intensity and eventually, it is increasing intensity;
- Next up is your 'U' word, which requires being Open-minded (72) at the level of Opening, Spontaneous (85) at the level of Transforming and finally, Extraordinary (98) at the level of Incredible;
- The next part of the acronym is Daily, which is essential so as to create new nerve pathways and also literally means actioning this new way every single day;

---

[3]https://thefinancialbrand.com/42323/advertising-marketing-messages-effective-frequency/

- The last part is Execution, which delivers the new knowledge and means following steps right through to the very end so they actually happen in practice;
- Decide which keys are most important to improve yourself;
- Life is an Adventure (66). Create yourself by which tile you choose to be. Start simple: choose a below-60 tile to overcome and an above-60 tile to bring alive. Include one, two or three keys to add to your life **right now**, immediately and be RUDE with it.

For Steve, RUDE means developing the ability to become relentless, like the Terminator on an unstoppable mission, and continually moving forward in a relentless way.

For Wayno, RUDE means daily 'having a go' at anything and everything that wisdom experiences as part of his higher calling. Wellness, growth and improvements sprint forth from his RUDENESS. This enables him to be more for himself, his family and all the teams that he is a part of – every day counts.

Corporate leaders in traditional companies tend to operate in weekly and monthly cycles for activities that could be done on a daily basis. This is why RUDE is so important to change mindsets and daily working practices.

RAW – The deeply resting part of a leader's life

Many leaders work hard (not often RUDELY) and **do not** balance this with deep rest. They may aim to 'relax and recover' through activities like a run, yoga, a walk, swim or bike ride. While these activities are great for our overall fitness and wellbeing, they are actually key 15 – moving the body – and **not** RAW.

So, what is RAW? No movement, just **being**. At the end of a run, lay down; at the end of a yoga session, do shavasana (a period of time at the end of the yoga poses where a person lies down on the mat with eyes closed, relaxing deeply and not moving at all); at the end of a walk, sit; at the end of a bike ride, have a hot bath; at the end of a work day, have a sauna.

R – Rest, recuperate, revitalize, rejuvenate, recover, reinvent, reset, reflect, relax, restore, refresh

A – Absorb – breathe in the ambiance, sunlight, sound of waves, time with no responsibilities;

Anchor in – let go of the worker, problem solver, fixer and over-thinker and anchor into spending time just being, not doing;

Affirmation – Look for Realizing Power (81) and reaffirm your positioning in the above-60 tiles by remembering the great parts of the preceding activity;

Acknowledge – the team's support, progress, growth;

Allow – any below 60 to arise and wave away. Allow any above-60 great feelings to wash through you;

Align – with what 60s, 70s, 80s or 90s look like for you.

W – Wisdom

The guiding principles for **RAW** include:

Ego has stories about RAW being a 'waste of time', 'unproductive', and has no 'KPIs' (Key Personal Indicators).

A leader needs to be above 60 for RAW to be a part of life as Ego Pride will look for another thing to do, achieve, succeed in order to promote itself.

R is for all/any of the words that slow you down and promote moving away from the Thinking, Problem-solving Mind and towards where the Witness and eventually Wisdom Mind resides. Your body might tell you it's overworked, over-stimulated or exhausted by signs such as headaches, skin rashes, lower immune system, hypersensitivity.

R is about giving the body an opportunity to start to come back into balance. Without it, the body may develop illness symptoms.

A is for deepening in the **R** state.

W is for the Wisdom Mind, which is associated with the 80s and 90s. Wisdom Mind is able to do its thing, which is to provide insights. Silence, nature or very gentle background sound can promote this state to arise. Some of your best 'ahh ha!' moments are from this part of RAW.

It's not possible to build a life or a business purely based on RUDE techniques as an individual is likely to burn out or the business would not be sustainable without RAW. Let's build daily and weekly plans and stick to them in a RUDE and RAW way.

Action you can take
- Identify the important keys and set weekly goals;
- Map a weekly schedule;
- Refer to your calendar on a daily basis;
- Is your activity balanced with stillness?

24. Personal retreat

At a certain point in your personal development the Witness Mind is more available so that in a given situation above-60 truth can be accessed rather than Thinking Mind programmes. This needs to be nurtured and personal retreat time is a valuable way to do this. Thinking Mind thrives on keeping busy so it creates activities, projects, addictions and other forms of distractions in order to gain temporary pleasure, satisfaction or relief from below-60 emotions and thoughts. Slowing down for an extended period can be very valuable to witness what happens in the stillness.

A personal retreat is one way to test how reliant you are on keeping busy to avoid what may arise in the silence. Alone and in the silence, you may be able to witness to a greater degree your inner world chatter, stories and emotional charge. You may need to be Ready (61) for the below 60 to flush up in the absence of distractions. People often start with a few minutes of meditation and later are able to be in the silence for a few hours with the mastery techniques. This can lead to spending a number of days alone according to what arises within you, how competent you feel with staying as the witness and your capacity to invite the Wisdom Mind to oversee and deal with what arises. Many people often have a mentor or another support person they can call on while on these long retreats.

Organizing a week-long mountain trek with your Ego constantly occupied is one type of challenge but a personal retreat, where the intention is to sit with the mastery techniques for days to watch what arises within while mapping it on the Awareness Code is altogether a different type of challenge. A level of maturity is required for this endeavour and is highly encouraged.

Action you can take
- Book a weekend away for yourself or with others;
- Book an organized retreat.

25. The Awareness Code App
The App allows team members, family, friends and colleagues to give feedback on your personal awareness and for you to give feedback on their awareness. You can plan actions and goals which will go into your diary. There is a library of 100 videos, one for each tile. There are meditations to assist you to understand aspects of the ACL such as how to access Witness Mind and Wisdom Mind. There are also 160 diagrams that accompany the 100 tiles, providing greater understanding and insight. Search Awareness Code in the App Store for iOS or the Google Play Store for Android.

Let's review

- The Code is a technique that invites use. With your devoted use of the Code, you will be called to action practices to maintain physical wellness, emotional stability and mental clarity.
- The 25 keys reveal the best practices available to support your journey towards balance, joy and becoming an inspirational leader.

PART 7

ABOVE-90 LEADERSHIP AND BEYOND

CHAPTER TWENTY

Above-90 Leadership and B.I.G.

What Does an Above-90 Leader Look Like?

An above-90 leader in many ways is invisible in the same way awareness is invisible to the naked eye. So, how then is an Incredible Leader recognized? Answer: by the gifts or the consequences that such a leadership provides to those he is connected to. The collaboration that exists through qualities such as patience, kindness, readiness, or any one of the above-90 tiles is the leadership. Qualities from the Transforming line and in particular, Integrity (88) stand out. Such leaders are naturally Inspiring (89) without trying to be and integrate the above-90 qualities so profoundly that their mere presence is the gift. They emanate the qualities through their beingness as much as through anything they actually do.

Hierarchical systems within a team can still apply in the presence of an Incredible leader in that some leaders have a more solid grasp of staying above the integrity line and so they become role models for the ones venturing out into new territory (Spontaneous, 85). An above-90 leader is one who is aware of his or her role at the top of the hierarchy but is very much a team player and finds his or her purpose in steering a team towards the full potential each is capable of. Meaning and purpose arise in inspiring others towards above 90, which has very specific traits and ways of functioning. Such a leader is profoundly connected to humility and there is no attachment to being perceived in a particular way as the seductions of glamour have long been relinquished. In such an energy field, people who are committed to supporting the company, team or life itself are instantly lifted into the realm where their highest calling or passions are felt to be possible and become an everyday reality. On the other hand, if there is work to be done on any of the tiles below the integrity line, the downward call of the negative thoughts or feeling of these tiles will alert the above-90 leader to address the call as soon as possible.

The above-90 leader sees challenges as opportunities and the exposure of limiting or outdated ways of working together is celebrated. There is no attachment to how things have been done in the past and a natural movement towards what is required in the present moment. This does not mean the wisdom of the past is discarded but rather it is integrated to such a degree that lessons of the past are immediately available in the present in order to affect the future direction of the company, family or any other group working together. Employees of such a leader are compelled to know themselves at a level of identity that is beyond their current experience of self. For example, if a person has mastered the tile Grateful (90), then there is a pull towards Sincere (91) or any one of the tiles beyond as the current tile becomes a launching pad for what is beyond once a tile has been mastered. An above-90 leader does not need to think about this process, they **are** the process.

The process has been integrated to such a degree that brain function and physiology match the process of evolution or growth. After practising Witness Mind at 60 to 89, it becomes more accessible and available. There is a presence that sees perfection in the moment and there is also the flow of life moving towards the flowering of a united global human consciousness. When they operate from Stepping In, it is Fearless (68) and Fully In (69). When they operate from Opening, it is from Wow (78) and Flowing (79).

Above-90 leaders sometimes come into the public eye during a crisis. They emerge from the chaos and the way they conduct themselves alerts us all to an error of thinking or entrapped way of being that has become ingrained in our structures. Such a leader is already living the new paradigm that the crisis asks us all to step into. A crisis simply means there is a forum for their skills to be integrated by a wider group of people through the example the leader offers. So, in a crisis where lower levels of functioning have come to a head, above-90 leaders who are otherwise fairly invisible begin to emerge as they have a very real and important role to play in steering a team towards letting go of qualities that bring destruction. Instead, they show us how to embrace life-sustaining principles.

During the climate of COVID-19 in 2020, there was evidence of the planet having time to breathe as destructive ways of using its resources were slowed down. There is a requirement for governments and people to collaborate in a new way and to address the crisis with any one of the tiles above 60. In this way, the crisis itself provides the training ground for new political, social, IT and economic systems to be born and to finally let go of the habits of leadership that create crises.

The B.I.G. (Beyond Incredible Group)

When the words of this book have touched you deeply and you are inspired to lift towards the realms of Beyond Incredible (100), there is a potential to become involved with a small group of people united in attaining this way of being. We invite you now to consider what it is to be Beyond Incredible. What it might be like to live there. What potential exists to be fast-tracked towards this outcome, not for your own sake but for the betterment of humanity, the planet and life itself?

The tiles seem to be portals into different worlds of experience. On the journey towards Beyond Incredible, we must enter the territory of every tile, map that territory, explore its secrets and come to a place of mastery where any portal can be moved into and through without becoming stuck or imprisoned there.

This mapping process brings the revelation that when a person is positioned in tiles lower than 60, they cannot understand the tiles above them. When positioned in an above-60 tile, they can come to understand its own level and those below it. Persons able to access the tiles of Incredible and who have practised the Awareness Code Mastery Techniques will be able to experience the sense of warmth, generosity and deep compassion that typically arises at this level. To go beyond this level is the exception rather than the norm. This activates experiences of Heartfelt (92) energy previously unknown and prepares the body for the changes required as it gets closer to Beyond Incredible.

As you approach 100, there is a truth that arrives that lets you know that you are so much more than what you do, and so much more than what you think you are, so much more than a physical, mental or emotional body. Humility arrives with this truth because the same truth applies to everyone and everything around you. Spirit shines out from the essence of beingness within everything the gaze falls upon. At this level you know yourself as a part in the plan along with everyone else. You are living a life where you have moved out of using only Ego Mind and into using more Witness Mind and then further again into using more Wisdom Mind. Eventually, you can access Unity Mind at 100. Beyond Incredible and living here is difficult to put into words. There is an ability to open a portal for someone else trapped in a lower tile, allowing them to experience a moment of Grace in the awareness of a higher tile. This can be life-changing.

Every tile must be understood and eventually mastered. The emotions of every below-60 tile are emptied out to enable the eventual ripening and ability to move through the portal of Grace. The deeper you go, the greater the possibility for others in your team or family to deepen as well. With each person who pops through to a higher tile, the greater the pull of entrainment upon those ready to move up from below. Hence, we can begin to see the potential for the exponential evolution of humanity.

Living at the level of Beyond Incredible accompanies a paradigm shift away from what one might 'DO' towards what one is to 'BE'. Doing the impossible without the need for validation is natural as the awareness is aligned with spirit, which simply is Beyond Incredible and Superhuman. In this state, what you do is secondary to what you are. Power is derived from being rather than doing – we might say 'Being the impossible' lives here.

At this level of awareness there is a clear and unfettered feeling that it is all for the greater good, that a greater intelligence is overseeing it all. Devotional wellness replaces personal gain. Indeed, the personal gain has been surrendered into an 'us'. You are moving towards directly experiencing yourself as a vessel constantly being filled and emptied in service to others. Your spirit affects the team in a powerful and immeasurable way.

Imagine living in a space beyond the dramas of life, beyond the duality of victim and perpetrator, even beyond the concept of good and evil, while still very much involved in all that is going on that is part of your 'responsibility'. Can you imagine seeing both the victim and the perpetrator standing in front of you and feeling a breathtaking awareness of the perfection of it all? It includes, but is deeper than, compassion. Can you imagine the profound witness ready to assist both victim and perpetrator to a higher awareness if they were to ask? Imagine not feeling compelled to interfere out of any judgement of what is unfolding, nor to take sides.

Can you imagine that simply witnessing unfolding circumstances in this way has a powerful and positive effect on the event and whatever is unfolding? Like a magnet, Beyond Incredible pulls on the polarized aspects of entrapped spirit within others, allowing their lower-tile awareness that is their Ego to be dropped for a moment of Grace. People can be left feeling, 'What just happened?' Living in this realm seemingly enables you to smile inwardly, blissfully no matter what circumstance is brought to your awareness for action or comment. It leaves you ineffably of service, witnessing the way that service is called.

It seems that below 60 we react to whatever is occurring from a self-motivated perspective. When we find ourselves above 60, we have learned to pause and respond from a soulful awareness of both self and other. At Beyond Incredible, an impulse arises from spirit and there is a sense of witnessing the body in action in service to the One Life, which is all life, and miracles can occur. This is why it's called United Mind.

Take a moment to reflect on the impact a group of people interested in being like this in the world could make. Our vision is to achieve that and to create a Beyond Incredible Group (B.I.G.), who would live and model a super movement to the world. This would help to assist a global reset, which feels imperative for our time. This group is already forming the opportunity to apply for membership. Each individual will be assisted on the journey through the Awareness Code from the limited and middle tiles to the deeper tiles and then to Beyond Incredible.

Picture this: you are a part of a group that consists of an economic leader from London, a future potential president from Zambia, a philanthropist from Mexico, a sporting hero from China, a corporate leader from Australia and an American actress. You all have one thing in common: it is an inspiration, a knowing that there is another level of being available. And you are trained to help bring that level out of each other and manifest it. From being Beyond Incredible, wonderful new projects and ideas will manifest.

People who are B.I.G.-orientated can be leaders from multiple disciplines, e.g. medical, economic, political, corporate, sporting, creative arts, religious/spiritual leaders and so on. Do you see your potential to become a Beyond Incredible leader? If so, check out www.beyondincredible.com.

Conclusion

For companies or other organizations to be successful and to perform at their optimal level it is imperative for leaders to operate from a space of awareness that has integrity at its core. The Awareness Code is the first tool that empowers leaders to identify their level of awareness. However, more importantly, it offers developmental guidance on how to transition from entrapped awareness to an awareness that reveals solutions to challenges and thrives in having the opportunity to do so. To aspire towards the next level of growth is in itself a very powerful state of awareness that will transform companies. Ultimately, you are encouraged to be Incredible and beyond as this is the most powerful form of leadership on the planet.

To function from Incredible and beyond is to accept a radically different approach to the levels that are below this way of existing and yet this style of leadership understands and has compassion for all of them. This level asks companies to become comfortable with paradox and let go of principles that have been long held as best practice.

A new approach is required to address the challenges of this century. Incredible Leadership and beyond understands that the highest potential solutions are to be found in collaboration and fellowship as a foundation. Integrating at the deepest levels creates an undeniably subtle but powerful energy field that remains solid, no matter where others are in the Awareness Code. Everyone has a role to play in the unfolding of human awareness. There is an understanding that any action from this space of Incredible and beyond will carry with it the spirit of aliveness. At such levels, all resources are experienced as a profound gift and they are used in service to support life.

This is an attitude that is awakening within us and will transform the planet. As a species, our role is to traverse all levels of awareness so as to learn from them. We have pillaged, raped, destroyed, coveted and found any number of ways to negate life only to discover that there are repercussions in the form of karma. The rate of change that is occurring is fast-paced and the technology available at our fingertips means that decisions have the potential to affect all of us at a global level. Let's make life-sustaining decisions.

Certain levels of awareness project doom because they are not aware of the solutions that exist at the core of the challenge. The solutions are profoundly beautiful and exist in a place that we all share. This place is our deepest nature and it transcends the human form. It is time to speak and live from a place that acknowledges the miracle at the centre of our existence. To consider, even for a brief moment, that life is a profoundly exquisite gift is to touch the awareness that supports life at its core. Real and lasting change is born out of such a place. Every person has a role to play in transforming their own awareness level simply because it is a potential of our species. Power comes with owning this truth and speaking and acting from this place with conviction and uncompromising diligence.

We wrote this book from our highest callings, born from witnessing first hand, through hundreds of company and private workshops, the toll on individuals and organizations when there is no alignment with the Revelation tiles. We have also witnessed world-class organizations with admirable purposes fall short of their dreams because of a systemic lack of leadership awareness.

We developed the Awareness Code for leaders as not only the antidote for these shortfalls, but also the catalyst for accelerating the shift towards a level of functioning that is profoundly sustaining of self and the globe we live on. Individuals, teams and companies now have a map and can align with the already existing movement towards the incredible solutions that exist at the heart of the challenges we face in this next decade. To become a part of this is a joyful experience. You have a role to play, it is a fundamentally important role and you are never alone in this.

With Gratitude

From Wayno

A huge inspiration for this work comes from the work of Dr David R. Hawkins. David's work affected me deeply, brought me to tears of joy many times as his series of books unveiled truth after truth for me. His work was central to the private consultations, retreats and workshops I have facilitated. I am deeply grateful for his outstanding contribution.

To the group of wonderful Mavericks, some of whom were the original participants on the 'Path of the Mystic' I offered over 20 years ago. These 42 people are dedicated to understanding and living the above-tile-60 version of life and I learn from them all in our once-or-twice-a-week gatherings. Thank you, Anaya, Anita, Barb, Barney, Bianca, Big Mav, Bri, Carlos, Cindy, Claire, Clara, Diddie, Georgie, Izumi, Jacqui, Janne, Jasmine, Jo Beth, Jojo, Justin, Katie, Kim, Linda, Lisa, Luke, Lynne, Marise, Matt, Michelle, Nicole, Philli, Randal, Rob, Robyn, Sal, Stevo, Tim, Tizmae, Trudi and Willie.

To my four children, Bj, Bianca, Jimmy and Elija, who have not only managed to give me wonderful opportunities to expose below-60 tile behaviour in myself, but have also shown me qualities and expressions of above 60 that continue to 'blow me away'.

To Steve Tappin for his capacity to deep dive into the unknown with me and strip away all unnecessary convention and just 'go for it'.

To my partner Sal, who provides such deep support and never-ending insight into spaces I am not developed enough to go.

From Steve

Dedicated to loving memories of the late Sylvia Tappin and David Henry Tappin.

To the inspiring teaching of Sir John Harvey-Jones, Mr Duncan White and Wayno.

Deepest gratitude to the Xinfu core team – Andy, Diddie, Laani, Liam, Luke, Kyna, Rod, Rowena, Victoria, and Racey – and our trusted practitioners and friends, Ed, Gianfranco, Brian, Mike, Julia, Chloe and Tracey.

Thank you to Wayno's Monday evening meditators for incredible insights. A special thank you to Diddie, Anaya, Marise, Claire, Sal, Bianca, Kitty, Trudy, Philli, Jackie, Bri, Izumi, Robyn, Jasmine, Stevo and Barney for your incredible skills and therapeutic practitioner work to create your first Maverick leader!

To my Chinese fellows, Joe Baolin, Joe Chen and Liu Donghua and Maggie Cheng.

To our past, current and future CEOs, who constantly inspire us to develop new and incredible work and our new global ambassadors – we love you all.

To the late Burgess Meredith and Sylvester Stallone for Rocky's inspiration and training.

To Olivia Newton-John for your inspiration in the words of 'Magic' and Angelina Jolie for your inspiration and for being an incredible female role model.

To Leeds United fans everywhere around the world: continue to go 'Marching on Together'.

To Jo, the most incredible ex-wife and mother in the world.

To my loving family: Emma, Mark, Harvey, Will, Ted, Mae, Miles, Jo, Felix, Dexter, Claudia, Auntie Betty, Jean, Debbie, Mark, Liam, Dominic, Justine, Mark, Koby and best friends, Les and Big John.

Finally, to my daughters Lauren and Hannah to bring to life what is possible as you give your best from love and work in true fellowship. I'm deeply grateful for Lauren's love and contribution to the book and Hannah's love and creativity.

With love,
Steve

From Wayno and Steve

Both would like to deeply thank Claire, Katie, Philli, Luke and Diddie for contributing their wisdom and skills in putting it all together, often from illegible scribblings.

Thank you also to Clara for capturing and expressing visually the tile Entrapments and Revelations with originality and finesse. Amazing insight for a 20-year-old.

And to Marise, who somehow pulled it all together, kept us on task, provided incredible insight and feedback and entertained us through her tears and laughter as the book moved her deeply.

Index

Capitalized entries, other than names, refer to tiles in the Awareness Code. Lower case entries are related to the use of general terms.

AWARENESS CODE

		United	Doing the Impossible	Breath…
Incredible		90 Grateful	91 Sincere	92 Heartfelt	93 Devoted	94 Thriv…
Transforming		80 Highest Callings	81 Realizing Power	82 Realizing Value	83 Fellowship Mindset	84 Embr…
Opening		70 Receptive	71 Witnessing	72 Open-minded	73 Trustful	74 Conn…
Stepping in		60 Realizing Truth	61 Ready	62 Preparing	63 Releasing	64 Reorie…
Egotistical		50 Narcissistic	51 Arrogant	52 Know-it-all	53 Self-centered	54 Dismi…
Controlling		40 Malicious	41 Enraged	42 Bully	43 Confronting	44 Dece…
Wanting		30 Infatuated	31 Perfectionist	32 Addictive	33 Over-ambitious	34 Sche…
Stressed		20 Numb	21 Terror	22 Dread	23 Trapped	24 Fright…
Despondent		10 Inconsolable	11 Hopeless	12 Unfulfilled	13 Lethargic	14 Wou…
Lifeless		0 Self-loathing	1 Self-hatred	2 Pathetic	3 Unlovable	4 Bur…

taking	Miraculous	Mastery	Superhuman	Profound	100 **Beyond Incredible**
ʃing	95 Compassion	96 Altruistic	97 Heart-bursting	98 Extraordinary	99 Revealing Grace
acing	85 Spontaneous	86 Off-the-charts	87 Integrating	88 Integrity	89 Inspiring
ected	75 Collaboration	76 Emerging	77 Agile	78 Wow	79 Flowing
ʃtating	65 Positive	66 Adventurous	67 Conviction	68 Fearless	69 Fully In
ssive	55 Defensive	56 Pretentious	57 Ego Confidence	58 Complacent	59 Not Buying In
iving	45 Resentful	46 Passive-aggressive	47 Annoyed	48 Frustrated	49 Sceptical
ming	35 Competitive	36 Attached	37 Narrowing Down	38 Identifying	39 Ego-requesting
tened	25 Worried	26 Anxious	27 Over-pleasing	28 Insecure	29 Hesitant
ʃded	15 Hurt	16 Saddened	17 Disconnected	18 Discontented	19 Disinterested
den	5 Embarrassed	6 Wrong	7 Regretful	8 Never Enough	9 Inadequate